Shakespeare in Space

Studies in Shakespeare

Robert F. Willson, Jr.
General Editor

Vol. 14

PETER LANG
New York • Washington, D.C./Baltimore • Bern
Frankfurt am Main • Berlin • Brussels • Vienna • Oxford

H. R. Coursen

Shakespeare in Space

Recent Shakespeare Productions on Screen

PETER LANG
New York • Washington, D.C./Baltimore • Bern
Frankfurt am Main • Berlin • Brussels • Vienna • Oxford

PR
3093
. C67
2002

Library of Congress Cataloging-in-Publication Data

Coursen, Herbert R.
Shakespeare in space: recent Shakespeare
productions on screen / H. R. Coursen.
p. cm. — (Studies in Shakespeare; vol. 14)
Includes bibliographical references and index.
1. Shakespeare, William, 1564–1616—Film and video adaptations.
2. English drama—Film and video adaptations.
3. Film adaptations. I. Title. II. Series.
PR3093 .C67   791.43'6—dc21   2001037676
ISBN 0-8204-5714-0
ISSN 1067-0823

Die Deutsche Bibliothek-CIP-Einheitsaufnahme

Coursen, H. R.:
Shakespeare in space: recent Shakespeare
productions on screen / H. R. Coursen.
–New York; Washington, D.C./Baltimore; Bern;
Frankfurt am Main; Berlin; Brussels; Vienna; Oxford: Lang.
(Studies in Shakespeare; Vol. 14)
ISBN 0-8204-5714-0

Cover photo of Julia Stiles in Michael Almereyda's
Hamlet (Miramax Films) by Larry Riley
Author photo by Pamela Mount
Cover design by Joni Holst

The paper in this book meets the guidelines for permanence and durability
of the Committee on Production Guidelines for Book Longevity
of the Council of Library Resources.

Printed in the United States of America

This book
is for
Kenneth Branagh

Contents

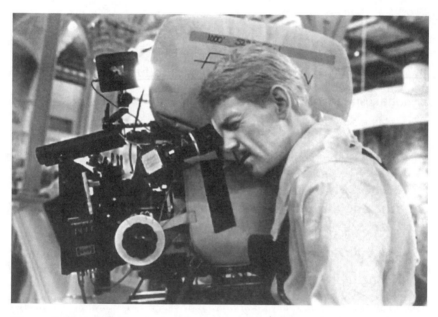

Kenneth Branagh lines up a camera angle. *Photo courtesy of Shepperton Studios.*

Introduction

My purpose here is descriptive and evaluative. Since many of the productions I examine are not commercially available, I hope to encourage them into circulation. In order to "see" Desmond Davis's *Measure for Measure* (BBC, 1978), for example, it is important to contrast it with David Thacker's 1994 version. The latter, though, cannot be found in any of the catalogs I have scanned.

I am not wedded to any theoretical position; indeed, I continue to find that theory has little to say about specific productions. The essays in James Bulman's excellent anthology, *Shakespeare and Performance Theory* (1996), for example, look briefly at only two actual productions, both susceptible to post-modernist analysis, but each also highly suspect as representation of the inherited script (Greenaway's *Prospero's Books* and LaPage's "Mud *Dream*"). While the recent Boose-Burt anthology, *Shakespeare: The Film* (1998), can blithely dismiss the notion of text, I believe that an inherited script (or scripts) exists and that it outlines the options for production available to actors and directors. The script is moving forward in time—it is not timeless, but seeks production *in* time. Production, invariably, will show us our own zeitgeist or episteme, linking what is construed as the "meaning" in the script to meanings we perceive in our culture.

Production of the script is a mode of interrogation. Thus, for all of its archaic early-modern English, the Shakespeare script is never anachronistic. Shakespeare is always our contemporary, though not hollowed out to merely modernist or post-modernist premises. A *production*, however, hurtles back in time as soon as it appears and is probably "dated" even as it emerges. It may discover that it cannot control its moment. Samuel Crowl (1994), for example, shows how the Mankiewicz *Julius Caesar* (1953), meant to evoke memories of Mussolini's Italy, instead picked up resonances of the McCarthy witch hunts of the early 1950s. The Royal Shakespeare Company's production of *Richard II* in 1972 arrived at the Brooklyn Academy of Music at the height (or depth) of the Watergate revelations and received a lot of unearned energy from that historical moment.

We are involved, then, in a paradox—the script itself seeks meanings as yet to emerge in society and culture. The production, having illuminated those meanings for a moment, falls back into that moment, which, in turn, recedes down lengthening corridors known as the past. An irony wrapped within this paradox is that productions that make a conscious attempt to equate our moment with what a director perceives in the play—*Romeo and Juliet* in Bosnia or Northern Ireland, for example—almost invariably fail. They cut the scripts off from their archetypes and their own history and present them as merely contemporary. Branagh's *Love's Labour's Lost* (2000) is consciously anachronistic. It uses the songs of the 1930s and the wide-screen format of the 1950s, and, whatever its faults, has the virtue of not attempting to cram the possibilities of the script into a merely contemporary context.

My own approach will be labeled "reactionary" (Traister 1999), but it argues, quite simply, that one cannot evaluate production until one accounts for the "space," actual and conceptual, within which the production appears. Shakespeare's plays were written for at least two stages and probably for a third (Globe, Blackfriars, and Whitehall). They involved little, if any, scenery and probably incorporated an acting style that addressed the audience directly on occasion.

The "framing" of stage is, of course, different from that of film or television, in that you have a proscenium enclosing "real space" (not a good format for Shakespeare) or a configured cosmos like that of Shakespeare's original Globe, where heaven, earth, and the underworld were represented even when a script such as *King Lear* might be challenging these visualized assumptions. A common misconception about theater is that "the eye [is] freer to roam" (Ranald 1999, 46). Not so—if the director is doing his or her job with lighting and sightlines, you look where the director wants you to look.

Even when the stage doesn't move or change its dimensions, however, the scenes upon it can "close up" or "open out" as a scene may demand. Compare the "big" public scenes in *Richard II* with the smaller "behind-the-scenes" scenes. (Indeed, the intimate second scene of that play tells us what the first big court scene was all about!)

SHAKESPEARE ON SCREEN:
THE CENTENARY CONFERENCE
Benalmádena, 21-24 September 1999

CONFERENCE PROGRAMME

Universidad de Málaga

Celebrating 100 years of Shakespeare on film. *Courtesy of José Ramon Diaz Fernandéz.*

Film has evolved from the photograph—which dates from the mid-nineteenth century—and then from a mode in which sound came from a live piano or orchestra and dialogue occurred on title cards. It is preeminently a *visual* medium in which sound and the spoken word are adjuncts to the image. Black-and-white film can achieve a considerable field of depth. Color film is limited in its depth field, unless a director mutes the colors (as Olivier does, for example, in the battle scenes for his *Richard III* and as Taymor does in her crossroads scene in *Titus*).

Television is not film (even if films are made for TV). Its image does not result from light shining through a sequence of moving images but from the bombardment of electrons within a cathode-ray tube. A videocassette is a magnetic, not a light-sensitive, mechanism. Television comes from radio—which dates from the early twentieth century—and was, originally, radio with a picture. It can contain more dialogue than film and needs more dialogue to augment its image. It is a close-up medium and uses three basic camera shots—close-up, two-shot, and reaction shot. To experience the difference between film and television, enlarge the standard television image to the size of film and notice the distortion. Television, with its reliance on the spoken word, should be a good medium for Shakespeare. "Big" scenes, though, can be difficult for television, since the medium's effort to enclose a large space merely shows how small the screen really is. As Mr. Wonka says in the film, "Whenever you transmit something by television, it always ends up smaller on the other end." Big scenes require careful editing to suggest size without really showing it (see the deposition scene in the 1978 BBC *Richard II* to see how this is done).

We know, of course, that television has been largely domesticated to our space. The set, when turned off, reflects our "living room" and tries to *affect* our living space when turned on. In that Shakespeare is a "special event," it does not sort well with our casual environments. A specific generic instance is the televised stage play—where stage acting can conflict with the "cool" medium (as in the recent televised Beaumont Theater *Twelfth Night*)—or the remake of a stage play for television, which often results in a splendid television production (Nunn's several such ventures and the recent Richard Eyre *King Lear* and Deborah Warner *Richard II* are examples of superb productions in this mode). The "offshoot" (a story based on a Shakespeare plot) is another area to be explored, and it includes films such as those of Kurosawa, Stoppard's *Rosencrantz and Guildenstern Are Dead*, and Branagh's *A Midwinter's Tale*.

Some of the plays have recently emerged in animated and silent formats. The Animated Shakespeare produced twelve plays in the early 1990s using one of three techniques—cel animation, painting on glass, or puppets. A generic question asks about tragedy in a "cartoon" format. Can that possibly work? The silent films, suddenly available to us on a cassette recently released from the British Film Institute, insist on further questions, particularly the acting style necessary to convey meaning and the use of title cards to atone for the lack of voices. The silent films (and some of the great foreign films) suggest that the action imitated is prior to the language of the scripts. The process involves much more than finding visual equivalents for the words. It demands that the director give us a glimpse of archetype beneath the action—the confusion of surfaces engendered by deep ambition in Kurosawa's *Throne of Blood*, for example.

If a "thesis" applies to my discussions of individual productions, it is this: production occurs in space. Physical space includes the wide screen and outdoor location available to film versus the smaller screen and the almost invariable studio of television. It includes the brief moment (ten or twelve minutes) in which early silent films narrated a much longer story. It includes the half-hour and the various techniques of animation for the animated Leon Garfield scripts. Conceptually, it includes the musical comedy format of the 1930s, which Branagh employs in his *Love's Labour's Lost* (2000), and the Elizabethan sub-genre of the revenge drama, which Julie Taymor embraces for her *Titus*. I have made an effort to "measure" production against the space it inhabits or attempts to inhabit.

The Shakespeare script moves forward in time, acquiring meanings as new possibilities make themselves available in a culture. In its latent form, the script will remain "timeless" as long as such constructs as "language" and "person" and such concepts as "history" and "love" remain in cultural circulation. The script or play text becomes implicated in time as soon as it is produced. Even productions done "in authentic Elizabethan costumes" betray their moment, as we can see when we look at photographs of Poel's effort at authenticity at the turn of the twentieth century. They represent a late-nineteenth-century conception of what Elizabethan England looked like. The "text," although "fixed" as of, say, 1601 (and granting the work of subsequent editors), is free to roam, and it does roam and will. Production, however modern, becomes immediately trapped in its time. It plunges backward in time at the moment of its emergence, passing the seeking script, which is going in the other direction. The Thacker *Measure for Measure,* for example, imagines a world that has become television but that directorial concept is already anachronistic in 1994, because the world since then has become at least as much a computer monitor and modem as it has a television set and camera. The play itself—*Measure for Measure* and the others—presses into the new millenium, seeking new ways of becoming "excitingly relevant" and becoming almost immediately anachronistic, but not irrelevant, since it permits us to reconstruct the history from which it emerged. Since the script itself offers an almost infinite number of options to actors and directors, the ways that different but simultaneous productions of the same script achieve their meanings will be very different.

By *space,* I mean not just physical area—though that is significant to my analysis—but conceptual space as well. According to the theory of relativity, no absolute demarcations can be made between space and time. Kenneth Branagh, for example, may imitate the 1930s musical in his *Love's Labour's Lost,* but he must avail himself of techniques either not available or seldom used in those musicals—the wide screen and Technicolor, for example. Time—the year 1999—impinges on the black-and-white art-deco world of Fred and Ginger. If we watch an actual film from the period—*Top Hat*—as did the cast of Branagh's film before they began rehearsal, we are aware of the time between us and the film's moment. That continuum is always stretching. Within "space" I include genre, which determines what can happen conceptually and imaginatively within a dramatic format; medium, which imposes physical controls on what can happen with a specific script; and even response.

However idiosyncratic and inevitably subjective a response to a production may be, it is *part* of the space of production, Aristotle's final cause. If, in the theory of relativity, one of the variables is the *motion of the observer,* response to a production is conditioned by the motion of the frame of reference. That is always changing, for many obvious reasons, including the response to new productions of the same script, which invariably changes the observer's stance, even if only slightly. The quality of the critic's response is, of course, open to debate, but the critic's movement through time and the thick but invisible atoms of experience are a given. I did not believe that

Henry V could be played as a reflective introvert until I saw David Gwillim's Henry for the BBC (PBS 1980). It was a performance calibrated to television, pulling us forward to a quiet voice and thoughtful eyes rather than riding us back with the rousing rhetoric that Olivier's camera, booming backwards and upwards, could accommodate but that television cannot. For the BBC *Henry V*, space dictated style and insisted that the critic at least evaluate the relationship between the small screen and the inherited script. The generic premises of the revenge play dictate much of the shaping of Taymor's brilliant *Titus Andronicus*, which is at its best when paying attention to the two revenge plots—Tamora's and Titus's—and their final collision.

Many other elements condition the "space" of performance. The transition from medium to medium can be a significant factor in production, as when a stage performance before a live audience is televised. The relationship between acting spaces can be crucial to production, as when a stage version is remounted for television. Our cultural response to "history" dictates our response to drama based on history. If the private lives of politicians, celebrities, and aristocrats are now open to public scrutiny, those lives always were open to our observation in Shakespeare. Exceptions, such as Henry V, reveal their lack of an inner life by painfully exploring that absence. Richard II as gay male—a possibility that hovers around the script—makes more sense in our culture than it would have in earlier moments, when Richard was the poet who could not rule, a prelude to Hamlet. As rendered by Fiona Shaw, Richard becomes a powerful characterization, at least partly because he is unabashedly out of the closet.

The historical moment is itself a space that invites certain interpretations, that reinterprets the script for us. Both Trevor Nunn's wonderful *Twelfth Night* and the Tom Stoppard *Shakespeare in Love* explore gender issues that our zeitgeist have made available to us. Nunn uses his camera so that Viola can show us some things that Cesario hides from "his" environment. The zone created by a one- or two-reel silent version or a half-hour animated production of a given script obviously conditions what story can be derived from a more complicated and obviously far longer script. In each case, time becomes an enemy of effective narrative but also insists on emphasis. The results are not always or even usually the shallowness that the time-versus-script differential might lead us to anticipate.

My use of the concept of space has limits. I do not mean the area within the frame, as Anthony Davies tends to mean it (1988), or the space between observer and object or person observed, as Lorne Buchman defines it in usefully distinguishing between film and stage in his book (1991). By space I do mean the sheer size of a given script. The conflated *Hamlet,* for example, is titanic, even if we disregard the mythology that has grown up around it and the inevitable weight of other productions that any new production carries with it. Part of the history of Branagh's two-hour version is his longer version, from which he edits and from which he cannot escape, except to completely eliminate many of his long takes. The initial film inhibits his options for reducing the film to a standard length. At the same time, Michael Almereyda's budget kept his film, fatally I think, from re-creating the "lifestyles of the rich and famous."

Another space into which the script can move is adaptation. That is, not merely placing an edited version of the script in a particular historical moment—just before World War II, for example—but the effort to translate the script into, for example, the southern United States, which called themselves the Confederacy, in the 1860s, as in the NBC *Tempest*. Such translations can work generically, as in the case of opera and ballet, and they can work as films: Woody Allen's *A Midsummer Night's Sex Comedy*, for example.

What follows is not an attempt to "break new ground" with a theory and accompanying jargon that, assuming incomprehensibility to begin with, will be obsolete as the ink dries. Rather, this is an effort to describe and evaluate in conventional terms what has appeared in the past decade. Designed for popular media such as film and television, these productions deserve a non-esoteric response and a placement in their time, before they are either forgotten or carried off into ethereal zones of theory where very few can follow or wish to tread.

Chapter 1

Editing for Film:
1990–1996

One of the clichés of the past fifty years—I heard it retailed recently at the Newport Film Festival—is that "if Shakespeare were alive today, of course he'd be a filmmaker." The assertion is far too kind to most films being made today, but it is a valid statement about the medium of film. Film alone has the capacity to absorb Shakespeare's genius. It is not that Shakespeare could have transformed film and shown us what it was and could be—film has its geniuses—but that film alone has space enough for his almost boundless imagination. Film moves easily from the grittiest documentary to the most ethereal fantasy, and we, the audience, accept the conventions of each sub-genre without blinking. We have learned to read the signals regarding the degree of belief or disbelief we are to exercise as we experience the film. The great Shakespeare films have given us a glimpse of what Shakespeare might have been as filmmaker. As his own scripts seem sometimes sui generis and certainly distinct, each from each, the great films manifest different visions—the script as played through the prism of another imagination. We see Kurosawa's warriors lost in a fog at the beginning of *Throne of Blood*, a mist that is partly in the eyes of the beholders. We see Kozintsev's Lear and Cordelia in flowing robes going off to prison amid the rigid spears and thick helmets of Edmund's army, and we see his incomprehension—"Don't they know they've lost?" He goes into his fight with Edgar with doubt still lingering in his eyes. We see Welles's Falstaff break through the layers of ceremony that hedge the new Henry V, believing that it is still Hal in those robes and under that crown and within those clouds of incense, and being educated to the difference between "the thing I was" and the sudden plurality of kingship. In another great Welles film, we see Desdemona walking on a quay, far from where Iago and Othello talk on the parapets, the distance between Desdemona and Othello becoming emotionally infinite and eternally unbridgeable at the moment the camera discerns her and Iago turns her into "ancient history." We see Hamlet losing himself as he plays with the puppet he has made of Yorick's skull in Ragnar Lyth's great film. Hamlet becomes a child for a moment within a parenthesis in the sentences of death.

It may be that only film can transmit the archetype, the basic configuration of the narrative that makes it at once familiar to the individual and common to cultural experience. The archetype is not "trans-historical," as it is accused of being: it picks up the colorations and emphases of a specific zeitgeist as the story moves forward in time. The Shakespeare script tends to do the same thing, particularly if not forced into some concept of "correct" historical staging or narrowed into a specific time and place. The physical width and depth of film is space enough for the images, and its light sensitivity is transparent enough to transmit their deeper meanings and not just their surfaces.

Television is all surface, with the rare exception—the BBC *Our Mutual Friend*, for example, which incorporates some superb location shots on the upper Thames. The shots do not reach for "field of depth" but they are effective, like the one of Lizzie in her rowboat in the mist. For all the occasional effort to be "socially relevant," stage no longer seems to reach for meaning. The Royal Shakespeare Company (RSC) is cued to the tourist dollar, as it admits, and often produces confectionery Shakespeare around its bookstalls. Most shows on the West End or Broadway are merely "entertainment," if that. Even a great stage performance is available only to the few who can get to one of the few places in the world where one may occur. What is communicated in the media, of course, is a function of audience expectation, and perhaps the only medium that we will allow any depth or power is film.

The media have different relationships to time that dictate the strategies and tactics involved in adapting the Shakespearean script to its space. Film involves a reel pulling images past a light, bringing them to light frame by frame and enlarging the frame for us. The image expands above our heads, and we sense that enlargement in the depth field that contrasts with the emotional depth of close-ups, which are themselves larger than life. On film, the story literally rolls toward an ending. We can sense the shrinking supply of narrative. The circular movement of the light-seeking images makes the flashback technique easy. Stage tends to move in time—a narrative inset, of course, can serve as "flashback"—and television tends to be fixed in time. The constantly changing commercials for one product, which, in time, is often difficult to identify when compared with the product in older commercials, tells us that television is "present tense." "Old" television tends to have a dated quality. It tells of its practitioners' struggle with the medium. Older films tend to show us the medium's intersection with an historical moment, a culture. The television image is literally a bombardment. Television tape conflates the media. It is linear. It passes in front of us. While the stage shows us time passing, and while we can sense time passing as we sit there, the stage can also ask us to suspend our disbelief. The stage, then, can show us things that transcend the literal. Television's ability to do so is severely limited. Its ghosts and witches tend to be very conventional, very "human." Television can seldom show us anything other than "now" or take us very far from the assumptions of the room in which we are watching it. Film, of course, has its grammar and rhetoric, in which "distance, perspective, and relationships can change with the fluidity and subtlety of a line of verse," as Jack Jorgens says (1977, 25). Film, then, is a kind of language, but it is one to which we cannot speak back. It is like the green face of Oz thundering at us. We can pay some attention to the man behind the curtain, but we cannot approach and demand reciprocity. Film is, then, a superb medium for the half-truth of propaganda—as in the films of Sergei Eisenstein or Leni Reifenstahl—and, it follows, for the transmission of much more than half-truth. The great Shakespeare films insist that we sense that truth, whatever it is, and however it varies with the individual responding.

The successful Shakespeare film captures an archetype that is also in the script but that predates the script and which Shakespeare treats within his own conventions and with his own language. Archetypes are plastic energies, not immovable icons. Archetypes are a priori. An effort to create one results in the Ozymandias statue syndrome, because false icons fall like the swastika over the Reichstag, or one discovers that the invention has already occurred. Great films, of course, narrate stories that emerge from archetypes. *A Place in the Sun* depicts the dooming desire for wealth and status. Its title alludes to Icarus. *Sunset Boulevard*, as its title suggests, emerges from the dooming desire to turn time backward along its one-way avenue. *The Wizard of Oz* deals with wandering far from home, in a dream, into a land of dreams, and the wish to go home again, so it goes back at least as far as Genesis and *The Odyssey*. Editing Shakespeare for film involves editing toward visual images that work from our eyes to our imaginations. That process inevitably moves away from language.

It is not the conventions and language that make Shakespeare continually relevant but the archetype that reshapes itself within new historical circumstances suddenly discerned in the Shakespeare script. This phenomenon is inevitable, because, as Louis Montrose says, Shakespeare "generates action by combining conflicts grounded in such fundamental cultural categories as ethnicity, lineage, generation, gender, political faction, and social rank" (1996, 33). Add to that list the dynamics that must exist in any culture of tension between father and son; father and daughter; man and woman; man and power; woman and power; the fact of love, which has its variations in different cultures, of course, including the rubbing of noses; the fact of sexuality, which has basic similarities in any culture; and the fact of death, which is common to all cultures—and one finds archetypes working beneath the conventions of Shakespeare's stage and the "fixed" quality of his language. The script imitates an action basic to humankind, regardless of the variations that different cultures inscribe on the action. The action is prior to the language that may illuminate it or that may be unnecessary to reinforce its visualization. The Shakespeare film succeeds when it communicates these depth structures. That sounds easy enough. You don't get in the way of the mimetic transparency—once you have decided what story the script is telling. It is surprising, though, how often the camera gets in the way, how often directors simply erase what is potentially there in favor of their own conception, their own reshaping of the materials to conform with what their own vision may be. In saying that, I do not deny the need for interpretation of the script. It is also true that only a rare director can approximate the level of genius that even the most humble of Shakespeare scripts invites. Sometimes, however, it is simple, like Olivier's camera booming out from Henry V's orations to include the army being incorporated by the words, or Welles's camera in *Chimes at Midnight* capturing the breath of people in cold cathedrals, the ghosts of dying people in a winter kingdom. In the great Shakespeare films, technique serves vision. The great Shakespeare directors discover, in their very different ways, how to translate the archetype into one of its images, and, in their films, into a sequence of images.

It is a good thing that Shakespeare did not become a filmmaker. The great interpreters of his scripts on film are very different. They demonstrate the options that a given script offers a director. They show us how different the same script, or praxis, can be when reshaped by the imagination of a Kurosawa, a Kozintsev, or a Welles. Furthermore, Shakespeare's *films* would be trapped in time, in the conventions, camera angles, actors, and editing techniques of a specific time, capable of knowing only the history available at the moment of production and embedded in that moment, whether consciously or not. Samuel Crowl shows how the Mankiewicz *Julius Caesar* insisted that its audience in the United States respond from its experience of McCarthyism (Davies and Wells 1994). If not coerced into a specific period or political configuration, the Shakespeare script will interrogate an instant in culture almost accidentally. Shakespeare the filmmaker would not have been able to do so. Films are invariably of their time. The script is free of time until the time of its production and, if it is effectively imagined, then it speaks *of* a time and that time's approach to film and script. Film as genre has the same quality, as does its ancestor, the photograph. We now see, however, how film and the Shakespeare script move forward in time to tell us with remarkable precision where we are. The combination of film and script has no predictive power, of course, but it is easy to predict that one or more of the scripts will be seen to be suddenly "relevant" in a future moment and that a film will be made of it. I am surprised that no one has made a film of *Troilus and Cressida* and will not bore anyone with the issues in the script that are "very much alive today." I was surprised that Julie Taymor did a film of *Titus Andronicus*, but I was pleased that she did. The film becomes irrelevant only when Taymor's images lapse into current clichés—the boy at the outset, warrior robotics, and the "hope for peace" at the end, the latter as stereotypic a political ploy today as it was for the Elizabethan ("and after, holiday!"), and is not to be taken seriously. As we Unknown Citizens learn, "When there was peace, he was for it. / When there was war, he went."

Essex's followers, who commissioned an "old play"—*Richard II*—on the eve of their rebellion against Elizabeth, were wrong about what the play says. However *Richard II* may denigrate its title character, it cannot be said to justify rebellion against a bad prince. Deposition, as Carlisle predicts, will bring on the Wars of the Roses. The play does, however, move forward to absorb the new meanings moving up from the seeds of time. That is what Essex's followers were trying to say. In that sense, they were ahead of their time.

The Films of the Early to Mid-1990s

I want to look briefly at some recent films in light of the space of performance—the problematic relationship between film and stage, the film and the archetypes in the script, and the film in time—the time of the script, the moment of the film's emergence, and the inevitably subjective response the film elicits from the critic, who is also implicated in time.

One would like to believe that the reason for all the Shakespeare films in the mid-1990s is that at last stage and film are communicating with each other. Kenneth Branagh did a *Henry V* on the stage in 1984 before he made the 1989 film that can be credited with starting the current welcome deluge, and he did a "complete" *Hamlet* for Adrian Noble before making his four-hour film version. Branagh's *A Midwinter's Tale* is about a production of *Hamlet* in a provincial town full of empty churches, empty pockets, and full pubs. It is a Mickey-and-Judy venture that succeeds because of its many built-in ineptitudes. Tom Stoppard's brilliant film of *Rosencrantz and Guildenstern Are Dead* is based on his play, but it is very different, not just as film is different from stage; it is a different script. Richard Loncraine's *Richard III* is a "historicized" version of the Richard Eyre production at the Royal National Theatre in 1990, which sketched in its fascist background against our suspension of disbelief. Noble's film of *A Midsummer Night's Dream* is based on his stage version. Branagh's new *Love's Labour's Lost* continues the amateur theatrical mode in a sense, in that it is constructed as if it were a Hollywood film of the 1930s; the wide screen and Technicolor are added, but Fred and Ginger are absent.

Although Branagh had played Benedick in a *Much Ado* directed by Judi Dench for the Renaissance Theatre, his film version has him engaging in slapstick sight gags with lawn chairs. His sentimentalizing of the Beatrice-Benedick story tends to squander a superb performance by Emma Thompson, a moving and vulnerable Beatrice. The film is further undercut by the irrelevant background music that Branagh cannot seem to avoid in his films. Peter Greenaway's *Prospero's Books* features a great stage actor in the late John Gielgud and a very conventional reading of *The Tempest*, but it is very far from any sense of the stage. The Oliver Parker *Othello* has no stage production behind it and is so heavily edited toward the imagery of film that it edits out the words that show why Othello is doomed, regardless of the malign workings of Iago. Al Pacino's

Looking for Richard is a documentary about making a film of *Richard III* in a city innocent of any knowledge of William Shakespeare (though that ignorance could be a function of the editing of the documentary). Trevor Nunn, director of *Twelfth Night*, has never directed the play on stage. Nunn bought four of his stage productions brilliantly to television—*Antony and Cleopatra*, *Macbeth*, *The Comedy of Errors*, and *Othello*.

Luhrmann's *Romeo + Juliet*

Baz Luhrmann's *Romeo + Juliet* is aggressively a film. One doubts that any of its participants have ever spoken in a theater, except perhaps to have caused a disturbance in the fourth row. Luhrmann's film does not attempt to explain the origin of the feud. It simply is, like a poisonous plant with a deep network of unseen roots. The film is not set in bitter cities such as Belfast or Sarajevo, but in a huge neutral metropolis—Ciudad Mexico—that serves, like the ancient feud, as a background, or subtext, for the aimless ebb and flow of teenage activity.

The film's major metaphor is religion, which is shown to be irrelevant. The originating script suggests the evisceration of Christian symbols and the ceding of power to those crossing stars of which the chorus warns. In a radically condensed shooting script, Luhrmann leaves in the line about "Some consequence hanging in the stars," and Romeo's "I am fortune's fool," his "I defy you stars," and his line about "shak[ing] the yoke of inauspicious stars." The pistol with which Romeo kills Tybalt has an ivory portrait of the Madonna on its stock. The church has a huge Christ on top gazing down on Romeo's murder of Tybalt. Romeo holds his arms out, echoing the Christ figure, as he shouts about being fortune's fool. The statue itself is under repair beneath its widespread arms. It is a decaying monument in a world of mere bad luck. Were we to infer backward like revisionists, we would conclude that Christ's crucifixion resulted from a random roll of the dice. Tybalt, his own arms held out, floats in his own spreading blood at the foot of the stony Savior. The pool is the fatal analogue of the one in the Capulet garden, where Romeo and Juliet bubble their unfathomable love in silence. Tybalt, standing in front of a Gruenwald crucifixion, sees Romeo and vows vengeance.

The Friar has a huge cross tattooed upon his back. He gives good advice about "violent delights hav[ing] violent ends," but he drinks, smokes pot, and betrays a liking of little boys. He fantasizes headlines of reconciliation. His imagery is that of this society. His is a tabloid imagination. The Apothecary's door is adorned with pictures of the Virgin and Child torn from magazines. The bandage on Romeo's wounded left arm is stained with a red cross of blood. A red cross rests later against a funeral wreath. Red crosses are painted on the Friar's medicine cabinet and on the unnecessary ambulances that come to pick up the bodies of the lovers. The Montague stretch limo sports a bronze cross behind the back seat. When Laurence says "My lady stirs!"—anticipating Juliet's awakening—the camera shows a quartz Virgin and Child, Christ and Mary as clock. Deity is now a commercialized subject of time rather than the point at which time ceases and eternity begins. The cross that links the names of the lovers in the film's title is an ironic icon, a signal of emptiness, not of completion.

A compensatory softness plays against these obscene images— of sheets, curtains, the clothes on the statuary of the Capulet garden, the gauze on Juliet's bier. The god Pan stands near the Capulet pool, a pagan god surviving into this overly Christianized culture representing energies that have no outlet where religion has lost its mystery and surrendered to the conventions of a meaningless feud. The lovers see each other first through a fishbowl. It is a mutual vision through the unconscious of desired completion, the archetype of the self, mirrored as a beloved alterego. Romeo and Juliet enjoy their moment in the swirling roil of the pool—bubbles full of words that cannot be found in the language—and in the grotto on the dawn of their wedding morning—these are lovers saying goodbye in wartime—then reach the sequel of the tomb. All of that is almost wordless here, a silence earned against the tumult of the whirl of meaningless noise around them. The film shows them yearning unconsciously for the silence they find, the silence of death. The strength of their love and its fragility are vivified by the environment the film provides for it.

If one responds to the *language*, as opposed to the images, then one's conclusion is likely to resemble that of Thomas Pendleton: "This is an extremely unintelligent work, and the fidelity to Shakespeare's language is often accompanied by ignorance about the language...[T]he effect is much like a *Monty Python* skit" (1998, 66).

The images show teenagers drifting toward death, as Peter Blos says they must in his classic study on adolescence. Historical circumstances suddenly make sense of the Shakespeare script—or it makes sense of them by holding the magnet of the narrative up against the undifferentiated sprinkle of filings that is the moment. In 1968, a very different film, Zeffirelli's version, explored the generational conflict that pervaded society (not just in the United States) as a result of the U.S. government's misguided activity in Southeast Asia.

Library of the Magus

Among the silliest of recent films is Peter Greenaway's *Prospero's Books*. Greenaway substitutes the crawling, squirming insides of books—as if their covers were rocks that had been lifted up—for whatever the script may be saying. He imposes television upon film, a blatant reduction of scale and artistic premises as he gives us a seemingly interminable Home Shopping Network sequence, in which actors so out of work that they have pawned their very clothes present fish and bananas to Ferdinand and Miranda. Within this misconception, Greenaway can do nothing with Caliban, giving us instead a standard new critical version of the play. Suppose he had pursued Caliban's suggestion that Prospero's books must be seized, that they are a source of power, and depicted a contest for control of the media. Seize his books—and then his television station! As it is, even Miranda's potential to bring forth a brave brood for Stephano is hardly an issue here. The isle is full of naked people presumably prepared to give delight and not get hurt. That this film has become the favorite of the theorists argues that it was not made to bring a new interpretation of a complicated script before audiences but to attract the avant-garde to its gimmicks. Not much time will go by before the film is seen for the travesty that it is.

Fascist with a Withered Arm

The Richard Loncraine *Richard III*, fixed as it is in an explicit 1930s London, cannot reach for the script's deeper register. Unlike Luhrmann's *Romeo and Juliet*, this film attempts to explain rather than to explore. "Oh yes—fascist takeover!" we exclaim, looking for the familiar signals. London under Nazi Germany is brilliantly depicted in Kevin Brownlow's gritty, black-and-white film *It Happened Here* (1966).

In the inherited script, Richard's experience triggers a response from within him. It explodes outward from the a priori principles at which he has sneered and will sneer again once he dismisses conscience as a word that cowards use. The film can only move toward a satire that it has not announced. A smirking Richmond watches a happy Richard drop into a bonfire inhabited by the late Al Jolson, warbling a 1925 song. While "I'm Sitting on Top of the World" is meant to remind us of James Cagney in a 1949 film, *White Heat*, the song is an optimistic hymn to the booming 1920s. James Loehlin suggests that "the specific use of Jolson alludes to a defining moment in film history, the introduction of sound in *The Jazz Singer*" (1997, 76). The songs that would have done *that* are "Dirty Hands, Dirty Face," "Blue Skies," or "Mammy." The year 1925 was the height of the silent film era, the moment of Gilbert, Valentino, and the debut of Garbo. If the allusion is intended, it punishes anyone who knows how to read a calendar. The archetypal 1930s song is "Brother, Can You Spare a Dime?" as rendered by Bing Crosby. Now that would have been funny, as Richard plunges away, hand held out. Unable to go where the script goes, the film settles for inanity and trusts that post-modernism's ample mantle will accept that category as well.

The film's best moment, when the royals view the newsreel of their elevation to power in a momentary conflation of the event and its observation, is isolated. It reminds us that the Nazis used film as part of their propaganda and that we know Nazi Germany by film. Goebbels was filming his epic about Frederick the Great, pulling troops from the front to serve as extras in the spring of 1945, even as Zhukov drove from the Vistula to the Oder, only forty miles from Berlin. Here we might have seen Buckingham screening an edited film of the population's less than enthusiastic *collaudatio* for Richard, à la Leni Reifenstahl's *Triumph of the Will*. Films about films can be exciting. This script was imported into a moment in history that obscured whatever may be going on in the script. Perhaps *overwhelmed* is a better word to describe the effect of the setting on the play, as Pendleton suggests: "The relocation of the action to England of the Thirties [is] pursued into incoherence. [The film] so grievously underestimated the power of the Nazi imagery that [it] ends up telling a visual story different from and at odds with the ostensible narrative of Richard of Gloucester" (1998, 65).

The stage version, directed by Richard Eyre at the National Theatre in 1990, pulled us into a nightmare world of black uniforms, klieg lights, and summary executions. The stage forces us to fill in the details with our imaginations, so that our suspension of disbelief became a powerful continuum in which we let belief take hold of us. The grim rooms around the single lightbulbs under which prisoners were interrogated became visible to us and were multiplied down a terrifying regress into other countries and other times. We could sense, just out of sight, the thousand outstretched arms, the clump of the goosestep down the Champs Elysées or Oxford Street, the triumph of the will. By trying to make it all "real," this film does not permit us to believe any of it.

Branagh's Footnote to *Hamlet*

Kenneth Branagh's *A Midwinter's Tale* (for non-U.S. consumption, known as *In the Bleak Midwinter*) trades on clichés—a threadbare group of actors going to a town called Hope to do *Hamlet* in a run-down church at Christmas: the director who threatens suicide in front of his company, and almost has to go through with it, since the counter-thesis is a long time in announcing itself; the cynical older actor who has never played Shakespeare; the ingenue who calls this ragtag group her "family"; the actor who cannot remember his lines; the designer whose "concept" is "space," then "smoke"; the agent who would pull her client out of the play for a three-film Hollywood contract; the Ophelia who actually slaps Hamlet during a performance, and so forth. Some of the configurations go back to the backstage dramas of the 1930s. Add to the stereotypical characters and situations that the actor who cannot remember his lines also drinks to forget the rest of his life (he drinks so much that he is likely to influence the next harvest, as one of his colleagues warns); that the ingenue is virtually blind but won't wear glasses and thus makes entrances that are bone-threatening crashes; and that the director will spend precious moments with Francisco to find the most frightening moment of his life, so that "Who's there?" will project the fullness of fear to the audience; and that the actor's subtext is changing a tire on a busy motorway, which he mimes before Bernardo's entrance, and you have unpromising material indeed. Then consider that the production of *Hamlet*—which does occur—brings a son to his father, a mother to her son, a father to his daughter, two lovers (Hamlet and Ophelia) together, Hollywood contracts to two minor actors (the male a wicked parody of the great Patrick Stewart), and Christmas bells sprinkling like crystal over the depressed village, and you cry, "Oh no!"

But out of this comes a funny and moving film that transforms the bleak midwinter into a Christmas card. The film is caviary to the general, almost all subtext, some of it having to do with the history of British theater, some with the play *Hamlet*. The film is superbly edited and timed, insisting in a Capotesque way that we overhear the lines as one sequence dissolves into the next. Nicholas Farrell develops a subtextual foxiness for his Reynaldo. Gerald Horan delivers his "And let him ply his music!" as if he were Coriolanus haranguing the Roman mob. The church in which the play is to occur is also the "digs" for the actors. Two sleep in the crypt—"cryptic actors," as one of them says. A cardboard Shakespeare watches the performance, and a cutout American Indian also observes, stonily absorbing the political incorrectness that Mickey and Judy are perpetuating with their extravaganza. But what begins as murder in the cathedral ends as a community of the spirit, as the setting gradually exchanges its irony for its sacramental values.

Stoppard's Play as Film

Tom Stoppard's *Rosencrantz and Guildenstern Are Dead* is likely to get lost in the flood of filmed Shakespeare, but it is brilliant. The camera moves fluidly in and out of various planes of reality, insisting that we as audience question the *level* of illusion at work during any given moment of what we know to be an illusion known as motion picture. At "Gonzago," a masked king and queen observe puppets. The King (Donald Sumpter) rises and looks back on masked players as a flash of recognition leaps back and erases all levels of fiction. The masks come off the players and Hamlet believes that Claudius has also been unmasked. Perhaps he has—but for whom? Rosencrantz interprets the King's reaction in aesthetic terms. "It wasn't *that* bad," he says, as he and Guildenstern exit through the wreckage.

As Hamlet and Claudius vie to impose their contradictory interpretations upon Elsinore, the film addresses the question of art itself and its relationship to other modes of representation, even that of nature itself, as Rosencrantz brilliantly but fruitlessly experiments with it. His discoveries include gravity, the principle of harmonics, the law of acceleration, the aerodynamic application of Bernouilli's principle, steam power, the laws of equal and opposite reaction and of conservation of energy, and aspects of vector theory and convection. In addition, he sets a new record of forty-two seconds for keeping a paper plane in the air, shattering the old record of eighteen and eight-tenths seconds set by Ken Blackburn. Rosencrantz is finding meanings a century before Newton, but he is a mute, inglorious Newton, because, as Elizabeth Wheeler says, "Perception both on an individual and a societal level is necessary for awareness of significance" (1991, 5). Since no cultural perception occurs, no reality pertains to anything that Rosencrantz discovers. To put it another way, Rosencrantz's observations do not translate to the two criteria that Stephen Hawking assigns to a scientific theory: description and prediction (1988, 9). Furthermore, as Bohr and Heisenberg have shown us, observation changes what is observed, physically and in translation into language and replicable modes. Here, the phenomena observed become alms for an oblivion to be given shape much later in a new physics that itself will move from Newton's static cosmos through Einstein's "cosmological constant" to Hubble's observation that the universe is expanding. In a sense, nature is like the Shakespearean script—the "meanings" are there, but the circumstances required for their articulation and formulation have not yet occurred. The script is expanding in ways that will come to be seen in retrospect to have been within the measurements of relativity and, as the changes occur, within the much smaller dimensions of quantum mechanics. Rosencrantz, even as he demolishes Aristotelian paradigms, cannot bring his insights to completion. His discoveries prove that probability *is* at work in his world, but the proof resides within a model yet to be defined.

Rosencrantz's disquisition on being alive or dead in a box comes half true. Neither state is reached, since their existential bodies have been hanged, but their roles as characters remain inside the Players' wagon on the stage that can be lowered at a moment's notice. They are alive *and* dead. They are inside the play, thus potentially inside a fiction that is their only "life" that will not recognize this time either. They are doomed to silence on rotting pages or to an endless repetition of the same questions without answers, a recurring nightmare. They may get a whiff of déjà vu now and then, but they are doomed to believe that each moment in this old and familiar play is always and forever the first and only time. They are in that script, their parts "written," as the Player says, as if the play were the book of fate. They are not dead exactly, but they can come alive only in the estranging world known as *Hamlet*. Guildenstern recognizes "Gonzago," but he does not recognize that "Gonzago" is a play within a play or that he is within a play, both Shakespeare's and Stoppard's. The snippets of *Hamlet* that Stoppard includes in his play suggest that a fate *is* at work, but it is the specific scenario dictated by Shakespeare. They can come out of the script box (even if other characters mix their names up)—"Hey you, what's your name, come out of there!" as Rosencrantz demands—but it is a movement from stasis, suspended animation into an unfree, scripted environment, where, as Guildenstern says, "There's something they're not telling us."

When Hamlet escapes to the pirate ship, Guildenstern complains, "We need Hamlet for our release." What he means is that they "need *Hamlet* for their release." They will not get Hamlet to England, but *Hamlet* will get them there and provide sudden closure. Hamlet has rewritten the commission, and *Hamlet* will not release them. That closure will occur in each production, after they have struggled through the same confusion, that is, unless a director such as Olivier erases them altogether. There never was a moment when they could have said "No," nor will there be. They will never understand the play in which they participate. Nor will we, of course. The existential commentary rides out, making us much more like them than Hamlet, who at least motivates much of what he does not understand either.

More Iago Than Moor

Oliver Parker's *Othello* moves to Cyprus without a storm. Oars pull onto an uncontested beach along a placid bay. The Venetians land, to the delight of the Cypriots, in scenes reminiscent of the newsreel shots from Sicily in 1943. Othello rides up the hill and into the square on a magnificent black charger. His superb and hubristic speech on landing ("Now have I my content so absolute") is almost completely erased in exchange for a long kiss delivered to Desdemona. The crowd is uneasy—the war is not officially over yet. If they "resent and envy [Othello's] triumphs," as Janet Maslin says (1995), the envy is muted. Racism, if present, is only subtly conveyed. In the Olivier film (1970), Frank Finlay's Iago keeps glancing at Othello's very black hand clasping Maggie Smith's very white one. We get the point. Here, Othello merely announces that the Turks are drowned. Perhaps their boats were leaky. Perhaps they all followed each other in formation into the rocks. We get no sense of Cyprus having had a close brush with a brutal occupation or any hint that Othello represents a version of invader. If that agency is removed, we get no sense of the Turk rising from the stormy sea (the "Pontic") within Othello to beat a Venetian and traduce the state. If the fatal absoluteness he vaunts as he sees Desedemona is cut, we get no sense that what happens is a tragedy. Here, we should have been allowed to pause for a moment to *listen* to Othello before the script began to pursue its pell-mell descent into darkness and error.

Our belief in what happens—and film does not ask us to suspend our *dis*belief—rests on Iago's four syllables —"I hate the Moor." We may get a hint of sexual jealousy, in that Iago mentions Othello's having done Iago's office between Iago's sheets, but we are meant, I think, to accept this hatred as motiveless malignity. Branagh follows Henry Irving's advice and plays Iago as extremely affable, a chap you'd be likely to invite to dinner after a brief conversation. What makes him believable to us is that he is permitted to address us directly in close-up. This is a stage technique, of course, seldom employed within the "distancing" lens of a film camera. It takes a confident actor to bring this off, of course, but the direct approach helps us to accept Iago's confidence. At one point, after Roderigo learns to his ecstasy that Cassio has been cashiered, Iago turns to us. Roderigo returns to clap Iago on the back. Iago gives us an exasperated look. The reason we believe in Iago is because he believes in us. Iago's only problem is Roderigo, who keeps leaping at him unexpectedly like Wile E. Coyote in a Roadrunner cartoon. One of the best scenes in the film is Roderigo's confrontation with Iago (4.2). Here Michael Maloney holds a dagger close to Iago's left eye. Iago is in danger, but he translates the threat into "Why, now I see there's mettle in thee." Iago is getting in over his head, and it is *Roderigo* who makes the point.

Parker's editing has one major payoff. The first part of 3.3, the long and central scene of the play, begins as a workout in the tiltyard, moves inside as Othello and Iago towel off, and then down into the armory. The "film moves," as Samuel Crowl astutely notes, "from the daylight world of military exercises, where Othello meets and parries Iago's thrusts, down into a murkier environment where physical blows are replaced by verbal ones" (1996, 42). Othello has heard of unfaithful wives, it seems, and jealousy. He does not think it can happen to him, but he is calmly prepared for it should it occur. Parker shifts the scenes and the time of 3.3, so that the pressure of Iago's manipulation of Othello from conceptual to experiential modes of understanding is plausible. The handkerchief *becomes* talismanic—Desdemona smiles at him from his fantasies to say that these stolen moments are hers. It is the taunting, not just the infidelity, that tortures him. Iago reshapes the past for Othello so that he becomes not just a stranger to Venice but a stranger to himself and what he knew. He becomes a voyeur peeking through windows in his imagination at something that happens only there. Thus Othello can "peak" in increments, fueled by cannily placed hallucinations of Cassio and Desdemona naked in bed. This imposed rhythm is powerful, particularly as Othello's rage begins to flow toward a "reasonable" conclusion—evenge for a "cause" larger than the personal. This sector of the film is particularly potent because Laurence Fishburne splendidly underplays the words. This film is underrated, I think, among the several Shakespeare films of the 1990s. It might have emerged from an understanding that one of Othello's great strengths is his command of language. Strength in a tragic hero is also doom, of course. We should have been permitted to hear Othello tread the fatal carpet of his own rhetoric as he lands at Cyprus. We needed that to sense the shape of Shakespeare's tragic structure.

Nunn's *Twelfth Night*

Twelfth Night is a difficult script out of which to craft a film—we cannot believe that the others believe that that's a boy! The play has seldom worked in a realistic medium—one can recall Joan Plowright's ludicrous attempt to double Viola and Cesario in a television production of the 1960s. But Nunn goes right to the gender issue, and Imogen Stubbs, in a brilliant comic role reminiscent of Harold Lloyd, shows how hard it is even to be a stereotypical male. And it is, of course. It is a learned behavior that requires constant energy and ceaseless vigilance lest the pose be revealed *as* pose. It does, finally, demand an escape into the feminine, either positively as psychic integration or negatively in a destruction of a fragile persona that cannot be put together again. The film splendidly depicts the psychology of gender issues—Stubbs chafes from riding a horse astride, turns green from smoking a cigar, watches a sure scratch turn into a superb snooker shot, and at the same time gets Orsino to fall for the androgynous self that lies beneath the superficial man so that her transformation into woman, which lies just beyond the film's ending, is a natural further step in a process the film has charted.

Viola's disguise becomes Nunn's metaphor within a naturalistic medium: What is gender? What are the limits of stereotype? How do stereotypic gender roles block communications within a psyche and, therefore, between human beings? In this sense, the film, for all of its fidelity to "the text," speaks directly to us. Shakespeare is asking the same questions that we are—or so it always seems when good acting finds a home in a context that works for the script. Nunn embraces wholeheartedly the boy-meets-girl-and-problems-result convention within which the interrogation can be launched. It is important, says Nunn, that spectators not "get off the hook of the play by dismissing it as an improbable archaic comedy" (Fineline 1996, 4), that they accept what they *share* with the characters. The "movie suggests that an essential sexual ambiguity exists in all of us," as Stephen Holden says, particularly, perhaps, "once the defining plumage of one sex has been exchanged for that of the other" (1996, C3). As in *As You Like It*, the exchange in *Twelfth Night* creates a psychological continuum within which narrow assumptions can erode and be replaced by the process of individuation. That is not true of all Orsinos in production, of course, but it seems to be true here.

Viola and Sebastian are shown early to enjoy playing games with their twinship, as they do in entertaining the passengers of the doomed ship just before it hits its rock. She has already learned to don a mustache in the game of identicality, so the game of interchangeability comes readily, if not altogether easily. Sebastian's clothes survive in a salt-stained trunk, so her assumption of a male role is part of an organic development. She straps down her breasts, adds a handkerchief to her pants. The transformation is consistent with William Wright's book on identical twins (1996). Wright shows (although he does not explicate the issue) that identical twins replicate each other's external habits—dress, preferences in food and drink, employment—and have similar scores on IQ tests and comparable results on personality analysis tests, but often contrast in basic values. The twins Jack and Oskar Yufe, one of Wright's prime examples, became respectively a member of a kibbutz in Israel and a member of the Hitler Youth in Germany. They had uncannily similar personal habits, but clearly the biological model does not account for socially constructed personas. While Viola and Sebastian may exhibit a tendency toward similar preferences, they also demonstrate marked distinctions based on gender. Viola wants a beard, all right, but not on her face. Her transgender behavior, however successful, is, as Orsino says "much against the mettle of [her] sex."

The camera closes up on the small moments when Viola responds to her masquerade and enforces our belief in her intrinsic gender and character—who she is and who she longs to be. Pendleton suggests that the opening sequence of Viola and Sebastian on shipboard "provides an emotional base for Viola's sadness, vulnerability, resilience, and hope" (1998, 66). Pendleton goes on to say that the "emotional climax of the film…is the reunion of brother and sister, not of their pairing off with their lovers" (66). In other words, as Jo Becker, the narrator of Sue Miller's *While I Was Gone*, says of "the mysterious dark twininess" of her twins: "They cared most about each other" (1999, 16). The importance of the reunion of Viola and Sebastian cannot be overemphasized in film or in the script, but the corollary of Viola's disguise is that Orsino takes her at face value, an assessment that makes her outer role easy but that complicates things for the woman beneath, in this case, the military uniform, particularly since Orsino is very attracted to the boy *as* boy. On stage, the effects have to be exaggerated—Orsino's clap on the back, his comradely arm around Cesario's shoulder. Here, the discrepancy in awarenesses is subtly delineated, so that instead of insisting that we suspend our disbelief, this Viola makes us believe that she can almost *become* a male, even against the increasing urgency of her womanhood.

The film occurs in early autumn, the time of Keats's "mist and mellow fruitfulness." The moment helps explain how Nunn "firmly attained the play's elusive tone of sweetness and sadness," as Pendleton says (1998, 66). Malvolio's deciphering of Maria's letter is accomplished with the help of a cold pastoral—an armless Venus—that he imagines to be warm and pulsing, eager to enclose him in its nakedness. Mist washes the empty choirs of the oak, and apples await their baskets in Olivia's orchard. It is not a cherry orchard. Olivia's potentially destructive sexuality will be socially absorbed. Helena Bonham Carter's snapping eyes suggest that she would like to free herself of her mourning. Malvolio has read her correctly, but he mistakes in reading himself as the agent of the release.

Orsino's castle is on an island, upon a causeway open only at low tide. It is a dream castle, often viewed from a distance, an outcropping of consciousness scarcely rising above the surface. There Orsino, having been wounded in a recent action, reclines, while his officers await orders. Toby Steven's Orsino is a version of William Meredith's Willoughy Patterne in *The Egoist*. Olivia, for all of her assumed melancholy, lives above a vast kitchen over which Malvolio presides, the duke of downstairs. Appetite lies underneath pretense, in Malvolio, in Olivia's house, in Olivia. Upstairs, the curtains are drawn against the watery autumn light, but the velvet hangings, painted Italian wallpaper, and sound-absorbing Persian rugs suggest, as Anthony Lane says, a "sumptuous relish in [Olivia's] mourning" (1996, 74). Hers is a Thackerayan world in which the widow's weeds must be carefully cut, the roast for the mourners rarely done, and the port so rich that mourners will beg a bottle now that the owner's shade has passed through the wine cellar. Between the castle and the country house is a fishing village, patrolled by Orsino's ominous mounted police. At one point, as they are chasing Antonio, the constabulary upsets a cart and slithers around a corner on a carpet of hake and seaweed, an image that links the ocean's abundant energy with the festive tables of the aristocrats and the fact that the linkage, at that point, has not been made. The piano at which Sebastian and Viola had sat becomes a tinkling set of keys on the tossing surf. They are ultimately washed to silence on the shore, but they suggest the coming of music to the Illyria peninsula, its many pianos and several songs, its harmonies waiting to be heard. The as-yet-unheard melodies of reconciliation and relationship are signaled by the opening episode on the ship and by the sounds that wash up on shore.

Nunn distributes the script to various locations, so that, as with many films of Shakespeare, knowledge of the script is not an advantage. Viola's soliloquy after Malvolio delivers the ring to her occurs in segments at different moments. The technique suggests how awarenesses and relationships can grow by increments over time and suggests, as film can do better than stage, that lives continue in spaces the camera visits only occasionally and that insights arrive randomly, often between scheduled activities. It is not that Shakespeare's stage cannot create private space or achieve a montage effect by shifting from place to place, which we identify by being told where or who the characters are. Often, in Shakespeare's scenes, we are told much that a quick camera can show us more economically. "Establishing shots" are verbal—"So this is the Forest

of Arden." "This is Illyria, Lady." Once Shakespeare gets his
characters out on stage, however, he likes to keep them there, as in
Viola's soliloquy, in which her insights develop with interrogation
but without much pause, and in which she tells us that she is in
love with Orsino. Nunn gives us all of this in psychologically
plausible snippets.

Loo[King] for [Richard]

Al Pacino's technique in *Looking for Richard* is to build areas of activity
that can then become points of reference. Few films are as self-
allusive as this one. Pacino cuts back and forth from Richard's
opening soliloquy to a discussion of what it means. He shows us
rehearsals and establishes the performance itself, a costumed drama
amid the Romanesque arches of the Cloisters, the medieval wing of
The Metropolitan Museum. He and his director walk the streets
around Times Square, interrogating the pedestrians and panhandlers
of the city. The effort to make the film also incorporates seeking an
elusive "Shakespeare." Who is he, or it, to the people thronging
amid the horns and police whistles? Will the film be made? One
Italian man, claiming ignorance of Shakespeare, leaves Pacino at a
"Walk" sign, saying "To be or not to be, that is the question!" For
one of the first times in the twentieth century, the line absorbs
meaning from its context. When a panhandler talks about
Shakespeare and *feeling*, we suddenly understand why Pacino leaves
in the lines about "a giving vein," "impotent and snail-pac'd
beggary," and "the famished beggars, weary of their bones." "Spare
some change?" the beggar has asked.

Once Pacino's system is established, and once we have been
educated to it, all the worlds of the film become available as points
of reference. As happens in the montage, the whole adds up to more
than the sum of its parts. Gritty city, tourist attraction, rehearsal,
and costumed performance move us in space and in perceived
time—not just the Cloisters' interpretation of the past, but the
pressure on the specific production of *Richard III* as well. The
dynamics are both spatial and teleological. Two Richards—one an
actor in rehearsal on the floor of the Cloisters and another sweating
in the dawn before Bosworth and death of life and soul; one in a
close-up, the other in a side shot, as if lying in state—alternate in
reading the lines. The sequence brilliantly suggests the split that
the character perceives within himself, worldly monarch versus

Al Pacino as Richard III. *Photo courtesy of Twentieth Century–Fox.*

truth-speaking jester; the debate between body and soul; and the technique that creates a character who runs up against an unalterable law oblivious to his consummate improvisational skills. Richard's dream looks ahead to his battle. The film incorporates glimpses of its own future as part of the shattered imagery of nightmare. The soliloquy is turned into a dramatic film. Since the film uses different moments as points of reference, it can suddenly permit itself to take upon itself the power of prediction.

Noble's Nightmare

I found Adrian Noble's *A Midsummer Night's Dream* on stage for the Royal Shakespeare Company in 1994 full of the ideas of other directors. If a criterion of the Shakespeare film is that it somehow reveals an archetype lurking in the script, this one fails. As film, as on stage, it does not edit toward any thematic or generic focus. It uses the doors of the stage production to little effect. Doors are the stuff of farce, of *Comedy of Errors* or *I Love Lucy*. Nothing is learned in farce. Situations are resolved. On the stage and in the film, the doors lead from nowhere to nowhere. They are gimmicks trying to disguise their irrelevance to anything in the script and they do not deal with the complicated issue of who the lovers are—if anybody—before, during, and after their experience in the woods. Here, the woods are lightbulbs. It is one thing to wish to avoid a conventional stage—or film—forest. If that is the director's wish, he or she must provide a substitute that is at least "a closely related idea," or something that permits us to link the words of the script to what we see. Lightbulbs on 4-foot-high flexible poles are simply silly. The film uses the stage's huge red umbrella. On stage, the umbrella rose with Bottom and Titania encouched within it. Here, it sails off on a sea of dew, so I add Winkin, Blinkin, and Nod to the other irrelevant associations the umbrella gathered to itself—Traveler's Insurance, "Pennies from Heaven," and "Up a Chimney Down." Noble borrows Mamillius from his *Winter's Tale* stage production for the Royal Shakespeare Company in 1992 to make the film a little boy's nightmare, thus overlaying a further story on a script already complicated by many narratives that call for contrasting styles and imaginative integration within the same production. M. P. Jackson says that the play "is unique among Shakespeare's comedies in its subtle interactions between different orders of reality and illusion" (1999, 29). At the end, the little boy

E GENTE / REFORMA, miércoles 12 de febrero de 1997

"Looking for Richard" in Mexico City. *Courtesy of Reforma.*

is integrated into the world of his nightmare, apparently never regaining consciousness. His mother, we assume, finds him cold in bed in the morning. Jackson suggests that the imposition of the boy on the script is "a bad idea. Shakespeare's play is far too adult a fantasy for this fresh-faced innocent, and the pajama-clad child becomes a mere irritant" (1999, 37).

While one must edit for film, Noble's televisual approach (as if he were televising a stage production) might have permitted more language to enter his shooting script. Hermia's plea for patience, immediately and amusingly countered by Lysander's plan for escape, is gone, as is Titania's powerful description of the vicarious pregnancy she has experienced through her votaress—a motive for her retention of the boy—as is Hermia's hilarious rationalization that Helena has "urged her height," as is Bottom's splendid parody of I Corinthians 2:9, as is Hippolyta's besting of Theseus about "the story of the night." Thus much of the dramatic give and take of the inherited script is simply erased. The film does nothing with the lovers, eradicating the superb role of Helena. Nor does the film establish any pace or rhythm. Instead, we get confusing cuts to the boy, who is by turns observing, manipulating, hiding, dreaming, and calling for his mother.

The film does not get beyond its premises as staged play. Why this stage production was selected to be filmed remains a mystery to me. In the film, the occasional metaphor of theater—the toy stage that becomes the real stage for "Pyramus and Thisbe"—suffers a midair collision with the metaphor of dream. The effort to fuse the two—the little boy as puppeteer—merely exposes "concept" as gimmick.

Hamlet at Length

The Branagh full-length *Hamlet* needed editing. Shakespeare's original production at the turn of the seventeenth century was no doubt edited for stage and did not run the full, conflated text past its Globe audience. Branagh adds an invading Fortinbras, perceived only by a concerned Horatio, so that the rightful claimant to the vacant throne takes over violently—and that's not what even the conflated script suggests. The film suffers from special effects that make the Ghost a ludicrous intruder from a Grade B horror film, from the most remarked-upon Marcellus in performance history, from the interminable tracking shots required to get all that language in, from a candle-lit mise-en-scéne in which the real lighting is palpable but just out of sight—the late-nineteenth-century placement in no way accounts for the material conditions of that period and thus becomes a set for *The Student Prince*—from an excruciating Ophelia, and from a musical score that slithers in irrelevantly to undercut some often excellent verse speaking. But it is not for verse speaking that we go to a Shakespeare film. When it is bad it can hurt—as in the Luhrmann *Romeo and Juliet*. When it is good it is not enough to save a film based on language and not visual image. I deal with the two-hour condensation of the longer version later.

A few failures—and some very good critics disagree with my assessment in that category, and with my evaluation of the films I label successful—do not diminish the accomplishment of these many new films. The translation from the verbal and rhetorical to the visualization of the word—something akin to an incarnation—continues, as filmmakers learn how to do Shakespeare. They are learning that no right way to do Shakespeare exists—as Shakespeare probably learned himself over the brief years of his own career.

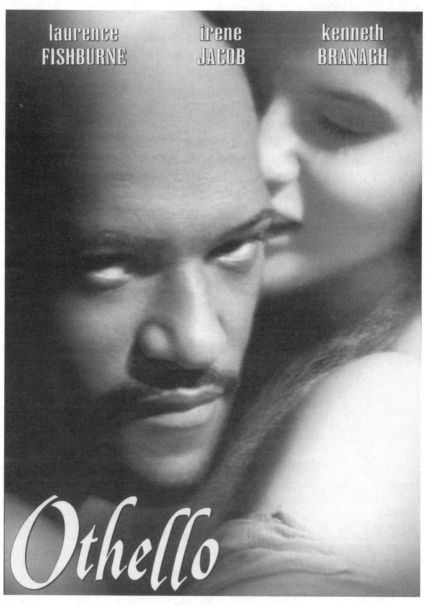

Othello poster, 1995. *Courtesy of Castle Rock Entertainment.*

Chapter 2

History and Television:
Two Recent Productions

The technical aspects of television have improved and are improving with new and better screens and pictures. One might ask, though, what is the use of improvements on that side of the set when the content remains as it is? Television images now imitate the computer screen, but is that not just another way of suggesting television's obsessive need to be trendy? Once, in the lifetimes of some of us, television was credited with ending the war in Vietnam by interrupting our dinnertimes with nasty images from rice paddy and jungle. I don't believe that. My own experience suggests that the war came to a slow halt only when the sons of the middle class started to be threatened. It was warm-body time and, suddenly, some of the bodies that would be bagged and stapled with a Purple Heart had some political leverage. Television was merely the bearer of evil tidings. Television's finest hour, according to Marshall McLuhan, was the Kennedy funeral. Some of us can remember staring at the black-and-white screen with our children for hours on end. We did, in those few days, become a national village.

Television is the way we get our history. Mostly, though, it comes in the quickly edited montages of candidates, of investigators treading or rowing over a crash site, of bleak shells of buildings in shelled or bombed cities. We know, of course, that an editor has decided which story leads off on any given night, and we have no choice but to accept that priority—that is, unless we specialize in financial or sports channels and are willing to wait through irrelevant material until we learn how our stocks or our teams have done. The very medium of television has changed in technique and range, giving us a way of measuring other changes that have occurred in our time. Obviously, we are linked in ways we were not forty years ago, and now we have only to tune in the news—on television— once the polls are closed to have the results of any given election

projected or mis-projected for us. This linkage and this instan-
taneousness may be responsible for the apparent need in affluent
Western cultures for immediate gratification—no waiting period
required or tolerated. Furthermore, television's artful concealment
of the ways it works may have something to do with our loss, as
a culture, of the values of structure, of what Aristotle calls
formal cause.

The question I raise is, How does our medium of instant history
deal with the history that Shakespeare presents to us? It is, in most
cases, as distant from his audience as the American Civil War is to
us, but Shakespeare's history is more malleable, less subject to the
precise details of a reenactment of a Confederate victory here and
there, or a Confederate defeat at Gettysburg. There is nothing "pure"
about Shakespeare's history. It has been edited and rearranged to
make a good play, just as surely as the disconnected bits of evening
news are designed around the products held out to us between
segments.

The Chorus to *Henry V* asks its audience to "piece out our
imperfections with your thoughts." The Chorus is right: history
requires an imaginative interaction, and no such thing as a correct
interpretation exists. The right wing now blames the protesters for
our not winning in Vietnam. I don't think we had anything to do
with the result one way or the other. Don't forget that two pro-war
candidates ran in 1968, when the country was being ripped apart
by protest and suppression of protest. The far right, however,
remains full of passionate intensity about the bad things that the
1960s spawned. They do not include their own war, of course, but
they certainly condemn the reaction to it. Candidates these days
say "Trust me," and ask us to fill in the blanks. As the Chorus says,
"'Tis your thoughts must deck our kings." I think that our
contemporary blank spaces have something to do with lack of depth-
field on television and with the sound-bite, 30-second-commercial
grammar to which we have become conditioned.

If we get our history via nineteen diagonal inches, that not only
shapes our expectations of what history is, but it shapes history as
well. We have small wars—however horrible—and small politicians.
Politicians are designed for television, as history seems to be. It may
be going too far to suggest that our addiction to television has
spawned the drug epidemic—as Pete Hamill argues (1990)—but
television's pervasiveness cannot be overemphasized. As Bill Moyers

says, "You can turn off your own television set, but you cannot turn off the environment of television. It goes on without you. It's not just the networks, it's the music video, the movie, the trailer—it's the culture that mediates between us and the world" (10 Jan. 1995). Add the Internet to the equation and one contemplates the paradigm shift that Swen Birkerts describes: "The familiar tradition of the book [is] destined for imminent historical oblivion, [swept away] by the technologies that will render it inadequate....[W]e are, as a culture, as a species, becoming shallower, [turning away] from depth...and are adapting ourselves to the ersatz security of a vast lateral connectedness" (1994).

To understand how television brings history to us, we have to understand that television is not film. Film on videocassette, that is film as it becomes television, becomes in the translation from a light sensitive to a magnetic mode, surprisingly unmagnetic. Notice what happens to sexuality in the translation. It becomes parody on television. No natural energy shines through—quite literally. We move from Marlene Dietrich to Zsa Zsa Gabor, from Garbo to Mary Tyler Moore. Television has no depth field, little variety of camera shots, and large studios but no location shots. It may be, then, responsible for our preference for the virtual reality of the video game, as opposed to the actual experience that the game simulates. The proximity of the television camera encourages a pulled-back style of acting that cannot hope to touch the range of most Shakespearean roles. A loud voice on television can go immediately over the top.

Space defines what can fill that space, and it is no surprise that large things don't occur anymore; our imaginations cannot accept them. TWA flight 800 goes down, but it is hardly the *Titanic*. Ethnic massacres do occur, but they are not the Holocaust. Invasions of Grenada or Panama happen, but they are not the Somme in 1415 or 1916 or D-Day or the Battle of the Bulge. Radio, of course, incorporated the listener's imagination. FDR was a radio president. Nixon and Clinton were television presidents. It may be that talk shows in which "the inhabitants of a parallel universe...do not mind sharing their most intimate secrets with millions of strangers" (as Cynthia Tucker says: 22 October 1994) insist that we know what went on inside that Oval Office. It may also be that O. J. Simpson represented not just the Icarian collapse of the American dream but the inevitable degeneration demanded by television, from the runner emerging from his envelope of blockers into the promised land to the murderer unable to fit those pesky gloves to his bloodstained hands while a nation watched. Television insists on being in every room–sometimes looking for criminals, usually showing us crooks, whether in fiction, documentary, or at the press conferences of politicians—and on reducing all space to its dimensions.

History "involve[s] a story" (Hodgdon 1997, 122). The first stories were told in words, augmented perhaps by cave paintings. Television, in fact, resembles the images of Plato's cave, wherein people accepted shadows cast by firelight upon a wall as "reality." People are apparently contented with those distortions and falsifications. But what is "truth" anyway? The story that television can tell is subject to certain limitations and perhaps strengths. It can contain no physical depth, thus no "big picture." It follows that television can reach for no large effects. It renders anything metaphysical—the appearance of a ghost, for example—merely psychological (see Dessen 1986).

The Warner-Shaw *Richard II*

Deborah Warner's *Richard II*, with Fiona Shaw, is a spectacular and moving production that compares favorably with the brilliant version in which Derek Jacobi starred over two decades earlier. That production (1978) has received little recognition, partly because the play itself is not popular, partly because the BBC series has been generally discredited, and partly because the subsequent *Henry IV* and *Henry V* productions in the BBC "complete canon" series are undistinguished.

What makes the more recent production moving is that Shaw plays Richard as homosexual male in love with his cousin Bolingbroke. It may be that in the stage production, Shaw played Richard as "girl," as she says (Rutter 1997, 314), or as "woman" (Berkowitz 1996, 9). Certainly the television version argues some ambiguity as to the King's gender, but I and other observers see this Richard as gay man. His clothes—trousers and gowns in white and gold—are unisex, similar to the garments of his male followers, "pretty youths dressed in Florentine taffetas" (Rutter 1997, 320). When Mowbray mentions the man without honor as being merely "gilded loam or painted clay," he glances at this gaggle. The King is called "King," referred to as "he," and married, even if he obviously despises his Queen. When Richard gives Bolingbroke a lingering kiss in the opening scene, the King seems to be flaunting his sexual orientation in the open court. He turns with a smirk and resumes a white, "designer" throne surrounded by the group of male favorites. Richard takes off his crown before the trial by combat to kiss (not just "fold him in [his] arms") Bolingbroke one more time, suggesting again a doffing of the political for the personal role. When the dying Gaunt gives Richard a long kiss later on, one that disgusts the King, Gaunt seems to be revenging himself for something he does not wish to put into so many words. Bolingbroke's accusation of Bushy and Green before he has them executed mentions, of course, the "divorce" that these favorites have wrought between Richard and Isabel, but it picks up further energy from the possibility that the two were Bolingbroke's rivals for Richard's affections. Bolingbroke was "near in love / Till [they] did make [Richard] misinterpret [him]." Bolingbroke's murder by indirection is powerfully understood here—it is not just political. It is intensely personal.

The production is splendidly scaled to its medium. The original stage version was set in the National's tiny 170-seat Cottesloe, which resembled, says Carol Rutter, an "elegant but austere antechamber to the gorgeous state rooms seemingly just beyond" (1997, 319). The television studio at Three Mills Island is a long rectangular space that can become Richard's throne room, the Duchess of York's spare chamber, a setting for a trial by combat (the only scene that fails here), a garden, and a mini-House of Lords for the exchange of gage scene (which the BBC cut) and the deposition scene that follows. When Richard lands on the stony coast after his return from Ireland, he stands against the blank wash of a seaside overcast. He receives the sacrament from Carlisle, but the elements are like the stones of Timon's banquet. Richard's effort at piety comes much too late. (The later ironic sacrament the anti-Henry party takes is cut here, as is the Aumerle subplot.) Richard's "salute" of the earth cannot be a kneeling and a sifting of soil in his hands. It is instead a wave of the hand at a rocky wasteland. A "fire-escape-like balcony" (as Berkowitz describes the stage set: 1996, 9) serves Richard for his confrontation with Northumberland at Flint Castle. The prison is dark, barred, and subterranean, but it offers a small upward glimpse of sunshine—a chance for Richard to look backward at the time he wasted. Most of the interior scenes are washed by candlelight that sends a golden texture across most of the faces. Bolingbroke, with his wild gaze and smashed warrior's face, thus seems very much out of place in this dreamlike, nocturnal space that Richard has created for himself. In the Cottesloe production, the candles were doused before the interval so that the space was invaded by floating, ghostly reminders of a ritualistic world just ending.

The Bolingbroke of the television version is Richard Bremmer, who played Exton in the original. David Threlfall, the original Bolingbroke, was unavailable. According to Rutter, Threlfall and Shaw shared an "uncanny physical resemblance" (1997, 318). The television version creates a powerful physical contrast between the dreamy Shaw, who is hardly delicate but dressed in flowing garments, and Bremmer, with his bulging eyes, sheer size, and armor. I do not agree with those who believe that Richard and Bolingbroke are "doubles" and can be interchanged, as in the famous—or infamous—Barton production of the 1970s.* As Joseph Price said of the production at the time, "The stage devices that were used to blur the personalities of Richard [and Bolingbroke] into one personality ran counter to the psychological foils these characters are to each other" (1977, 262). The relationship between the two can be expressed through Jung's metaphor of Shadow, which represents the personality formed by elements repressed by conscious orientation. In the television production, the two are physical and psychological opposites, who, taken in the aggregate, make up a whole. They love each other here. There is no doubt about Bolingbroke's reciprocity in the television production. This is a love affair canceled by political imperative, a matter of two body naturals yearning for what their bodies politic deny, indeed a love that politics destroys. Even in the deposition scene, Richard seeks comfort from Bolingbroke as Northumberland urges the petition upon the ex-King. Richard's "They shall be satisfied" follows from Bolingbroke's "Urge it no more." The two lovers are doing what they can for each other even here at the eleventh hour. Never, I would wager, has that subtext been brought to that scene, or, at least, never so powerfully. The relationship—and its failure—reaches deep into human experience. As in Aristophanes' metaphor in *The Symposium*, each yearns for the completeness the other represents.

In the opening scene, Richard and his courtiers laugh and begin to move away when Bolingbroke accuses Mowbray of "all the treasons for these eighteen years / Complotted and contrived in

* For a strongly negative reaction to this celebrated production, see my Shakespearean Production as Interpretation (Newark: Delaware University Press, 1992), pp. 141–43.

this land," but turn as Bolingbroke goes on to mention Gloucester's murder. Richard's mouth trembles for an instant. Bolingbroke smiles slightly. Has that got your attention? The point of Bolingbroke's later adjudication of the same issue is not, as Rutter suggests, that Richard and Bolingbroke are "doubles" (1997, 317). The later scene extends Bolingbroke's pose as "justicer" and shows us how differently he handles things. *He* will assign the "days of trial" to the contending parties, meaning that he has them under his control. If they cross him, the assignment of trial will be immediate. As it is, the trials never occur. Percy becomes Henry IV's enemy. Aumerle becomes Duke of York and dies in the van at Agincourt (though Shakespeare does nothing, as far as I can tell, with York's previous manifestations as Aumerle or Rutland). It is Northumberland's idea to arrest Carlisle here. In the BBC version, he does so only after a nod from Bolingbroke.

The trial by combat (1.3) is interrupted by Richard's apparent panic at the commotion the men are creating. The contrast between Richard's effete gay court and the brawling that "real men" want to enjoy is nicely drawn, but the scene becomes chaotic and incoherent. Furthermore, Richard's underscoring of stereotype here—the gay man as limp wristed, lisping, and upset by violence—undercuts the political point. Richard cannot afford to have Bolingbroke win. He is usurping the King's role by posing as the bringer of justice to England. Nor can Mowbray be permitted to defeat the most popular man in England. Mowbray is Richard's stand-in here, regardless of his denial (in this play and in Holinshed) of his guilt in Gloucester's death. Richard has to intervene and craft his frail compromise. His speech on "peace" is self-refuting ("peace" ends up frighting "peace"), a kind of Neville Chamberlainian "peace in our time" declaration, emerging from a desperate and improvisational politics. Mere "gay fright" in no way suggests what is happening here. A basic point the script is making—that, since Richard is the guilty party, the trial by combat can deliver no true verdict—gets lost in the jumble. If Richard *is* being played as a woman, some of the same stereotypical baggage pertains. Carol Rutter paraphrases Richard's reaction thus: "When 'womanish' Richard threw down the warder, it was because she couldn't stand any more...Her gesture read as a wholesale indictment of male 'order,' male protocol" (1997, 323). Either way, the issue of gender obscures the point about Richard's precarious *political* position.

Richard's frivolous attitude toward Gaunt's illness is particularly telling. Richard kneels and crosses himself as he prays to "make haste, and come too late"—an anti-prayer that shows how far Richard is from understanding the spiritual issues the play explores. Richard arrives with a funeral wreath and a mourning band in place, a reminder of Ian McKellen, as another Richard, wearing a mourning band to the scene in which the death of Clarence is revealed in the 1990 National Theatre *Richard III*. Shaw interrupts the Queen's prayer for the repose of Gaunt's soul: "So much for that!" York's complaint, splendidly delivered by the fussy Duke of Donald Sinden, is merely another old man's interruption of Richard's oblivious agenda. In the BBC production, Northumberland's revelation that Bolingbroke is at hand is delivered after Gaunt's funeral. Some time has passed. Here, the inference the scene presents–that Bolingbroke has made his move *before* Richard has given him a pretext for it—is possible. In the BBC version, though, David Swift's Northumberland is much more subtle and cautious as he sounds out Ross and Willoughby. In the Shaw production, all are in agreement from the start, so that the scene merely imparts information as opposed to dramatizing the formation of a conspiracy.

The production belongs to Shaw. She graphs Richard's manic surges and depressed drops superbly in the seaside scene: "keeps death *his* court" suggests what the poetry is saying. A king may have a great court, but King Death surrounds and pervades it. The lines are read as if Richard is actually thinking them as he speaks. The deposition scene is this production's high point. A sudden feminine voice intrudes upon male game-playing and asks "Why am I sent for?" Aumerle, who has refused to kneel to Bolingbroke, kneels to Richard. Richard sits down between an uneasy Hotspur and Northumberland. He puts the crown on the floor. Bolingbroke won't pick up it ("seize" it). Richard then insists that Bolingbroke and he "seize" it together. It is a child's game. And, of course, that is what Richard is demonstrating to the new King. None of this is worth anything anymore. Richard removes an invisible crown from his head, suggesting that the spiritual, intangible qualities that he inherited as King are gone. "Ay, no, no, aye," as Shaw reads the line is "Yes. No. No I," and then "Therefore no, know." What Richard knows, as Rutter has Richard saying, is that Bolingbroke has "shattered the fundamental contract that keeps me king" (1997, 321). Richard's demonstration of what Bolingbroke does *not* get with the crown is devastating, of course, but Richard's has been the prior destruction of sanctions and continuities. Richard puts the crown on Bolingbroke's head, then prostrates himself at his feet. He rises to embrace Bolingbroke for the "mockery king of snow" speech, a brilliant physical reinforcement of the destructive interaction they have experienced.

The garden scene ends with the Gardener (John McEnery) wishing that his "skill were subject to [the Queen's] curse." The earth, though leased out, though wounded with traitor's hooves, though devoid of its sacramental resonance, will continue to be fruitful. The BBC version of 1978 ended with the Queen's curse ("Pray God the plants though graft'st may never grow!"). That is illegitimate. It suggests that she has power within a play in which women are subject to the decisions that men make. The Duchess of York's appeal for Aumerle is granted only because Bolingbroke, on top of the fragile feudal system he has set up, needs friends. This is not a play where the curses of queens have efficacy—even unwittingly, as in the case of Lady Anne's curse of whoever becomes Richard Gloucester's wife.

The moment at which Richard capitulates would seem to come after Salisbury tells him that the Welshmen have defected to Bolingbroke: "They are fled," Richard says. It is an acceptance of fact and of relief—I don't have to fight. Richard's aversion to combat has been established. Jacobi makes the statement a question: "And they are *fled*?" He is still incredulous as he absorbs the completeness of his abandonment. Here, as Berkowitz says of the stage production, "Bolingbroke himself turned out to be the last person to realize the full implications of his insurrection" (1996, 9). Bolingbroke is a legalist who returns under a different name than that he carried into banishment in this play about the loss and the gaining of names and what they represent. Bolingbroke never states an objective beyond that of gaining his inheritance. York sees "the issue of these arms," as Richard does. We infer that Richard's resistance to a coup would merely create a conflict that *this* Richard would avoid at all costs. To play Bolingbroke as unaware of the end result of his return, however, is to ignore the careful formula he provides for Percy, Ross, and Willoughby in 2.3, where he pleads present poverty but future largesse. His words and the response to them constitute a feudal contract—the only available basis of power left to Bolingbroke. He cannily shows that he knows as much. The distance between

Lancashire and Northumbria, after all, argues more than a local arrangement. The play renders some interpretations simplistic. This production tends not to understand the politics of the play.

One of the strengths of the production is that Sian Thomas's stalwart words as Queen to the deposed Richard ("The lion dying thrustest forth his paw") emerge from a woman who would have opposed Bolingbroke regardless of the consequences. This production emphasizes the Queen's piety, suggesting that she represents that dead or dying sacramental context that Gaunt describes that might have resisted Bolingbroke's incursion. That this despised Queen adores Richard makes her words even more poignant here. She would have been Richard's natural ally had he not abandoned her for the male favorites who helped bring him down.

This production cuts the moment after the execution of Bushy and Green, when Bolingbroke politicly asks York to send "kind commends" to the Queen. It was very strong in the BBC production—Jon Finch's Bolingbroke effortlessly switching gears, Charles Gray's York shocked and heartbroken, scarcely listening to his nephew. Both productions cut Carlisle's description of Norfolk's career—he has fulfilled England's chivalric tradition as a banished man during a long lifetime that has somehow occurred during a few short and brutal months in England. The speech belongs in any production. It brings back an important character from early in the play and informs us powerfully about what Richard and Bolingbroke have conspired to exile from their country. It reminds us of the "timelessness" of Gaunt's vision no longer available to *"this* England."

The finale is a possibly confusing conflation of Richard's prison soliloquy and his assassination. "Music" is the splashing of Exton and his accomplices through the sewer that opens into Richard's cell. As Richard struggles on an existential level with his killers, the words argue that he is more than "half in love with easeful death." In an "all-hating world," Richard can love only death. He falls face down into the water and the scene shifts. Bolingbroke takes *his* crown off and leans into Richard's coffin to kiss the corpse, expressing a final reflex of body natural beneath the trappings of recent kingship.

The framing allusions—"like sacrificing Abel's" and "With Cain go wander"—are gone. In the first, Bolingbroke sees himself as a biblical avenger. In the last, though he assigns the guilt to Exton, he is the one who is guilty (as Richard was of Gloucester's murder) and who will pay a price for his role in regicide. The murder of Gloucester is now irrelevant. Bolingbroke has rushed headlong into the guilty world he claimed he would redeem at the outset. The editing here, toward the love of former King and new King, excludes some of the deeper resonances of this superb script.

As we enter a millenium of mumbles, one must pause to remark that this production is beautifully spoken. It should be made commercially available. This is a wonderful play. It deserves to have two splendid productions representing it. The new television production emphasizes *personal* relationships, as befits the scale of the medium. The triangular conflict—Richard passionate about Bolingbroke but entangled in a political marriage—is movingly depicted. The death of Richard ends this version. No further history is to unfold. No wars will spin into time from these events. No further plays are to be performed. This treatment of *Richard II* differs radically from that of the BBC, which knew, as Shakespeare did, that more was to come. The Warner-Shaw production serves then as a generic contrast to the 1978 version and helps us see it, as it helps us see the newer one, as a separate work of art emerging from this neglected script. It may be that the complexity of the language in the play, the myriad thematic linkages that the poetry makes, and the complicated political context have kept the play in the dark. It is not often produced on stage. No film of it has ever been made, and only three recent television versions of the single play exist (the third an undistinguished Bard production of 1982 with David Birney). The Warner-Shaw version edits toward an emotional dimension that neglects the political but that also turns the script into a moving personal drama. The cultural moment in which a "gay" Richard can come out has been predicted, of course, by Derek Jarman's *Edward II*, but the moment represents one of those spaces that culture opens up for the exploration of an old play that suddenly discovers an environment in which to come alive again.

Caird's *Henry IV*

John Caird's is a difficult production to evaluate, partly because it is hard to describe. Part of the problem is generic. Caird's habit of jumping in and out of scenes written for the stage, and therefore intended originally for a complete treatment *as* scene, is a filmic technique. Caird tends to use dissolves. The transition is often based on a verbal echoing of one part of the script by another. The effect is of "montage," where the sequence adds up to more than the sum of its parts. The production is designed for television, however, a much more limited, much more normative mode than film. Montage on television brings us history as a sound-and-vision bite. That may be the way our "history" comes at us these days, but it is not the way the plays were written for the stage. The BBC-TV *Henry IV* plays of the late 1970s, directed by David Giles, though doggedly straightforward and often dull, present the inherited scripts clearly. Giles's productions have the negative merit of accepting the few camera shots that television affords and of embracing the medium's limited field of depth. Caird "interprets" the plays much more heavy-handedly than the BBC does and probably in ways that television cannot accommodate. He is right to suggest that television is a linguistic medium, asking us to *listen* as opposed to merely watching, but the constant changes in scene sometimes take us away from a moment we thought we were understanding. I asked myself whether it was useful to know the plays and answered, yes—one *has* to know the plays to follow this reordered, chopped-up version. We must know the history already in order to grasp the history that Caird is giving us. And knowing that history is not always an advantage.

Perhaps because Caird wants to concentrate on the fragility of personal relationships, the magician Glendower is erased. Falstaff's confrontation with the Chief Justice early in Part 2 is juxtaposed against Henry's castigation of Hal in Part 1. Falstaff seems to march toward Gaultree Forest but ends up at Shrewsbury. At times I had to ask "What *is* this adding up to?" At other times, Caird grants his audience the supreme compliment of letting them figure things out for themselves. The result of this montage, on television, has the effect of "collage" but without a frame that permits any sense of gestalt or overall design to emerge.

The production begins with little boys playing at swords, then looking in on "history." They are the ones who will grow up during the course of this sequence, from 1398 to 1413 or so, to die in battle as the hideous god of war looks at them. This is a Kottian view of history. Richard II descends a set of steps, the sun gleaming behind him, to play a fragment of the deposition scene. He demands that Bolingbroke "seize the crown," then crowns Bolingbroke and sarcastically wishes him "many years of sunshine days." Roger Allam, who plays this cameo of Richard, is one of the best actors of sarcasm extant.

Ten years pass. Henry IV asks for the prince. The scene shifts to the tavern. This establishing of historical context and physical location takes less than five minutes and is brilliantly done. The camera moves to Northumberland and Hotspur. The latter is seen almost exclusively against an ominous gray sky—a northern sky presaging storm. As Falstaff talks about "his vocation," the scene dissolves to Henry IV laboring at his, remarking on young Percy's pride, tearing up Percy's demand that Mortimer be ransomed. We then go back to the tavern where the Gadshill robbery is being planned, then to Northumberland, who explains why Mortimer is such a threat to Henry, who did "seize the crown." After Worcester explains the genealogical chart leading to the crown to Hotspur, the camera cuts to a map of Gadshill. Rebellion and robbery are paralleled, as is the rebellion's emulation of Bolingbroke's original seizure of power. Poins's "I will stuff your purses full of crowns" becomes the operative phrase for this sequence.

The tavern scenes are sometimes hard to see. Since candles illuminate the foreground, we can't get past that bright light. One of the production's best shots shows Hal looking at hilt of his dagger, at the bronze sun there that he will imitate. He has already made his plan, but here he displays some of the improvisational skill that he will master with Falstaff to make that plan work. He pounds the dagger into the table. It also imitates a cross, of course, so ironies accrue as Hal outlines his plan with a nasty satisfaction that, for me, undercuts him for much of the rest of the production; he is too much like his brother John as the script shows that prince to be (but not here—here John is just a younger brother needing comfort). Firth delivers his plan so softly that those who do not know the words and their intent are likely to miss this significant speech. The textures of the tavern world are composed of warm fires, inflamed fleshtones, and the rich brown of hogsheads and timbers that tend to pull Hal's voice into them.

A high-angle shot looks down a gray column at Hotspur talking of honor. The camera moves from Hotspur's "sport, " which is battle, to Gadshill and robbery. One of production's few long shots shows Falstaff's girth as he stands in empty space before the robbery. "Have you any levers?" The King complains that "many thousand" of his "poorest subjects are now asleep," while he suffers sleeplessness (this arrives all the way from 3.1 of Part 2). Some of his subjects, though, are on the London–Canterbury Road, others are about to rob them. The King's soliloquy touches on the sleeping "ship's boy," and we see a boy sleeping near a rain-lashed window under a model ship. This is Falstaff's Page, who leads us to the play extempore. It is composed of close-ups, two- shots, and small-group shots. Falstaff thinks but does not stammer as Quayle did in the Giles production, destroying our sense of Falstaff's virtuosity. The scene shifts to Hotspur and Lady Percy sparring. Does he love her? This unresolved love carries over through the scenes adumbrating Henry's doubts about his son. Hal talks of Hotspur, then the scene develops into the play extempore, providing a *sequence* at last. Twice the response "Falstaff" is left to the tavern crowd: "his name is..." "that villainous abominable misleader of youth..." Falstaff and Hal vie for control of the debate, and each gains it in this early rehearsal of rejection. We move from Falstaff asleep to Henry IV waking up and remarking on the "foul...body" of his kingdom, back to Falstaff, then to the King talking of the "revolution of the times" (also from Part 2). As the King discusses a "history in all men's lives," Hal appears for "private conference." Caird does not show Henry's crucial adjustment of Richard's accusation. What Richard said was, "Northumberland, thou ladder wherewithal / The mounting Bolingbroke ascends my throne." What Bolingbroke says Richard said is "Northumberland, thou ladder by the which / My cousin Bolingbroke ascends my throne." Bolingbroke emphasizes kinship, not ambition. Hal's entrance introduces the confusing series of cuts to Falstaff and his encounter with the Chief Justice (meant, one assumes, to show the contrast between Hal and Falstaff—the former always on the side of "law and order" regardless of appearances) and to set up the confrontation between the brand-new King and the Chief Justice later on. The scene is often cut, but it works very well here, as Henry V permits himself to be convinced of the "justice" of the case. Falstaff follows the Prince "up and down like his ill angel" just as Henry claims Richard "ambled up and down, / With shallow jesters and rash bavin wits." Caird might have provided a more telling echo. Hal, talking of the sun's breaking through the clouds, says, "That when he please again to be himself, / Being wanted, he may be more wonder'd at..." Bolingbroke, complaining to Hal, says of himself, "By being seldom seen, I could not stir, / But like a comet I was wonder'd at."

Bolingbroke's heavenly body is—though he does not intend this—a portent of disaster ("Comets importing change of times and states": *Henry VI*, 1.1.2). The echoing suggests that Hal's approach is similar to Bolingbroke's, except that Hal achieves a kind of invisibility by being too often seen. The King's "vile participation" equates to Falstaff, so the metaphor Henry is making sticks to Hal as well. Falstaff talks of England making "a good thing...too common," and here the King echoes Falstaff: "Not an eye / But is aweary of thy common sight, / Save mine, which has desir'd to see thee more." Caird might also have reminded us of Hal's "I know you all" in King Henry V's "I know thee not." The echo underlines the degree of calculation that lies under even Hal-Henry's most spontaneous moments.

The scene between King and Prince is edgy. Hal's defense is merely loud. We are not convinced. Henry IV's "sovereign trust" is itself fragile. The concerns of the kingdom are immediately undercut by a shift to the tavern, where Doll and Falstaff are curtained off in bed. Then the camera cuts to Lady Percy asking why she has been "banish'd from my Harry's bed." Her efforts at love undercut Percy's monomaniacal insistence on war. It is the conflict between politics and private life again, with a different emphasis.

"I love thee not," says Hotspur, to martial music. We see Hal preparing, then move to the scene in Part II (2.4), (the greatest of the tavern scenes, to my way of thinking), in which Hal anticipates Falstaff's excuse: "You knew I was at your back, and spoke it on purpose to try my patience." Then Hal says, "I know how to handle you." The issue, expressed in an infinitive phrase is "how to handle Falstaff." Falstaff turns the issue into "the wicked" and forces Hal to "say that which his flesh rebels against." Hal is saved from rhetorical defeat only by Peto's interruption. Hal can wax moralistic about "profan[ing] the precious time" and leave. This production plays the scene as mere fun and games, neglecting the ongoing contest between Hal and Falstaff that sets up the rejection, where Falstaff is denied a "reply." Caird attempts to contrast the aimlessness of the tavern and the necessities of staving off rebellion. But the tavern is not without purpose; it is energetic and it is where Hal learns to be king. Part 1 of this production ends with a contrast between Lady Percy, asking Hotspur whether he loves her, and Doll, rushing "blubbered" to see Falstaff off to battle. In the plays, of course, the battle is not just Shrewsbury, but Gaultree Forest—a non-battle. Here Gaultree Forest is conflated into Shrewsbury. Gone, then, is the wonderful episode of Coleville's capture by Falstaff, and Coleville's subsequent defiance of Prince John that sends him to the block. At Shrewsbury, Walter Blunt goes smilingly by Falstaff and draws the line about "grinning honor." This treatment makes nonsense of the inherited text, which shows Douglas killing Blunt. Grinning honor is the rictus of a corpse. Why the role of Blunt had to be preserved is a mystery, since, although he keeps reappearing in his production, he has no role to play in it.

Part 2 brings us to Shallow and "the days we have seen," then to a sleeping Henry IV, wasting away physically, as Hotspur is militarily, as Richard did earlier, when all his followers deserted him for Bolingbroke. Hal's rise is prefigured in Vernon's speech, which arouses Hotspur's anger. His "die all, die all, merrily" plays across the faces of Falstaff's recruits. Thus, two versions of illegitimate activity are related. Hotspur's chance for legitimacy is canceled by Worcester. Kate Percy's indictment of Northumberland is left in. It gives the previous sequence between Kate and Hotspur an ex post facto power. She shows that she knows Hotspur loved her.

Caird erases Henry's knowledge that he won't be going to the Holy Land, in spite of his long and pious opening. It is not that Westmoreland brings news that forces Henry to "brake off" his purpose, it is that Henry has to deal with Hotspur and the hostage crisis. We learn that Henry knows as much before his long speech. Perhaps it is impossible to dramatize the ex post facto sequence here. It is like the opening of *Richard II*—we only learn what the first scene was about by going on to Gaunt and the Duchess in the second scene. These plays can be a kind of jigsaw puzzle where relationships between the pieces do not come into focus until time tells actions what they have meant. To lose the hypocritical opening of *I Henry IV*, though, is also to lose the wonderful irony of the end of *II Henry IV*, when Henry learns that the prophecy of his crusade has shrunk to the four walls of the Jerusalem Chamber in Westminster. Henry greets this reduction of the divine to the finite with piety: "Laud be to God! Even there my life must end." Henry IV falls ill here after Shrewsbury. As Hal returns the crown to him in their final confrontation, the old King's mind sees Richard handing him the crown instead of Hal. In a millisecond his reign passes before his eyes, even as the image recapitulates history for us in a brilliant dissolve back to the face of Hal. The moment creates that instant of awareness between sleep and waking where time becomes elastic and where past hope and present regret coalesce in ways that can be experienced but not described. Since this Henry IV sequence is self-contained, we get no words from Henry or from Prince John about France and "foreign quarrels." The production's theme of corruption—open profligacy and disguised disease—shows a fattening Falstaff and a thinning Henry IV. It does not convince me, however, that the beneficiary of the two fathers—this callow Hal-Henry V—has learned how to become King.

The rejection scene is strange. Henry and a group of four monk-like friends (John, the Chief Justice, Warwick, and Blunt) come past the place where Falstaff and company are standing. The moment contains no public aspect, therefore no political element. And thus is Henry V denied a chance to show that he knows, at last, "how to handle" Falstaff and, it follows, how to deal with the likes of Cambridge, Scroop, and Grey by being politic, not just nasty. The Orson Welles film remains the touchstone for the rejection scene. Television will never come close. Then, in a series of tableaus around Henry IV's tomb, the Hostess and the Eastcheapians gather to mourn Falstaff, while Henry V tells his followers that his father "has gone wild to his grave." The new King ascends into the sunlight from which Richard had descended so long before. Again, boys observe the comings and goings of the great men. These boys will die somewhere among the many fields of the Wars of the Roses. These boys are not playing at war—war games are no longer popular. These boys are like the children of Auden's poem, "skating on a pond at the edge of the woods." They do not care one way or the other what is happening, but they will be yanked into the destructive vortex that changes in kingship create even for those who do not care.

The acting is often superb. Ronald Pickup's harried King is much more convincing than the compulsively hand-wringing Bolingbroke of Jon Finch in the Giles version, and Calder is a far more powerful Falstaff than the stammering Quayle. It is a treat to see wonderful veterans like Woodvine and O'Conor so confidently at work. Redgrave, though, tends to whisper inaudibly, and Firth has none of the introspective depth that Giles's David Gwillim brings to Hal. The Giles productions also contain some superb smaller depictions— those of John Tordorf as Feeble, Robert Eddison as Shallow, and Salvin Stewart as Coleville, a country gentleman dragged by feudal obligation into the crossfire of modern politics. Caird's Rufus Sewell brings a sinister quality to his Hotspur, where Giles's Tim Pigott-Smith is merely an immature hothead. Michele Dotrice, a passionate redhead, and Josette Simon, a brooding African, bring separate strengths to the great role of Kate. Caird's deletion of Glendower may result from his sense that the magician is not "televisual."

As a teacher, I would recommend the Giles productions as a prelude to Caird's conflation and restructuring of the scripts.

"We assimilate facts within patterns," says Peter Saccio, "and when those patterns change, we rewrite history" (1988, 210). This tendency is what Hayden V. White calls "metahistory." What Caird does is to change the patterns with which the plays are usually delivered on stage or television, intermixing scenes, changing the chronology of the scripts, letting the kingdom become a place in which certain words and phrases are available for repetition, as is always true at any time in history. The metaphor here is the power structure that floats certain phrases out to be repeated as if they constitute the original thinking of the citizenry: "If we don't take him now, we'll be facing him five years down the road" (said in 1990 of Saddam Hussein). Words and phrases, though, turn on their inventors, as do actions. The economy of these scripts is that if theft occurs at the top, it replicates itself there and at all the levels of the society that suddenly open up when the older, hierarchical system disintegrates. Assuming we can follow the narrative, the dissolve technique, which by design is never instant, gives the effect of time passing: time for information to travel, time for minds to be made up or to change, time for kings and fat knights to age and die. This production demonstrates the limits of the thematic approach, one I prefer to a post-modern disintegration of the script into unrelated performance fragments that have nothing to do with each other. Too often, that latter tendency is the "style" here. When the technique works—as it often does here—the effect is brilliant, and these great plays are reshaped before our eyes for a fresh consideration.

Chapter 3

Shakespeare on Television: *Four Recent Productions*

Dennis Kennedy makes a distinction between metaphoric and metonymic modes of production (1993, 266–267). The metonymic approach sets the play in a world meant to reinforce meanings in the script. The metaphoric technique is neutral or eclectic about where or when, but supplies specific suggestions of concept or theme within the production, often through a "single or detachable image" (266). Kennedy's example is Peter Zadek's 1987 *Richard III,* where "the semicircular arena look[ed] like a cutaway barrel, with wooden slats curving upwards from the sawdust floor to the flies, making a graphic metaphor of claustrophobic space" (275). This "suggestive" approach usually works best for television, which lacks a field of depth that can accommodate either a location or a detailed set and which relies on editing of close-ups, two-shots, and reaction shots that virtually defies analysis.

The Jonathan Miller–Lawrence Olivier television version of *The Merchant of Venice* (1974) is an exception to my generalization. It is full of things. The metonym is the relationship between material Venice and opulent Victorian England. The proof of the generalization is Trevor Nunn's 1974 *Antony and Cleopatra,* where the contrast between the filmy curtains and deep cushions of languid Egypt and the march of martial Rome contextualizes some great performances from Janet Suzman, Richard Johnson, Patrick Stewart, and Corin Redgrave. Another example of the metaphoric mode is Jane Howell's 1982 *Henry VI* series for BBC, with a playground set that ironizes the plays' political machinations and, again, provides a space for the superb acting of Julia Foster, Peter Benson, David Burke, Bernard Hill, and others.

Of the productions I am considering here, Richard Eyre's *King Lear* (1998) uses metaphor superbly but too sparingly. Nicholas Hytner's *Twelfth Night* (1998) has neither an overall concept nor any smaller details to suggest what the director and actors have discovered in the script. Like so many recent sets in British theater, the design seems unrelated to the script. It is as if a group of strolling players said, "Let's do our play here, where all this water is!" The Thacker *Measure for Measure* (1994) dances on the line between metonym and metaphor with relative success. The NBC *Tempest* (1998), produced by Bonnie Raskin, is all "closely related idea" that swamps the originating script.

Eyre's *King Lear*

Richard Eyre's *King Lear,* televised on the Mobil Masterpiece Theater in October 1998, is a remounting of the 1997 Royal National Theatre production at the tiny Cottlesloe Theatre. Ian Holm who was sixty-six when he played the role in 1997, won the Olivier Award for his stage performance.

This production is scaled to the medium and has the stage experience behind it that almost invariably results in a good remounting for television. The actors command both the verse and their characters, as they did in the Jonathan Miller *Merchant of Venice* and the Trevor Nunn *Antony and Cleopatra, Macbeth* (1979), and *Othello* (1990). This is probably the best television *Lear* since the Joseph Papp–Edwin Sherin version of 1973, a skillful rendition of a performance at the Delacorte Theater in Central Park in which the audience became part of the texture of the production. It is more gripping than the 1982 BBC version, which had overcrowded frames and Michael Hordern as a fussy old CEO, and is more calibrated to its medium than the Thames version of 1983, which was an act of homage to Olivier accompanied by intrusive music.

The Eyre production uses a unit set—a large room with a table for conferences and meals, torches on sconces, and doorways—but little detail. It uses overhead shots to establish groupings before the camera closes in. Changes in lighting signal changes in mood. Like Nunn's small theater productions in The Other Place, Eyre's was scaled to television from the start, as Margaret A. Varnell says of the Cottlesloe version: "The barrenness of the stage lends a surreal quality to the production. The spectators are forced to concentrate on the language and the family quarrel unfolding before them because there is simply nothing else to look at" (1998, 22).

Some of the television shots involve simultaneous speech and reaction, as in Lear's rejection of Cordelia and his invocation of sterility upon Goneril. This can be an intense and complex experience, since we are reading two characters at once. Lear's blast at Goneril—which can bring a gasp to a theater audience—describes her own deepest fear. Her face contorts in agony as the terrible words pour from her father. Barbara Flynn's superb Goneril is never sympathetic, but we can understand what Lear has done to her within the fierce and dangerous space between father and oldest daughter.

The major sacrifice of this production is Finbar Lynch's Edmund, here a slight, balding eavesdropper with little to say. He loses the entire "excellent foppery of the world" speech (I.2.121–136). A fragment of his great "Thou nature" soliloquy (1.2.1ff) is voiced-over the opening scene (after Gloucester says "who is yet no dearer in my account"). Gloucester's roguish "good sport at his making"—which can provide Edmund with a grievance—is cut. He does seem surprised at Gloucester's statement that he will be going out again to wherever he has been for nine years. He gets "I grow, I prosper. / Now, gods, stand up for bastards" later, in its usual place (1.2.20–21), but to lose the soliloquy is to lose the trajectory of the character. Edmund seems at the outset no more significant than William Osborne's calculating and insolent Oswald. Lynch has none of the hooded menace of Raul Julia's Edmund in the 1973 Central Park production, where Julia's Puerto Rican nonchalance projected a threat to a New York audience, and little of the understated calculation of Michael Kitchen's superb Edmund in the BBC version, where Edmund is one of Arendt's clerkish Kommandants. Lynch's Edmund is a victim caught in the crossfire of warring sisters, hardly their seducer.

Cordelia's asides in 1.1 are cut to give impact to her "Nothing, my lord," but her sudden assertiveness toward her sisters ("I know you what you are," to Goneril here), which must be a combination of intuition (Goneril's "plighted cunning" has not been established) and repressed anger at what has just happened, seems strange here. Perhaps we need a glint of calculation and fewer tears from Cordelia to balance the confrontation at the end of the scene.

The married couples are surprised by Lear's "reservation of an hundred knights" and seem instantly to be figuring the costs involved. The opening scene is dynamic, not just because of Cordelia's refusal to go along with the auction but also because it makes much of the responses of people who have not been informed of the plans made for them as extroverted males such as Lear and Gloucester bang down their agendas.

Holm gives a biting performance as Lear. He has always been a king and he has lived without a wife for a long time. His emotions have atrophied, even as his intelligence has sharpened. He controls his environment completely. At the outset, he laughs at the word "death." *He'll* never die. Then he stops laughing. It isn't funny. "What are *you* laughing at?" his glare asks. This is an intense, as opposed to a "grand," *King Lear* (as the Elliott-Olivier version tried to be), and, most of the time, it is scaled to television. When Lear goes over the top, as when he awakens after the storm, the sound system threatens to burst a woofer.

The production uses several brilliant metaphors. Lear enters for 4.6 (his reunion with Gloucester) wearing the Fool's woolen cap. Lear has gained an identity since the Fool said "I am a fool, thou art nothing" (1.4. 190–191). Lear has become the Fool, who "by imagination grasps a value that cannot be demonstrated rationally" (Heilman 1948, 186). The hat is a simple borrowing from previous scenes that remarkably deepens one that follows with all the meanings that apply to it, including the equations of wisdom wtih folly, substance with nothingness, presence with absence.

A basic metaphor is accomplished by lighting. The production begins with a visual eclipse of the sun, an image of Gloucester's line about "these late eclipses" (1.2.106). The opening scenes are shaded in gold and rose as torches burn. The interiors grow grayer, grimmer, until finally the bars of a giant prison shadow the hallway outside the set. We recognize that a police state has ridden in under the movement of the script. The eclipse recurs at the "cheerless, dark" ending. Suggestiveness can work on television. It is not the medium itself that is banal—though its lack of physical depth invites aesthetic shallowness—but the way it is used.

The storm scenes are too rain-swept. The lines are hard to hear unless you know them already. We have not been prepared for the intrusion of a "filmic" literalization, but the stony expanse on which the characters execute their dance of death does show us that we are in a zone outside castle walls, a place where both kings and wretches "feel." At the end, Kent tugs a wagonload of bodies out into that landscape. We are in the twentieth-century world the play predicts.

The production needs more definition toward the end. Portions of 5.1, in which Edgar and Edmund are put on course for their trial by combat, are placed before 4.7, the reunion of Lear and Cordelia. That means that only a snippet of the scene between Edgar and

Gloucester—who lost "And that's true, too"—intervenes between the reconciliation of Lear and Cordelia and their going to prison. When Lear awakens in 4.7, he is in a violent rage that modulates unconvincingly. His reappropriation of Cordelia in 5.3 is an uncomfortable solo. Holm reads it beautifully, but that is all that happens. Eyre builds nothing into the scene to suggest that Lear's fondest wish ("to set [his] rest / On her kind nursery" [.1.1.123–124]) is itself suspect and, in the script, is surrounded by and interrupted by threats to that vision. Sometimes a Cordelia—Lee Chamberlin opposite Jones, for example—resists Lear during this scene. In that instance, Lear was Uncle Tom. His daughter had marched at Selma. The Eyre production needed *something* to challenge Holm's sensitive treatment of the lines. The two film versions, in powerful black and white, contrast with the Eyre version—Peter Brook's in 1971, with all that smoke and a smoldering Edmund, and the Kozintsev of 1970, with all that weaponry and an Edmund who could not comprehend the happy indifference of Lear and Cordelia.

Eyre excises much of the Fool. Here, he is another older man, but Michael Bryant's is a moving characterization, showing that another way of living a life during the same span of time can grow toward wisdom, what Jung calls "individuation." This Fool is particularly powerful as he tries to continue to function—to serve Lear—even as he is dying. Much of Edgar is gone, including all of his asides, but those are welcome deletions. Some people, however, must wonder what he is doing with Gloucester. Is the allegory into which he coerces his blind father Edgar's revenge for Gloucester's disinheriting him? That motive makes sense, and, without the mawkish rationale, it does here. The major cuts in Lear's part are "Take physic pomp…And show the heavens more just" (3.4.33–36) and the speeches on "adultery" and "justice" in 4.6. The latter scene concentrates on Lear's interaction with Gloucester. The speeches would have underscored Lear's new status as a seer into things— ironic, of course, in view of his own role in endangering Cordelia a few scenes later—but they may have been deemed too long and complicated for today's audience or, in the instance of Lear's misogyny, too offensive.

Hytner's *Twelfth Night*

Why was Nicholas Hytner's *Twelfth Night* televised? I recall wanting to see Peter Hall's 1994 *Merchant of Venice*, with Dustin Hoffman's quiet Shylock and Geraldine James's racist Portia, taped for television. It had a unity of design and an understated style of acting that would have translated splendidly to the medium. Now, it is lost.

Hytner's *Twelfth Night* was televised because it was there—at the Vivian Beaumont, Lincoln Center, New York. *Twelfth Night* is potentially a good play for televised live performance. The presence of an audience helps us suspend our disbelief. More than most of Shakespeare's plays, this script calls for that suspension. Trevor Nunn's 1996 film version attacked the gender issue directly by having Imogen Stubbs's Viola show how difficult it is to play the male role. The implication is that it is difficult for *males* as well, trapped in the stereotypical assumptions they must uphold and manifest. Thus is the comic ending of plot reinforced on the level of the characters' awarenesses—particularly Orsino's. Hytner's bland production gives us little to believe in the first place, therefore no psychological misapprehensions or emotional blind spots to show the way to the clarification of the comic ending.

The production "emerges" from a vast upstage ocean, intersected by wharfs and walkways, and features a downstage pool. Paul Rudd's Orsino offers little with which Helen Hunt's Viola can fall in love. He is a layabout who can paralyze his dukedom simply because he is the duke. Philip Bosco's Malvolio has sunk so far into the depths of his pompousness that his sudden lust is not credible. Kyra Sedgwick as Olivia is giddy, even before she meets Cesario, and splashes past whatever signals might reside in her prose or verse. Hunt's squinting and anxious Viola struggles with her emphasis. That difficulty might have been a subtext for her uneasy pose as young man, but here it seems just an actor's inexperience.

A few good moments—Cesario entering to a circle of dark and veiled women, and the threat that a gigantic Maria poses to Cesario—do not make up for the production's overall pointlessness. "The three younger actors [Rudd, Sedgwick, and Hunt] haven't the vocal technique, the stage presence, or the innate personas that would give character to some of the loveliest, wittiest romantic language in the canon," says Vincent Canby (1998, 2). David Patrick Kelly's Feste is apparently an out-of-work rock singer who shows too well why he lacks advancement. Why must directors of this play cast Feste with actors who cannot sing? Toby and Andrew, Brian Murray and Max Wright, do some good work as a comic twosome—and, I am told, were good on the Beaumont stage—but effective acting in an auditorium can become overacting on television, as it does consistently during this production.

Director Hytner says of the "locational high concept"—Vienna in August 1914 or the Wild West—that "this approach has the virtue of consistency, but also its drawbacks. The provision of a solid social context is often illuminating, but always to some degree confines the plays to a place much narrower than Shakespeare's imagination" (1998, C4). Most places are narrower than Shakespeare's imagination, of course, but Hytner provides no imaginative space in which his production can develop. Mel Gussow argues rightly that "water is the central motif—more than 10,000 gallons at every performance" (1998, B1), but sheer volume of water is not a set for anyone but Esther Williams. Its only effective use is a cut from the ornamental pool outside the Beaumont to Orsino's outsized, onstage bathtub. Water, cushions, and vague late-nineteenth-century Bombay motifs do not help the actors establish who they are in their world. No such "world" exists in this production, nor do any "closely related ideas" to create resonances with an audience. The "eclectic mix of costumes," says one reviewer, "helped to transport the audience to a plane where East and West blend as smoothly as hosts and guests, men and women, fools and fanatics" ("Midnight at the Oasis," *Shakespeare Magazine* 2, no. 3 [Fall 1998]: 6). If so, the production manages to avoid whatever conflict resides in the script and trades drama for an unwillingness to create useful contexts for actors and audience.

Thacker's *Measure for Measure*

David Thacker's televised *Measure for Measure* (1994) comes close to a metonymic approach to the script, but it works as metaphor because its "closely related idea" is television itself. While it shows us Vienna as police state, its technique suggests the nightly news's montage of horror—from images that reflect a "decline of morality" to the draconian effort to combat that perceived degradation—wars on drugs, for example, that serve right-wing posturing and whose outcome has already been bought by the enemy. Thacker's state uses television as a central component of its controlling environment. This is not precisely "metaphoric," however, since metaphor involves *unlike* things. Here, television shows us its own image, perhaps suggesting that the mildly futuristic world of the production has become televisual, a kind of virtual reality in which what is seen on the screen and what exists in "reality" are identical or in which what we used to call "reality" has become imaginary. Dr. Johnson could only "refute it, thus" by smashing a screen that showed a rock. Everything is seen through a camera's eye and reprojected onto a screen. In 1994, such a concept might have seemed to predict a "logical" next step for Western society. Now, the "world as television" has to surrender to the world as computer screen, or to some combination of television and computer, as in the Almereyda film of *Hamlet*, with which I deal with in Chapter 8.

Since 1979, when Desmond Davis directed an excellent version of this script for BBC-TV, we have needed another production for the purpose of contrast. We "see" the former production in the mirror held up by the new one. Olivier's masterful *Henry V*, seeking a way to demonstrate his mature skills, is much more vivid in light of Branagh's insecure young king, testing himself against the vast unknown of warfare.

Davis's *Measure for Measure* features a stiff, puritanical, lace-collared, leaded-glassed Vienna that holds out no promise of an emotional messiah. Isabella can find only cold statuary to which to "complain." As with the other BBC productions of that period, this is a "straight" version that shows the Duke as impresario, methodically staging the final scene so that his tawdry machinery will make him look "like power divine." Isabella's only edge of control is to keep the Duke waiting at the end before the final triumphant procession. Kate Nelligan's Isabella, says Graham Nicholls, is "a refreshing essay at a plain performance, but one cannot now return to the pre-1970 Isabella who can be accepted on her own terms and who will leave the stage smiling on the arm of the Duke" (1986, 79). Nicholls alludes to the Isabella of John Barton (Estelle Kohler), who turned the Duke down at the end, as did Jonathan Miller's Isabella (Penelope Wilton) in 1975. But Angela Carteret at St. George's (1977), having made a vivid mistake in deciding to get herself to a nunnery, accepted her Duke (Joseph O'Conor) with alacrity. In John Retallack's Oxford production of 1990, John Mitchie knelt before his Isabella (Carla Mendonca), humbling himself as he had asked her to do only moments before. She accepted him as the *exception* among the Lucios, Angelos, and Claudios of the world. The ending depends on what a production has shown us.

The script, like any of Shakespeare's, offers options from which directors and actors must select. The choices are dictated by a host of factors—the "concept" of the production; the actors and their relationships, both as people and as characters; the genre (is *Measure for Measure* a comedy or a problem play?); the desired effect of that genre; and the zeitgeist within which the production emerges. Thacker's version shows, for example, how quickly zeitgeist can change by what we would now have to call an overemphasis on televisual "values." Even if the "concept" (as in the Thacker production) is on the alienation and isolation that television is said to induce, no reason exists for a smiling Isabella's *not* leaving on the Duke's arm if that is the inevitability toward which the production has built. Here, as I will suggest, the production builds toward the inevitability of the next show on the program.

Graham Nicholls suggests of the 1979 production that "with no emotional or psychological basis for [the Duke's or Isabella's] behaviour, the play loses its way in a maze of tedious intrigue" (55). I agree that Kevin Colley's Duke did keep himself obscured in his dark corners. As I have argued (Coursen 1984, 65–69), the medium dictated the ending, as opposed to any convincingly imitated development between the Duke and Isabella. The play is a soap opera that can achieve conventional "happy-ending" closure on prime-time television. Television is seldom a site for the ambiguity that we can discuss and ponder on the way home from the theater. Nelligan's tentative exploration of the roles thrust upon her by Lucio and the Duke does, however, permit her final decision to take the Duke's hand to reflect the maturity she has gained. It is a cool performance for the cool medium.

Thacker's version is much "warmer"—no cold blues or leaded windows—with the crucial exception of Tim Wilkinson's portly, soft-spoken Duke. We observe the Duke observing his city on his giant-screen television. It shows that icon of riot, a burning car. Whores walk the streets. Gay males cavort in public entertainments. Vienna is Gomorrah, Medici Rome, Times Square. Thacker cuts from the arrival of Angelo ("I come to know your pleasure") to Overdone's brothel (where she cares for the son of Lucio and Kate) back to the gray and chilly room of state, to the red-hued whorehouse again, to Angelo, who has cleared away the Duke's pile of books and now gazes at a single law book, to the shocking arrest of Claudio as he and Juliet hold hands in a bistro (trying to live out a "last time I saw Paris" moment within an anachronism known as romantic love), to the whorehouse, to Claudio being strip-searched in front of a group of voyeurs ("why dost thou show me thus to the world?"), to a brutal raid on Overdone's establishment, and so on. Davis's technique in the 1979 production is very different. He gives us long shots and full scenes, with a voice or a sound occasionally coming in over the set for the previous scene or the noise of a previous scene echoing into the next (suggesting the continuous flow of the Shakespearean stage) and with the ironic reinforcement of having the convent share the architecture of the brothel, but with a less lurid paint job. Thacker's camera is paced to brief glimpses of a police state attempting to reassert control over a licentious society. The camera's inability to pause simulates the mindlessness of power, a terrifying unwillingness to consider consequences once certain policies have been put into action. It is the process that Barbara Tuchman documents in *March of Folly*. It is very important here—particularly for television's potential suggestive, or metonymic ability—that Thacker not identify his police state. These thugs are not members of the Falange or the Gestapo. They could be the boys next door. The production does not tie itself down to a distracting set of historical analogies.

Thacker suggests motivation by images, but that technique is often insufficient. When the Duke says "Lord Angelo is precise," we see Angelo looking at his law book. The Duke is testing Angelo—but why? This mild Angelo, hardly presented as a public exemplar of virtue, poses no challenge to a permissive Duke. That the Duke merely wishes to reimpose dusty statutes is to take the script at its most superficial level. In spite of Thacker's having directed the play for the Young Vic in 1988, he has not asked the basic question. Why is the Duke absenting himself? Furthermore, Angelo has hardly forgotten his desertion of Mariana. He looks at a photograph of himself and a woman and puts it in a drawer. We see a woman standing behind a rain-sluiced window. People who don't know the play—and that would be a goodly number of the audience—might ask, Is she a former lover? Is Angelo's harsh judgment of Claudio some projection of Angelo's own self-hatred? Is the Duke's plot an effort to reunite Angelo and this mystery woman? If so, it goes awry when Corin Redgrave's dour and middle-aged Angelo discovers that Isabella has reignited the torch he has been carrying for the discarded Mariana. His is not the repressed fire that Tim Pigott-Smith brings to the role in the BBC version but the subtext of a man who has given up on sexuality until it is suddenly presented to him again—quite unintentionally—by Isabella's "prone and speechless dialect." He gives her a rancid kiss, which she tries to wipe away from her mouth. In the convent, a single candle burns with incandescent ambivalence in a scene borrowed from de La Tour's seventeenth-century portrait of Magdalene. As Isabella wishes a more strict "restraint," her dark locks fall to the floor of her spartan room. As Claudio is thrown to the straw of his cell, the imagery of "restraint" is repeated. Are we to infer that brother and sister inhabit opposite segments of the moral spectrum but that each extreme imposes restriction? Later, in 4.3, the Duke takes a long look at Isabella in Lucio's comforting arms ("O petty Isabella!"). Does that vision kindle the Duke's passion?

Perhaps, but this ponderous and humorless Duke seems as ill-suited for Isabella as she for him. She is a gamine with luminous eyes, which are set off by the deletion of her long hair. The eyes hint of madness as she clenches the strange plurality of "More than our brother is our chastity." But this is a play of extremes, and the production captures them. Religion itself is extreme here, not merely an option for a young woman of the early seventeenth century (even if the "Poor Clares" would have been a radical choice within the available options). The play is also "ambiguous," as critics used to say, and the production is nuanced in the direction of fruitful uncertainty. Does the Duke display a hint of voyeurism as he gazes at the television tableau at the outset? If so, the production suggests how "pleasure"—legal authority—can become "pleasure"—sensual license. Is the Bible at which the Duke points in the final scene upside down or rightside up? If the former, he indicates the Sermon on the Mount. If the latter, he is invoking the *lex talionis* of Old Testament law. Does Isabella accept the Duke's proposal at the end? Having had everyone else exit from his chamber—Miller did the same thing in his brilliant 1975 production—the Duke, checking to make sure that the television crew covering his return has packed up its cameras, ends with "What's mine is yours." The camera rises to show him and the novice standing on the chessboard floor of the ducal room. Hers is the next move, but she does not have a chance to register even the flicker of an eyebrow as the frame freezes and the credits roll. The fact of external production takes over from the drama of inner decision, appropriately for this production about restraint and control— and television.

In Miller's production, the Duke pulled a brilliant public relations coup, but when he wanted something for himself, Isabella turned him down. The response of Juliet Aubrey's Isabella to Wilkinson's

Duke would seem to make little difference, since nothing has occurred between them. My inference is that her answer will be no. He presses his advantage too soon, as the script seems to suggest ("But fitter time for that"). He recognizes as much here in her startled, possibly angry, gulp on "say you will be mine." His proposal seems to spring unexpectedly from his ennui and therefore lacks conviction. An early shot with Francesca and a later scene with Mariana suggest that Isabella's hugs and kisses may be more than pro forma. She makes clear that her plea for Angelo in 5.1 is for Mariana. Her legalistic excuse for Angelo is thus permitted to contrast vividly with the New Testament argument that had kindled Angelo's passion ("Go to your bosom...") in 2.2. It may be, though, that the Duke has misread her gender preference. Because Thacker gives the characters no edge of innocence on which to stand, he gives us no certain place from which to assert "meanings." Ambiguity is hardly television's forte, but it functions here. The deliberate, "old-fashioned" decision based on one's sense of morality and self cannot be made in a world that does not permit those kinds of distinctions. Again, the production shows us where we have arrived and, to some extent, where television has brought us in 1994, as opposed to 1979, where Isabella was at least clear-cut and wronged, even if a bit rigid in her righteousness. She could find no one to whom to complain because the Duke was absent. The latter Isabella can find no one to whom to complain because the Duke is there—in Angelo, in himself.

Thacker himself toys with us when the Provost uncovers a chalky cadaver. Is it Claudio? No. It's Ragozine. Again, Thacker permits us, as the Duke seemingly permits Claudio, to believe that Claudio is being led to execution. Our own expectations coincide with Claudio's, and they veer between extremes. The possibility of execution shadows the ending, which, of course, is a motionless tableau containing the "yes" or "no" on which Claudio had balanced.

In a production as rapidly intercut as this, a lot of the script is gone. The Duke sets up the bed trick so adroitly that we never hear of that "garden circummur'd with brick." Nor is it necessary in a modern medium for him to use the "O place and greatness" bridge in 4.1 as Isabella and Mariana talk, a soliloquy that is either wildly out of context or that tells us exactly why the Duke is engaging in all this machination. Here, the Duke does not claim a "complete bosom" for himself to Friar Thomas, an omission that takes away the later irony of his falling in love. Juliet's anger at the meddling

Friar, so well registered in the 1979 production by Yolanda Palfrey, is lost here to the urgency of Isabella's giving birth. Elbow and Froth are gone, though Pompey is permitted to inveigh against the law, to glance briefly at the variety of men dragged into gaol, and to name Overdone's overdoing ninth husband. His best line—"Your honors have seen such dishes"—is gone.

The underparts here are splendid. Sue Johnston (Overdone) brings a dignity, almost an aristocratic grandeur, to her role, thus decentering any moral certainties we might try to apply to the depicted world. Rob Edwards's handsome Lucio is a playboy, but no fop. He had played the Duke previously for Thacker, and his placement in that role would have radically changed the dynamics of this production— for the better, I think. It is unfortunate that Lucio's "Carnally, he says" and "Enough, my lord"—both funny lines, get lost in the rush of the final scene. Henry Goodman brings a joy to Pompey that this dark telling of the story needs. Margot Leicester's Mariana, though limited by heavy editing, provides a steadfastness of purpose that also benefits a production that makes so many rapid transitions. David Bradley's Barnadine is superb. He *wants* to repent, but to do so is to be executed, and so he lives on in an anguished limbo. The Duke's pardon at the end is necessary and moving. It makes sense as I have never seen it made before. Ben Miles's Claudio is a young aristocrat in love with Juliet. While he lacks the hint of weak sensuality that Christopher Strauli brings to the 1979 Claudio, Miles delivers a sweaty "Ay, but to die…" that sets up Aubrey's powerful rejection of him. In a sense, it is to Claudio that Isabella complains, in that he receives the full brunt of her unexpended anger toward Angelo. This production made sense of Isabella's overstated indictment of Claudio by suggesting that he is being blamed for what Angelo would have done to Isabella. Thus were the emotional dynamics of the second interview between her and Angelo and her meeting with Claudio powerfully linked, the former scene explaining the latter.

Thacker makes sure that we watch television within this production. Some of Overdone's customers are televised for "exhibition" purposes, perhaps even for a cable channel to which the Duke subscribes. The Duke observes Isabella and Claudio on a monitor. The Provost picks up his cues by watching the Duke's televised return to Vienna. But has the Duke, master of the media, learned more than to make sure the cameras are off when he proposes to Isabella? Does the stasis of the ending tell us that action and decision are impossible unless they are televised, unless they are a function of someone writing a script? The Duke's script has gone as far as it can go. It propels him and Isabella into that frozen moment at the end. This is that rare television production that questions the premises of the medium by leaving things hanging at the end and granting respect to its audience by not tying up all the loose ends.

That we have a contrast with the earlier production is a blessing. The Thacker should be made commercially available so that this rich and intriguing play can be brought more centrally into the teaching canon. Carefully conceived and edited, this script would make a great film. I suggested as much years ago to Kenneth Branagh, when Emma Thompson was available to play Isabella. Ah well!

The NBC *Tempest*

The NBC version of *The Tempest*, which aired in December 1998, is set in the Confederacy of 1865. The thematic links with the American Civil War would seem to emerge from the "freedom-bondage" concept that runs through the play and illustrates in different ways the conflicts of Ariel, Caliban, and Ferdinand. Here, we have an irrelevant Gator Man, played by J. Pyper-Furgeson, who wants his bog back, and an Ariel, played by Harold Perineau, who combines Caliban *and* Ariel. The "spirit" can become a crow at any moment he chooses, but he also does a lot of the domestic chores. As an unfreed slave, who learns about the Emancipation Proclamation two years after it has been issued, he wants to join Grant's army on the way to Vicksburg.

The production resembles a story of voodoo thrust upon a Civil War reenactment, or perhaps a nightmare of Mr. Hightower, Faulkner's preacher in *Light in August,* whose sermons keep rumbling off into the dust of one of Jeb Stuart's cavalry columns. The voodoo is promising (à la Gloria Naylor's *Mama Day*), but the production places the narrative in a specific 1865 and makes Ulysses S. Grant a sub-hero, thereby introducing a host of issues the script does not raise and blurring beyond distinction what the script does invite a production to explore. A specific time period is seldom a good environment for the translation of a Shakespeare script to any medium, and that is particularly true for television, where a limited field of depth cannot accommodate a lot of details. Here, it doesn't matter.

Kyra Sedgwick as Olivia and Rick Stear as Sebastian. Lincoln Center Theater. *Photo by Ken Hoard.*

The special effects "from the same masters who dazzled in last spring's miniseries, *Merlin*" (Williams 1998, 2), are tame and tiny, as they must be on a medium that lacks the scale for the spectacular and that usually translates the supernatural in to the psychological (see Dessen 1986 and Coursen 1993). We learn all that we need to know when we are told that "the teleplay is by veteran TV writer James Henerson, whose work [includes] 'I Dream of Jeannie' and 'Bewitched'" (Bobbin 1998, 2)—two shows that emerged from the very different personae of their resident witches. Had Prospero been played by Vanessa Redgrave, as in a recent London production...

The major problem with the production is its remarkable lack of believability. Television is a medium of soap operas that treat in tedious detail the reasons for meaningless actions, or that show persons who narrate stories that reveal the poverty of the human experiment. Peter Fonda's Gideon Prosper is a victim of both strains of these twin displays of futility. The sudden effort to lynch him— he is, after all, chief landowner of the area—is as improbable as his deliverance from the rope.

His motivation to stay in the swamp grows more and more implausible as pressure is brought to bear on him to develop a conscience. The effort here is to parallel the development of Shakespeare's Prospero, but NBC's Prosper is more a puppet of the plot—a Pinocchio—than recognizable character struggling with a moral or ethical dilemma. Why does he object to his daughter's elopement with her handsome Union officer? Prospero has reasons for slowing the romantic pace of Ferdinand and Miranda, but to change the motive into an apparent hatred of Yankees is to introduce yet another irrelevancy to the story. Since the swamp is right around the bend from the old plantation, Gideon can go after his brother at any time. His excitement at hearing that his brother is near is incomprehensible. After Prosper's storm, Katherine Heigl's Miranda, little homemaker that she is, gets herself off-camera by saying that she is going to check on the house. We remain breathless until she returns to report that nothing of the vine-woven, bark-covered Tarzan treehouse has perished. At another moment, after Gideon is plugged through the breastbone by his brother, Anthony (John Glover is a terrible shot until asked to shoot offhand from a rocking boat), I thought that we were going to be asked to clap our hands and say that we believe in "Dat Ole Black Magic."

At the end, rewards are handed out. The production answers the still-vexed question of Caliban by showing that Gator Man gets his swamp back because he had courage. It is a wonder that Gideon does not hand the cowardly blusterer a Purple Heart. As Prosper, Miranda, and Fred leave the island, Gator Man stands on his deck. No one waves goodbye. What does work is Anthony's sneering refusal to accept his brother Gideon's hand at the end, even though a firing squad awaits him. But we wonder, given this blank Prosper and this perfidious Anthony (who has committed far worse than *The Tempest*'s Antonio), why the hand has been offered in the first place. Since the action is heavily influenced by a voodoo priestess appearing as a face out of flames, the sudden advent of a "Christian" set of values has not been prepared for. *The Tempest* may be more pagan or cabalistic, more Giordano Bruno or Cornelius Agrippa, than a reflection of Richard Hooker and the reformed church, but it does have a strong Christian rhythm. How could it not? "After all," as Barnaby Dobree, writing of the final plays, says, Shakespeare "belonged to a Christian country; he had been brought up on the Bible; so its ideas, its familiar phrases, would naturally occur to him" (1961, 148). Here, we cannot believe in either pole of the play's syncretic value system (see Coursen 2000).

I sought some equation between Gideon Prosper and the Bible's Gideon. In the Book of Judges, Gideon is one of the citizens oppressed by the Midianites. After a lot of negotiation with God, which involves tearing down the altar of Baal, tests in which a fleece left out over night is alternately wet with dew when the ground is dry or dry when the ground is wet, and the reduction of his army from 22,000 to 300 (so the Israelites can't brag about what *they* have done), Gideon drives the enemy out, killing most of them, including the princes, Oreb, Zeeb, Sebah, and Zalmunna. It is a great story, but I could not find any parallel between it and this version of *The Tempest*.

The production reminds us of our own dispensation by constantly interjecting it, at what the directors must have deemed moments of unbearable suspense, with commercial breaks. Many of them were for what must be the worst television shows imaginable. If the spots selected to promote these shows are so crashingly unfunny, for all of the artificial laughter that floats around them like dead leaves, why would anyone be tempted to watch them? At other moments, since the production appeared only a dozen shopping days until Christmas, the mosquito-buzzing swampland of the Mississippi Delta was juxtaposed against the snowflakes, balsam trees, colored lightbulbs, and other clichés of a white, middle-class Christmas.

Freeing the slaves was necessary and overdue, but it was only a secondary reason for the American Civil War. I assume that the production meant us to infer the knowledge that the "brave new world of Reconstruction" became a version of the old world very quickly. What on earth is executive producer Raskin talking about when she says, "We loved the banishment and the isolation, in this case, in terms of North versus South" (Williams 1998, 2)? That statement signals incoherence at the heart of the project.

I asked myself a) whether the production would have been successful without any knowledge of *The Tempest* to get in the way, and b) whether the production enhanced our sense of the source. In each case, I answered no. The production itself is tedious, elongated beyond its intrinsic content and centered on a mere Scrooge. Its connections with the original script are so tenuous or simplified that it distorts rather than illuminates. Unlike other works of art—painting and sculpture, for example—the plays of Shakespeare permit us to inhabit them in our time and, inevitably, *with* our time. This production simply abandons its originating source and gives us a far lesser thing in its place.

It will be objected, rightly, that my critique would not even occur were it not for the production's linkage with Shakespeare's play. True—without that connection this *Tempest* would have passed unnoticed, its radical inconsistencies merely those of television melodrama. Our expectation of the medium is a fragment of Aristotle's "final cause"—the effect of the work of art on the observer. This *Tempest* can be said to have met our expectations for television, which are low. Television is in its infancy—and likely to stay there. We learn about it, however, as it encounters the Shakespearean script and struggles to find the right balance between a heavy concept and a bare stage.

Chapter 4

The Use and Misuse of History:
Two Recent Films

Any production occurs "in history," even if the production tries to escape a recognizable moment in the past. Some productions do, of course, and are often praised for their "post-modern indeterminacy." *Shakespeare in Love* survives some of its earlier lapses into anachronism, such as the silly 1970s trip to the shrink, which trades on self-congratulatory recognitions on the part of members of the audience, to move into a late-1990s vision of Elizabethan London, as if Sam Wanamaker's Globe had spread down Bankside and slid its tentacles across several bridges to the City, there to replace the steel and glass towers with squatter structures of timber, mortar, and brick, and gridlocked avenues with muddy lanes. The architecture, streets, and costumes convey "authenticity" and are not really much different than the black-and-white mise-en-scéne of the opening of the 1929 *Taming of the Shrew,* though the latter features more live dogs. Most important, the settings for *Shakespeare in Love* contextualize the love story and its conflict: an arranged marriage versus romantic love, which, in turn is the conflict central to the play-within-the film, *Romeo and Juliet.* Conceptual space and the story told within that space coincide perfectly. The film emerges from a tradition of films about the production of plays or musicals or films in which backstage and onstage worlds tug at each other. In this genre, the onstage world sometimes resolves the offstage dilemmas. Marion Davies's wonderful silent film *Show People, Singin' in the Rain,* Mickey-and-Judy flicks like *Babes in Arms,* and Cole Porter's masterpiece, *Kiss Me, Kate!* are examples of a genre that seldom fails, though it can do so, as in *Goldiggers of 1937,* which consistently trespasses beyond the boundaries of credulity. *Shakespeare in Love* benefits from its *not* having a happy ending. Unlike the examples I give or almost any other instance in the genre, the two young lovers don't end up together. That separation lifts the film above its generic counterparts. It is, as the comparison with old-fashioned films suggests, an old-fashioned film, doing what film has always done well and, above all, it is thematically unified from its depths to its surfaces.

The same cannot be said for Michael Hoffman's *A Midsummer Night's Dream*, which is a waste of money and, possibly, of good actors, and certainly of time for its audience. It is a good example of what happens when a shallow understanding of post-modernism overtakes the production of a Shakespeare script. Here the mode is further compromised by that old nemesis called "Hollywood," a term for any film that seeks only to be popular, to fill the screen with "stars" and count on them to make a banal production profitable. The film reveals no sense of whatever its generic premises may be. Apparently, that is an intentional absence, as some of the director's nonsensical utterances suggest. The historical moment that the film selects collides with whatever the script may still have to communicate to a late-twentieth-century film audience.

Dennis Kennedy notices a trend in staging Shakespeare toward "a trans-historical or anti-historical use of eclectic costuming and displaced scenery, creating through irony, a disjunction between the pastness of Shakespeare's plays and the ways we now receive them" (1993, 166–167). Ron Daniels's 1995 *Henry V* for the American Repertory Theater took this tendency over the border. "Whereas the English are very much these mud creatures," said Daniels, "the French are sky creatures" (quoted in Graham 1995, B30). This is as if Daniels (or J. R. R. Tolkien or Frank Herbert) were making a fiction, not Shakespeare, as if the contrast between the French and British, a "given" the play invites a director to explore, invites a reductio ad absurdum. "We're looking at these French creatures as very beautiful creatures," Daniels gushes, "very wondrous creatures. They walk on shoes that are 1 foot high, they ride these beautiful horses" (Graham 1995, B30). The French did walk around on high shoes and later were pushed around on wheeled platforms, from which they played chess or rolled dice on trays held high by servants. Later, they pranced inside toy horses borrowed from *Equus*. The "ideas" go back at least as far as John Barton's 1972 *Richard II*, where Mowbray and Bolingbroke appeared inside toy horses, as on an amputated merry-go-round for their trial by combat, thereby trivializing the profound issues involved in their dispute, and where Northumberland (the "ladder") grew into a giant upstage crow. These isolated images forced me to keep resuspending my disbelief until I gave up trying. The issues of this difficult script were sponged up by the distracting pictures Barton kept presenting to us. They belonged to no coherent world. In science fiction, although things happen that cannot happen in "reality," the writer creates a world in which they can and do happen. I think particularly of the *Dune* trilogy, where Herbert's imagination challenges our own.

It is true that tribesmen with spears charged Mussolini's columns in 1935, that a squadron of Polish uhlans attacked a Panzer division in 1939, and that an army without an air force defeated the United States in Vietnam. History is full of anachronisms and, even today, different parts of the world live in different, if parallel, times. Daniels, however, put his fantasy Frogs up against automatic weapons. While the French misunderstood the lesson of Crécy about the superiority of the longbow and charged headlong into it again at Agincourt, this contingent was from another time and another world. We were asked to plunge our disbelief into deeper places than it can go in order to accept what was happening on stage. We were being asked to imagine the charge of a group of armored knights against the machine-gun nests of the Somme in 1916. In that instance, the superior numbers, of which the inherited script makes so much, would mean nothing. By moving into *non*-history, the play made no link with our moment, except to suggest that *Henry V* and its title character represent a boy's fantasy as played out at a video arcade. It may be that my assumption that a director attempts to discover coherence in the script and to deliver that coherence to an audience is untenable within post-modernist criteria.

In 1935, Warner Brothers trotted out their stars and produced a black-and-white *Midsummer Night's Dream* that took advantage of the field of depth that color makes impossible and of the filmic silence that Warner Brothers had almost single-handedly destroyed. The Indian boy tries to follow his wafting friends, but pauses at a pond because he cannot fly. The donkey who pulled the props into the woods for Peter Quince bolts at the sight of his brother, Bottom, one of the film's images of monstrosity that contrast with fairies who dance up ramps of clouds as unicorns graze below. Oberon and Titania fly in from a far star and land gracefully on the parapets of Theseus's sinewy palace. The special effects that seem to rise from Korngold's adaptation of Mendelssohn are beautiful these many years after for all of the Hollywood auspices of the film (see Crowl 1992). The black-and-white format gives the film the feeling of an antique, which, in turn , erases discrepancies in casting and technique that would have been clear to a 1935 eye, still learning to tune its ear to film. Time has been kinder to this film than to other early sound manifestations, such as the 1929 *Taming of the Shrew*, which began as a silent film and still has the feeling of one; the 1936 *Romeo and Juliet;* and the 1937 *As You Like It*. Perhaps that indulgence results from the film's ability to do some things that films of any era can do well, perhaps because in some meta-cinematic way, it seems to be enjoying itself as it is being made, and as it is remade for us, frame by frame. By way of contrast, Peter Hall's 1969 version, with its jagged and self-conscious camera work, looks strained and dated only three decades later.

It is too easy to blame the lunatic excesses of the post-modernist approach—which prizes the eclecticism that Kennedy describes— for the almost complete failure of Michael Hoffman's star-laden 1999 *A Midsummer Night's Dream*. Post-modernism is a mode that offers options, after all, not iron-bound directives. Other failures—of casting, lighting, and that subtle but vital element called rhythm, which we recognize when it *isn't* there, but feel when it is—are also grossly palpable.

For all of its brevity, *Dream* is a difficult script. It insists on the delineation of several different worlds—of the aristocracy, adolescence, the working class, and the fairy kingdom—and on at once distinguishing between them and allowing them to inhabit the same stage and to interact with each other. It might seem at first to be a good play for post-modernism, in that it incorporates radical anachronisms: elements of deep mythology, Elizabethan sprites, and artisans. It demands, however, an integrative imagination like that of the Elizabethan syncretic imagination. These anachronisms do inhabit the same time, even if the fairy world verges on timelessness. Theseus can sneer or smile as he says "'Tis almost fairy time," not believing a word of it, but the others—Bottom, Hippolyta, and the lovers—in their different ways, know that something is alive in the shadows. We know that, too. The script demands, says Wilhelm Hortmann, an initial decision about the forces at work in Athens wood. "Is it the domain of creative Eros, stormily, even grotesquely upsetting, but finally life-enhancing? Or is Athens wood the place of ultimate self-confrontation, where we are made to recognize the human depravity which no manner of magic can gloss? A further factor that makes for diversity would seem to be what kind of lovers

Michelle Pfeiffer as Titania. *Photo by Mario Tursi, Courtesy of Fox Searchlight Films.*

errant (roues or ingenues, contemporaries or historical figures) and what sort of strolling players the director decides to send into Athens wood to be transformed" (1984, 217–218).

Rightly or wrongly, Hortmann makes the *woods* the focal point of the drama. Hoffman, wrongly I think, makes the town the center, or at least begins his consideration of the script there (Searchlight 1999, 10). For *Comedy* or *Shrew* perhaps, but not for *Dream*. Hoffman's town is an Italian square and marketplace that convinces us, with its bustle and buildings, of its solidity. We spend too much time there. The woods incorporate "Etruscan temples and tombs`...over-grown with roots and greenery" (12). It looks like the ruins of the Mayan city of Tul, north of Ciudad Mexico. I expected an angry maize god to spring out at any moment, but, to forestall that prospect, Hoffmann cuts Titania's line about the decay of the green corn. That great speech, so potently delivered by Judi Dench as the seasons altered behind her in the Hall film, is virtually excised here. And that is the problem in the Hoffman film. It lacks any sense of *change*, of a transformation that makes the known and the unknown quiver within the same object in a supernatural symbiosis. The film, then, does not do what film *can* do, and must do, with this script. Hall achieved it randomly, Reinhardt-Dieterle consistently. The Hoffman film does not suggest the imagination of *another* cooperating with or creatively resisting that of Shakespeare. Shakespeare's imagination, for example, shows that Oberon's love-juice affects more than just the eyes. Titania, awakening and before she sees Bottom, believes that she *hears* an angel singing. Our own imaginations must adjust immediately to a report for which we have not been prepared. The film director must make similar adjustments as he creates his or her translations. Producer Leslie Urdang compares the play to *Oz*, where a Technicolor dream world rises from the dusty winds of brown Kansas. But the contrast vivid in that film is lacking in Hoffmann's, as is the Oz-like reinforcement in a production of *Dream* described by Gerald Berkowitz: "The doubling of the machanicals and the fairies created a charming...*Wizard of Oz* effect, the characters in Bottom's dream becoming magical versions of his real-life friends" (1983, 90). The use of the consistent Shakespearean device of doubling does not, in fact, take much imagination. The theatrical technique, however, can have a powerful effect on our own participating imagination.

Alex Jennings as Oberon and Lindsay Duncan as Titania. *Photo courtesy of Channel Four Films and the Arts Council of England.*

Inside one of those Etruscan ruins is a smoky bar that looks like a dive in Marseilles—no reach for any magical effects here! This "magic forest occupied a whole soundstage at Cinetta" (in Rome), but it is hardly "the production's masterpiece," as the studio handout claims (Searchlight 1999, 12). The murky ruins do not contrast with the surrounding countryside, primarily because the latter is not effectively established until after the forest scenes, as the hunt hooves its way across the morning fields and the wheat moves back and forth in the wind like a section of violins. For how to get the country/woods contrast effectively into a film, see Woody Allen's *A Midsummer Night's Sex Comedy*. Here, the First Fairy's recognition of Puck is upstaged by the pungent dark and the nasty-looking denizens of this iniquitous den. Are we to infer that Puck is not supposed to be here—that, like Joyce's Farrington, he is sneaking a nip while supposedly on duty? This sequence epitomizes a film "cluttered nearly into claustrophobia with *stuff*," as Lisa Schwarzbaum says (1999, 48; her emphasis).

I could not discern Hoffman's editorial principle. His script seems to be made up of words that will prove that "this is Shakespeare!" or, perhaps, lines enough to placate his panoply of stars. He accomplishes none of the exploration of the script that good directors have accustomed us to—I think of John Barton's "Playing Shakespeare" series and of the tapes of Peter Hall rehearsing his repertory of the final plays for The National. Good ensemble acting can work on film, which has the ability to pick up the cues in the language that Barton has shown us how to discern.

The role of Hermia is gutted. Her plea to Lysander to "teach our trial patience" evokes his apparent agreement: "A good persuasion," therefore (and I paraphrase) let's get the hell out of here! That can be funny, and it sets up their later debate in the woods about where he will lie, but not if the exchange is not there. Upon awakening out there, Hermia loses the lines about her combat with the serpent. That is too Viennese perhaps for Tuscany, but it is a précis of Titania's experience with bestiality, a psychic payback perhaps for Hermia's having fended off Lysander and possibly a signal that she is ready for a less threatening contact with the knowledge the serpent represents once the marriage vows have been spoken. Another potentially illuminating moment goes by unrecognized.

Stanley Wells says of the lovers that they are "constantly subjected to parody and caricature in a manner that you find hilariously funny if you regarded them as no more then puppets, or wearisomely effortful if you thought of them as human beings" (1991, 201). I would amend that by suggesting that the women's attempt to behave as humans while puppets can be funny, as when Christine Baranski's Helena, having been partially disrobed, pulled on her gloves while trying to make a decorous exit from the woods in the 1982 Joseph Papp production in Central Park. The key to their characterization is that they are trying to behave like themselves, particularly like the self expected of them (they have yet to detach from the social pressures experienced by adolescents), within a dream. That never works, but the effort often produces the conflicts that we experience in dreams. Our conscious sense of persona objects, helplessly, to the embarrassment we are experiencing within that dream world. Hoffman tells us what goes wrong with these lovers: "A lot of productions treat [them] as interchangeable tools of the farce, but I really tried to get people grounded in their problems" (Rochlin 1999, MT44). This is to prepare for Chekhov and to ignore the control that *situation* exerts over whatever their problems may have been before they became interchangeable. It is situation, for example, that evokes Hermia's latent sense that she is short. It is situation that translates Helena's emotional insecurity into a belief that she is the butt of an elaborate practical joke. Here, Helena's only effective moment occurs *before* the love-juice is applied and misapplied as she pursues Lysander into the woods. Flockhart plays the "spaniel" amusingly. Hoffman's direction, though, undercuts the role. We *watch* her rattle her bike down the steps. We do not listen to her complaint about being considered "as fair" as Hermia. Helena's subsequent response to Hermia occurs against a pillar while, camera right, a sweeper works. We learn at the end that this is Puck, sunlighting apparently to earn some extra drinking money, but it makes no sense later and is upstaging earlier. Helena's conviction that she is the victim of a "confederacy" is rushed. Her assignment of Hermia to the hazing party is not a function of a dawning awareness here, just another product of a foregone conclusion. What makes it funny is that she is responding *as* Helena within a farce that contradicts any sense of individual identity. Her character "develops" step by step in response to her own negative and stereotypical vision of herself— but not in this film. Hermia's parallel effort to ascribe sudden defection to her stature, as opposed to the quick attraction that baffles Helena, is lost in the mud into which the lovers slop. This is an uncomfortable reminder of the LePage version at the National in 1992, which is fashionable to praise these days, but which remains an awful production by any criterion.

Branagh's *Hamlet* refuses to admit the late–nineteenth–century world to its purview. His is a Ruitania attempting to float free of any material premises. It remains a shallow film made up of images and language, but it has little of the physicality that film can lend to the Shakespeare script. Here, the effort to imply an early–twentieth–century placement gets in the way—with one exception. Flockhart is upstaged by her bicycle bouncing beside her down the steps of the town. "It gave me an incredible obstacle to work with," Flockhart says (Searchlight 1999, 11). It does indeed. Typical of the film's incoherence is Hoffman's "concept" for the bicycle. Hardly a means of transportation, it "becomes this thing she carries around with her, like all the negative concepts of herself…which make her a victim" (ibid.). In other words, in trying to be trendy, she displays her awkwardness. In trying to move, she ensures her psychic stasis. But this is at the expense of the words that are lost to the prop. Hoffman later alludes to the Italian film tradition by making Puck a bicycle thief. Initially, Puck thinks it some strange animal. Lord, what fools these spirits be! Puck does some sight gags with the bike—silent screen stuff that Chaplin would have made amusingly inept and Keaton acrobatically splendid (each would have ridden off backward, Chaplin having solved the problem, Keaton frantically aware that he had not). Here, Puck slows the film down with irrelevant and unfunny byplay. For a long stretch, the film is a film about a bicycle.

The one place where the cultural moment of the film contributes to its texture occurs when Bottom shows the fairies how to operate a Victrola. Bottom puts the arm on top of the record automatically, unaware that he is doing anything unusual. Music floods the woodlands, and the fairies say "Hail, mortal!" This moment where human technique is superior to pagan power, and where the movement of "civilization" is contrasted with the stasis of the world of the demi-gods, is isolated, however, unintegrated with any other theme or pattern in the film. The Red Seal records that the fairies have been stealing and toting out to the woods are intended to "upgrade its technology" (Searchlight 1999, 12). What? The Fairyland *has* no technology, and that is the point the film makes superbly at this moment, against the "logic" of its conception. Here is the "cultural logic of late capitalism" run amok.

Rosalind King asks how one "translate[s] the anachronisms and temporal circularities which characterize so many of Shakespeare's plays [to] contemporary" productions (1999, 299). Trevor Nunn shows how in his 1996 *Twelfth Night*, by taking on the gender issue, both in Olivia's denial of sexuality and Viola's assumption of the masculine role. It becomes the film's primary source of comic complication and amusement—as the script suggests it is. Nunn places his film in a late-nineteenth-century culture, where gender roles were strictly and stereotypically observed. That placement sharpens the difficulties that Viola faces in transgressing boundaries. If, of course, Elizabethan or Jacobean commonplaces are too obviously circulating through a given script, the modern director simply excises them. Branagh, for example, does not retain much of the "topical" script of *Love's Labour's Lost*, but the major elements of the praxis are there. In Hoffman's film, anachronisms introduced into a script laden with so many of its own tend to pull the production into a historical moment that confines it.

Film—Bergman and Fellini aside—tends to demand a "realism" that stage does not. Elizabethans apparently were not troubled by anachronism. Nor are we in Shakespeare. It does not matter that clocks strike in Julius Caesar's Rome or that characters from deep mythology, who can drop names such as "Hercules and Cadmus" appear in a play full of Elizabethan sprites. Victorian England works well for the play on stage—with Lysander a young Tennyson jotting down his better lines—and a modern Italian setting can work for *Shrew*, as Stratford, Canada showed in 1992. It can also be a disaster, as Bogdanov proved a decade earlier at Stratford, U.K. *Richard III* as fascist takeover on stage in 1990 was chilling. As film, the fidelity to 1937 produced a documentary effect that stifled the heavily medieval premises of the inherited script. Our age cannot tolerate anachronisms in realistic media, and so we have to accept that Richard's line about Stanley's "horse" (cavalry) tells us that Richard has forgotten in the comings and beheadings of his staff that he has put Stanley in charge of the Royal Air Force. Many cavalrymen became pilots in the early days of flight, including von Richthofen—the lesson of Balaclava having been learned by soldiers by 1914—but that was World War I. Richard is presiding over a version of World War II. The Stanley anachronism, where the allusion to cavalry is incomprehensibly retained, drops a bomb on the film as devastating as the one that Stanley releases from the single plane in Richard's air force.

Hoffman introduces a village square in Tuscany, early-twentieth-century technology, Etruscan ruins, and Woody Allen out-takes that collide with each other and drop debris down upon the script. To be fair to the film, the problem is more a conflict of styles—design and acting—than it is a function of anachronisms. It is merely typical of the production that no one is wearing "Athenian garments," though they are mentioned twice. The lines about the garments, including Puck's excuse, can be excised without confusion—Oberon does not know about Lysander until he sees that Puck has made a mistake—but if the lines are there, they must find some manifestation in the production. I expected Oberon to add, "You will say they are Persian."

At moments, the actors, torn between naturalistic motivation and the poetry, give us both word and action separately, thus tediously. This tendency is particularly noticeable in Dominic West's Lysander. A few times the actors misread their lines. Anna Friel swallows the word "fair" when she addresses Helena, so that Helena's "Call you me fair?" is really a question about what Hermia has said, not a bitter self-deprecation. Later, Demetrius says "Melted as the sun"—as opposed to "Melted as the snow"—so that the line as rendered means, "Melted as the sun (melts things)." In a production where the lines are not meant to convey meanings, these lapses themselves are meaningless. Hoffman does, to his credit, transfer some of the lines of the courtiers (one each) to Hermia and Helena during "Pyramus and Thisbe," but do the lovers see in that inner drama any reflection of their own recent misadventures? No, even though the play-within-a-play is a bad dream that the actors take seriously. The discrepancy, as Bergson suggests, is what makes it funny.

Perhaps the most damaging editing occurs when Theseus—having left out the dismissive equation of lover, lunatic, and poet—*wins* the debate with Hippolyta. The script, I believe, shows him being bested and as delighted to be interrupted ("Here come the lovers, full of joy and mirth"). Here he wins because he is the patriarch. Gone is the subtle juxtaposition of official versus intuitive voices. Theseus's discourse, says Howard Nemerov, is "rational, civic-minded, discursive, and tends constantly to approach prose." Hippolyta's is "magic, fabulous, dramatic, and constantly approaches music." The excess of one is that "art is entertainment," of the other "that art is mystery" (1964, 23–24). Here, Shakespeare's superb orchestration becomes chitchat between the Sauterne for the mussels and the Chablis for the salmon.

It can be hard to identify elements of pace and rhythm in a production, even when one feels them go awry. Luhrmann's pell-mell *Romeo and Juliet* plays out against the cauldron of Ciudad Mexico and seems to coincide with what happens in the play, in his production, to *make* it happen. Zeffirelli was condemned for a rushed *Hamlet* (Rafferty 1991), but I think his film pursued the "Claudius rhythm," a brisk effort to explain away ambiguity with easy oxymoron, a pace that trapped Hamlet within it. The animated Shakespeares can be extremely effective when their condensation imitates a lack of pause or hesitation, as in the *Othello*, which describes its title character's rush to judgment. Hoffman's *Dream* rushes past some signals and slows down for others that are not there.

Perhaps the best way to suggest the film's failure to achieve effective pacing is to mention an exception. When the film pauses to consider its material, the quality of that material shines through and shows the rest of the film what it might have been. Titania's speech in defense of her retention of the Indian Boy suggests the vicarious pregnancy she experienced through her vot'ress. Oberon's "How long within this wood intend you stay?"—a change of subject—is an admission of defeat. In this film, Pfeiffer establishes Titania's resolve with the "embarked traders" speech, and we are ready for some exploration of the play's central conflict. Titania is completely undercut, however, by Oberon's lack of any motive for wanting the Boy and thus, subsequently, for punishing her. Does she commit a kind of hubris in wishing to become a mother, and is her coupling with a beast the trip down the chain of being on which hubris insists? If this were the configuration, Oberon would be the chastening and correcting god. Or is Oberon merely jealous of the attention she gives to the Boy, as fathers can be when their wives are suddenly at the beck and call of infants?

Rupert Everett's Oberon is one of the bored pantheon in Sten Nadolny's *The God of Impertinence*, fighting vainly the old ennui. He is mildly upset that Titania won't give him the Boy, but it's a game to play. No response from her motivates his subsequent pity. She is just a product of his moods. He does release her, but his report of the "mild terms" which elicited his "patience" is omitted. Thus the *reason* for the comic resolution is not there. Has anyone learned anything? The question of the Boy—the removal of the obstacle between Titania and Oberon, a removal the necessity of which both finally recognize (it is the source of deep disturbances in nature, after all)—is simply dropped. The script as edited educates us away from basic issues in the play. We are told that although Oberon is profoundly bored, he cannot, like George Sanders, simply blow his brains out. He can only play silly games, the Donald Trump of Fairyland. Modern analogues do not illuminate the script, they revenge themselves upon it for being so damned complicated, that is, for being what our demi-gods—the superrich—strive to avoid.

Bottom is miscast and certainly misdirected as a lazy boulevardier. He flirts with the local girls and hides from his wife, but he has to go home again. Here, he goes home twice, once having had his white suit and brocaded vest doused with Chianti by mischievous boys (when I was a kid, my buddies and I knew not to waste the precious stuff!) and, the second time, after his woodland idyll. He stands at his window and watches wistfully as Tinkerbell becomes the third star to the right. We recognize sentimentality when it requests a response that has not been earned. Director Hoffman asks, "What if Bottom, as the king of amateur dramatics, has delusions of grandeur about himself because he doesn't have any love in his life?" Director Hoffman answers, "I started to build a story for him—a frustrating life and an unhappy marriage" (Searchlight 1999, 9). To build yet another narrative into this complex play is to add confusion, not clarity, as Reinhardt and Dieterle apparently decided when they cut an identical subplot from their 1935 version (see Jackson 1998, 29–31). Adrian Noble made his already eclectic and disjointed stage production even less comprehensible on film by making it a little boy's dream. He borrowed this concept from his own stage version of *A Winter's Tale,* but the effort at synthesis merely added a further bewildering element to a post-modenist mishmash. The director's job is to discern how the script translates to a coherent production at a historical moment, of which the production will make sense and that will make sense of the production—not to overlay or to undercut the potential story or stories already there with his own, or to change the potential unity of the script into isolated moments that may or may not work by themselves but do not work together within the completed work of art.

Kline looks like the latter-day Errol Flynn in *The Sun Also Rises,* and, even with donkey's ears, he is no "monster." The unhappy marriage story makes "sense" of Bottom's tumble with Titania, when in the script the episode makes no sense at all, even to him, except as a fathomless defiance of sensory experience. The rest of the acting troupe, particularly Roger Ree's woebegone Quince, play against Bottom's problem, not against the confusion of art and life which lends so much life and art to the rest of the play. Quince's company, says Desson Howe, resembles "the somber cast of 'The Iceman Cometh'" (1999, 35).

Hoffman has no idea who the audience is for "Pyramus and Thisbe." Are we part of the on-camera audience? Are we to laugh at the play directly, filter our responses though the ducal audience, or maintain a double vision in which we audit the play-within-the-play and its onstage auditors? "Pyramus and Thisbe" invariably poses a tricky problem in staging—or filming—since so much byplay occurs among the audience members and between Theseus and Bottom. The play-within-the-play usually works best when the onstage audience is downplayed. One moment that can work is to have Hippolyta ask how "Moonshine is gone before Thisbe comes back and finds her lover?" Quince, trapped on a panicky ledge between art and life, can shoot a glance at Theseus, who says, reassuringly, "She shall find him by starlight," thus entering into the game of solving problems in staging. But Hoffman does not solve the problem of presenting the material to us. His play-within-the-play is full of tedious business that gets repeated and repeated, as if, unfunny at first, it will somehow *become* funny, like a punchline that, having fallen flat, keeps getting repeated. What makes repetition funny, as Bergson says, is *interference* with the sequence, so that our expectation itself is interfered with—the target ducks and the bishop's wife enters the room in all her bosomy pomposity to catch a pie in the face. Hoffman lacks an education in the silent screen and thus does not know how its techniques still work on the post-modern screen.

As she mourns Pyramus, Thisbe yanks off her wig, as if to say, "This is *real!*" The removal of the wig, however, erases any sense of willing disbelief at precisely the moment when some fraction of dramatic faith might develop. Any opportunity we have to accept an emotional subtext within the fiction is squandered, in contrast to Papp's version of 1982, where Pyramus suddenly sees Titania slipping past a birch out there in the shadows of the dream forest and realizes—as when the truth of a dream floods consciousness—the truth of his moonlit fantasy. The live performance in Central Park, even if rendered televisually, opened up relationships and appealed to our imaginations as Bottom recognized that his adventure had been more than imagination set free in a dream. At that point, the play-within-the-play earned its suddenly serious quality. None of that nuanced, hypothetical balancing between intangibility and physical reality gets into Hoffman's inset. Instead, we must endure an extended gag about the length of Pyramus's sword and its threat to Wall's manhood.

"Pyramus and Thisbe" *is* serious. It strips away any illusions about nature. The artisans' inability to distinguish between art and life underlines the red-clawed quality of that which lies between man's romantic conception of nature. In Ovid, the lion is crossing the terrain to fetch a drink of water. In "Pyramus and Thisbe," that motive is eliminated. The lion is not thirsty, but *there,* and Bottom's question about why Nature framed lions is valid from a human standpoint (see Herbert 1977). Here, though, the fact that the onstage audience suddenly takes the play seriously merely underscores the unfunniness of this version. The play-within-a-film typifies what Janet Maslin calls "a wildly uneven range of performances with no clear style holding them together" (1999, C12).

Mendelssohn sounds at beginning and end, replaced at times by simple-minded theme music (as that behind Bottom's awakening, perhaps a portion of Simon Boswell's score), and at other times by Puccini and Verdi. Bottom gets a lugubrious oboe with vocal accompaniment (something about tears) as he returns, wine-spattered, to his shrew. Oberon's reconciliation with Titania is lost amid the offerings of a lyric soprano. You never voice-over another voice—unless the interruption is intended—something disc jockeys know but that film directors have yet to learn. As Lisa Schwarzbaum puts it mildly, the "random hunks" of music "clash" (1999, 48). We can be thankful that the musical director had not heard of von Weber's *Oberon.*

As *The New Yorker* critic says, the film "lacks taste and rhythm" and is "hard to endure" (D. D. 1999, 23). Does this effort to cash in on the Shakespearean moment set the overall effort back? Artistically, yes. Like any bad production, it suggests that Shakespeare is boring and irrelevant. If it makes enough money, however, maybe not. Hoffman's film may suggest to directors that, although post-modernist disintegration of the the text is "in" everywhere these days, the plays of Shakespeare demand an imaginative reassembly after their demolition.

Gwyneth Paltrow as Viola Des Lesseps in "Shakespeare in Love."
Photo courtesy of Miramax Films.

In Love In London

Shakespeare in Love is almost pure fantasy that grows beyond its initially sadistic premises—that debtors in Elizabethan England could be tortured with impunity by their creditors. An evening of pseudo-Python seemed to lie ahead. In spite of other moments of silliness—London watermen behaving like New York cabbies, for example—the film prospers on the premise of winning performances by Gwyneth Paltrow as Viola de Lesseps, Joseph Fiennes as Will (see Wolf 1998, 2A, 4A), and Dame Judi Dench as a crusty old Elizabeth. She says her final words to a rumble of would-be Raleighs who go for their velvet capes as she splashes through a London mud-pond. "Too late! Too late!" It is also too late for the young lovers. They don't end up freshly dead in a tomb, but parted by dint of marriage to someone else. "Those whom God has joined together not even I can put asunder," says the Queen. Based on one divorce, her church cannot condone another. Until the end, however, it is a great love story intercut with scenes from other love stories, particularly *Romeo and Juliet* and *Twelfth Night*. Stuart Klawans sneers at the film's "Cliff's Notes prestige" (1999, 35), but the rest of us seem happier.

After many actors have auditioned for Will's new play with Faustus's speech to Helen, Master Kent, the disguised Viola, shows up reciting Valentine's soliloquy on Sylvia (3.1), which looks ahead in its "banished" and "banishment' to *Romeo and Juliet*. She takes on a male role here, even the role of stereotypical lover. Her brief recitation, though, pulls Will's soul toward her. In love with his own verse, he begins the movement from a paralyzing narcissism through other layers—of clothes and of awarenesses. Will's writer's block dissolves in a flash of lust.

That Shakespeare encountered the occasional dam along the river of his creativity is probably not true, as any compulsive writer would agree. Furthermore, only a few of his characters are anything but voluble (Nym, Dull, Silence). The idea of his writer's block is an old one, however. Georges Melies, in his 1907 film *A Dream of Shakespeare*, depicts Shakespeare, stumped and pacing around the room. He sits down, puts his head in his hands, and dreams the conspiracy and assassination of Caesar, this time without feminine inspiration (see Ball 1968, 35–36, and the still opposite page 96).

In Ian Judge's 1994 *Twelfth Night* for the RSC, Orsino kissed Cesario before "his" embassy to Olivia, then backed away, touching his lips in puzzlement. Who am I? What am I becoming? The homoerotic experience was a prelude to a heterosexual relationship, of course. We knew that. Orsino did not. He had begun a necessary questioning of his own arrogant assumptions about himself. In a film of many borrowings, *Shakespeare in Love* steals this moment. As Will rows master Kent, his boy-actor, across the Thames within a superbly visualized nightscape and rhapsodizes about his love for the "absent" Viola, he falls in love with the stand-in, Master Kent, and kisses "him" just below the mustache. It may be homoerotic to a confused Will-Orsino, but we know what lies beneath the strapped-down breasts, so that the instant is a bit of foreplay in what becomes a fiery romance, conducted in moments stolen from the prying eyes of a rival. Viola has been Virginia Woolf's Judith Shakespeare, but instead of waiting futilely at the stage door, she borrows a page from Will's previous play (*Two Gentlemen of Verona*) and comes inside in doublet and hose.

The issue of gender is neatly carried forward into what is probably the film's finest sequence, a series of cuts between the actual romance and Will's new play, with boy actor playing Juliet and girl, disguised as male actor, playing Romeo. The lines of the balcony scene flash back and forth across the river, from Viola's bed to the rehearsal at the Rose, which entrances the assembled company. The sequence may show, as Janet Maslin suggests, "the bond between tempestuous love and artistic creation" (1998, B16). It *does* show how montage can suggest much more than its parts, in this case the instability of gender, perhaps the fusion of gender at some level deeper than the physical. The words refuse to stay within their gender designation. "Wilt thou leave me so unsatisfied?" says Will, in bed with Viola. "That's my line!" she protests, as actor and as woman. Will's appropriation of "I will come again"—Juliet's line in the play—has a different meaning here. The sequence culminates in Will's unwrapping of Master Kent backstage. All of this demonstrates passion most convincingly. Whether it convinces anyone of the equation between sex and artistic creativity is another matter. The backstage bout of concupiscence is spied upon by a young vagabond named John Webster, who is thinking that "The gates of heaven are not so highly arched / As prince's palaces. They that enter / There must go upon their backs." Elizabeth has the last word on the issue of gender: "I know something of a woman in a man's profession."

Tom Stoppard moves the scenario in and out of planes of reality, as the camera does in his film of *Rosencrantz and Guildenstern Are*

Dead. As the Montagues and Capulets square off in rehearsal, a rival party of actors, Burbage and the Admiral's Men—enraged that Will is letting Henslowe do a play promised to them—storms the Globe. The groups engage, Capulets and Montagues suddenly united against an invader, to the delight of Mr. Fennyman, the backer (Tim Wilkinson), who thinks it's part of the show. He becomes concerned when valuable props begin to shatter.

The film should not offend cultural materialists. Hierarchy—a greater power than can be contradicted—informs the film. Class differences are demarcated throughout, as are the newer power relationships always threatening class structure. "Who's he?" Fennyman asks, looking at Will. "Nobody," says Henslowe, the impresario (Geoffrey Rush). "He's the author." Simon Callow's tyrannical Master of the Revels bows to Wessex * (Colin Firth) and trembles at the voice of the Queen. A dog is obeyed in office, but only when his betters are not baying at him. Wessex can say to his unwilling bride, after he has told her that they are to be married, "You are allowed to show your pleasure," but he must grovel before Elizabeth, even if he thinks she's an "old bag." She, icon of worldly power, cannot untie the knot twined by the hand of God.

At the end of the film, Will takes on the role of Romeo because Master Kent has been found out. The boy actor assigned to the role of Juliet discovers that, overnight, his voice has become that of a bullfrog. Viola—having absconded from her marriage to Wessex— rushes down to play Juliet. She knows the part, of course, because it is a product of her love affair with Will and it has been recited to her even as the ink on the parchment dries. The words have been waiting for *her*, as woman and as actor. The film anticipates the Restoration, when women were at last permitted on the public stage. Will's love has permitted him to write both parts for the stage because he's been inspired by his backstage romance, which has been more than mere infatuation. (Will's previous play, *Two Gentlemen of Verona*, has been a hit only because of Crab, the dog). Master Kent (until opening

---

* *"Wessex" is a sly allusion to Hardy, whose novels—often set in his invented shire of Wessex—incorporate triangular, rectangular, even rhomboidal relationships. Wild crosscurrents of emotion eddy and flow as married persons fall in love with someone else, or a person tumbles passionately in love with the wrong person while the right person looks helplessly on. I think particularly of* A Pair of Blue Eyes; The Trumpet-Major; The Woodlanders; Tess of the D'Urbervilles; The Return of the Native: *and* Far From the Madding Crowd.

afternoon) has been playing Romeo. The transition and their own impending separation allow them to play the scene in the Capulet tomb with remarkable conviction. It is their last scene together, on stage or off, and they know it, so subtext and script coincide powerfully.

The ending is more satisfying than the conventional "ever after," because Will and Viola's passion is at its height, like that of Romeo and Juliet. Will and Viola part sorrowfully, but they will never know disillusionment at the decline of the first splendid flood of love and lust. It is, as Will writes it, "too rash, too unadvis'd, too like the lightning," but not (to borrow from Keats) like "All human passion / That leaves a heart high-sorrowful and cloy'd / A burning forehead, and a parching tongue." Theirs will always be first love, with the ache at its loss turning gradually to the memory of yearning that every spring will bring. The film has the grace to grant us our own sense of what passion is all about.

The film employs a variety of vividly imaged clichés about Elizabethan life and a number of useful half-truths—the effort of censors to close the theaters down, the simultaneous rivalry and cooperation of the theaters, Will's "friendship" with Marlowe, the death of Marlowe in a "tavern brawl," where the mistake that Will makes is closer to the historical truth than the version the film provides, that is, if John Nichols's splendid *The Reckoning* is accurate about Marlowe's death. The film depicts a hot-off-the-quill transition from parchment to rehearsal, "underlining the immediacy and spontaneity of Shakespeare's art" (Gussow 1999, B1). A necessary untruth here is that the Queen, even in disguise, would venture to the Liberty of the Clink to hear a play at a public playhouse. Ben Affleck, who plays Alleyn, is about the height of the other men in the play. Alleyn was so tall that they had to move a tree to bury him. He gives us a touch of Bottom in the afternoon, though, as he pauses before he accepts the role of Mercutio. Will believes that everything he has done so far derives from Marlowe. As Marlowe dies, Shakespeare is born. That is true, even if the cause and effect that the film implies is not. Stoppard says, "I have a special take on historical accuracy, which is that all supposed historical truths are temporary, meaning that they're always there to be modified in light of subsequent discoveries" (quoted in Lyall 1998, 22). While Stoppard carries his theory of revisionism to extremes, his modifications serve a wonderful film.

Regardless of superficial inaccuracies, the film coheres at the deeper levels. We believe in the love of Will and Viola. And the surface is brilliant. A small blonde girl from Rembrandt's *Captain Cocq and Company* rushes into the scene, showing that for all of Will's dual quests —toward love, toward artistic triumph—there must always be children who did not care whether it happened, as Auden says. Will makes an amusing entrance as Banquo's ghost to Wessex, who thinks that Will is the dead Marlowe—another hint of sexual reversal in the mistaken identity. Wessex flees, screaming for mercy. "Nightingale" and "lark" in Will's play emerge from the rooster and owl that sound across the lover's bed. Bette Davis returns for a cameo as one of the Queen's ladies-in-waiting. It would have been sheer genius if Joan Crawford had been on the other side as a commentary on queens.

The film tells us that "being in love" is a cure for writer's block, a source of almost divine inspiration. Perhaps for Dante and Petrarch. For "Shakespeare," love is not a destablilizing and distracting experience but a spur to poetry. My own sense is that Shakespeare works out the conflicts and ambivalences in his sonnets and that *Romeo and Juliet* is his objective view of young love. He writes the play as playwright. In the film, the play emerges from a personal transaction between Will and Viola, a private set of communications that lend themselves to a dramatic form beyond the existential love story. It is beautifully done if we do not wonder how a young man like Will could exist for days with no sleep, riding only the surf of sex and blank verse. Even young poets get tired, and even young lovers peter out. Paltrow, with her mouth partly open as if breathing in a new atmosphere of wonder, is splendid, particularly at the brilliant "Capulet" ball, at which Will-Romeo and Essex-Paris vie for Viola-Juliet. For her, the love of poetry and the poetry have begun to coalesce.

The innermost fictions of the film become "the truth" the film delivers. Viola, now Lady Wessex, bound for Virginia with her colonist husband, will remain forever young for Will. She will be the inspiration for a host of young women playing boys and played by boys in plays to come. It would be better, admittedly, for the film's thesis, had Shakespeare not already exploited this device through Julia in *The Two Gentlemen of Verona*, but not too many filmgoers will launch this quibble. While the next play that Shakespeare will write is not *The Tempest*, as the *New York Times* reviewer says (Lyall 1998, 22)—that cuts out a few good scripts between *Romeo* and 1610—we can sense an older Will, whose every third thought may be on the Avon, ceding a young Miranda (a still young Viola) to Ferdinand, the two to live out the life denied to Viola de Lesseps and Will Shakespeare. The brief romance has been the seedbed of Shakespeare's genius, the one love affair that remains the one. First times have nothing to compare themselves with and so invite their constant reinvention, at least until *Macbeth* and *Antony and Cleopatra* explore the far side of marriage. Kenneth Rothwell calls the film a "farce" (1998, 28)—that is, a complicated series of situations in which "the truth" is concealed from at least one of the characters in the frame. John Lardner labels the film a "fantasia" (1999, 62). I prefer to see it as a "romance," full of improbable but pleasing coincidence that becomes synchronicity. The ending becomes not a parting but a merging of Shakespeare and the creativity that would carry him for the next decade and a half—and a lot of us since then. Shakespeare was more a product of a craftsmanship deployed within the very specific architecture of Elizabethan theaters than of a sudden crystallization around a girl of his dreams untimely snatched from his embrace, but the latter scenario makes a better story and a much more sensuous film than could be made from dust, goosequills, and the slow, secret process of mastery.

Do "you have to know Shakespeare" to appreciate the film, as Marty Meltz says (1999, E1)? If so, some of the other recent films should help. *Romeo and Juliet* is the play most completely incorporated within *Shakespeare in Love,* and its "authentic" recreation will find a ready audience. Baz Luhrman says of his post-modernist film version that "when cinematic language can replace stage conventions it may help the telling" (Crowdis, 1998, 51). Students can engage in the game of "compare and contrast" with the two contemporary final scenes of *Romeo and Juliet,* one "on stage," the other aggressively a film. In each, a subtext works beneath the words—Will and Viola are parting; Juliet is alive, as Romeo's observation tells him—complicating and at once ironizing and reinforcing the spoken words.

At the end, Will is working on *Twelfth Night,* in which he makes Viola a boy coming to an infatuated Duke, seeking in language and music what he cannot attain in life. At the end, of course, Viola is to return in her woman's weeds to wed. It is the ending that Will can write but cannot attain. *Shakespeare in Love* borrows a storm scene from Trevor Nunn's wonderful *Twelfth Night,* so among the fringe benefits of Stoppard's film may be a drawing of attention to Nunn's film, which deserves more attention than it has received.

Imogan Stubbs and Helena Bonham-Carter in *Twelfth Night*, 1996.
Photo by Alex Bailey.

Chapter 5
Silents

The release in early 2000 by the British Film Institute of six silent Shakespeare films provides a wonderful opportunity to look at very early filmed Shakespeare without traveling to London or New York and going through all kinds of bureaucracy. The six films vary in quality, but they insist on a basic question: How important are the words to an understanding of the play? Or to put it in Aristotelian terms: in drama, is action prior to language? I think the answer is yes, and would argue on the basis of great foreign films: the Akira Kurosawa *Throne of Blood* (1957) and *Ran* (1984), the Gregori Kozintev *Hamlet* (1964) and *King Lear* (1970), and the Ragnar Lyth *Hamlet* (1984). The evidence provided by the silent films is mixed, in that title cards summarize the action that we are about to observe, so that our experience is similar to that of reading an outline of the plot before going to a play. The play, perhaps, should explain itself, but silent film (almost) always relied on titles, which have to be considered part of the artistic product. The silent films rely on comprehensible action and continuity between actions. I would argue that any production of a Shakespeare script demands the same. Jonathan Bate comes close to saying the same thing: "'Silent Shakespeare' does sound like a contradiction in terms: isn't the sound of Shakespeare—the glory of his poetry and his linguistic invention—essential to his genius? Yet there is a long theatrical tradition of adapting the plays into such modes as pantomime and ballet. These crude but strangely compelling films are in that venerable tradition" (2000, Arts 26). They reach back, I would suggest, to a pre-linguistic tradition, like that of sympathetic magic. Furthermore, as Jack Jorgens suggests, "Distance, perspective, and relationships can change with the fluidity of a line of verse. Static theatrical space becomes dynamic" on film. "The rhetoric may be very strong" or "it may be invisible," but the rhetoric of the camera substitutes for the verbal rhetoric of the stage (1977, 25).

The silent films, far from being an amusingly inept effort to condense a play into one or two reels, tell us much about the inherited scripts, their appeals to the imaginations of the earliest film directors, and the ways in which the translation of the plays to film has developed and continues to develop. The twenty-first-century filmmaker faces many of the same problems that the silent films attempted to solve—primarily, how to transform a medium in which almost everything is done with language into one in which almost everything is done with visual imagery. The "space" of the early silent film was severely limited. The camera tended to be fixed. Music was provided live to accompany the film; thus the films were seldom "silent." The story had to be told in one or two reels. No spoken word could be heard, so that title cards appeared before each new scene and sometimes in the middle of a scene, insisting on a very different activity than that given to a sequence of moving images. Early audiences, however, probably moved from title card—the "literary" experience—to photograph with greater ease than we do as we watch these old films today and perhaps resent the necessity to do the reading by ourselves.

As the century turned on its hinge, filmmakers did what they have also done at the turn of the millennium. In the early 1900s they showed, though Shakespeare, what the new medium was all about. Shakespeare helped define its possibilities and limits. That Shakespeare is suddenly so frequently on film as the new millennium begins is not an accident. Shakespeare shows us where we are and where we are not as we explore the scripts through film. By pushing against the edges of time as it moves, Shakespeare reveals centrality, which is also moving. The center cannot hold because it is part of a complex continuum. As the current cliché has it, we are not reading Shakespeare. Shakespeare is reading us. It would be easy to extrapolate and say that the British silents looked at Shakespeare from within a stage tradition while the American films took him outdoors, on location. There is something to the thesis of enclosure within a proscenium versus expansion into nature, but the best of the early films are those from Italy, which had neither the long and wide Shakespearean stage tradition of Great Britain nor the huge and developing continent stretching westward of the United States.

Given the complexities of any Shakespeare plot, the question to be asked of the silent versions is, What story is told? Secondarily, of course, one asks, How effective is the narrative the film renders? The story emerges from the archetype—the deep configuration that

"A rare opportunity to see these beautiful early films."
— Martin Scorsese

SILENT
SHAKESPEARE

Such stuff as dreams are made on...

DIGITALLY MASTERED FROM THE ORIGINAL 35MM NITRATE MATERIALS

Cover, "Silent Films." *Courtesy of Milestone Films.*

captures a basic element of human experience. The Romeo and Juliet story is not just one of young love. It is of young love attempting to overcome the objections placed against it by parents, society, or culture, and that opposition makes it archetypal, since the narrative seems to exist in all cultures at all times. The Othello and Desdemona story is not just one of love gone wrong, but of jealousy, which seems to have its roots deep in prehistory, when a man would not spend time and energy protecting offspring that were not his (see Buss 2000). Jealousy could be mimed so that anyone of sexual age would understand the story. Othello's jealousy is real, even if Desdemona's infidelity is not. The archetypal story of Hamlet is not just of revenge, but of a son's effort to revenge a father's death, a story that picks up inevitable Oedipal resonance. Some of Shakespeare's comedies emerge from archetypes that insist that identity is not to be discerned in assumptions based on stereotype; *As You Like It* and *Twelfth Night*, for example, and, to some extent, *The Merchant of Venice*. The archetype of *Much Ado About Nothing* is two people in love who do not know it. The archetype invariably involves something that is hidden, whether love from society or love from self, or gender, or even, in the case of *Othello*, the truth of another's identity. In most cases, the archetype is "visible" to the audience. We see what the others come to recognize, whether in love and the ending of comedy or in the *anagnorisis* of tragic insight. The exception may be Hamlet, of course, since we don't know how he would inscribe the "silence" of his ending. What we believe about any production of *Hamlet* is a function of individual insight, even if the experience of the play is communal. What Lear sees at the end is debatable, of course. The play, through Lear and Gloucester, has worked variations on and challenges to the archetype of "wise old man." Bate puts it this way: "The simplification of structure offers the potential of taking the viewer to the core of each play, revealing the primal quality of Shakespeare's stories. The combination of brevity and exaggerated acting style makes one see how the tragedy of King Lear is built on the model of a fairy tale gone wrong (two ugly sisters and a Cinderella who ends up being hanged)" (2000, AR 26).

Tempest

The earliest of the silent films on the tape is the weakest, a 1908 *Tempest*, directed by Percy Stow in Great Britain with an unknown cast. It begins with Prospero in a small boat at the side of a larger boat receiving Miranda and a large book. He "seeks refuge on an island" and appears in front of some patently phony rocks with Miranda in one arm and the book in another. Immediately, we notice film's reliance on the iconic tradition that preceded the printing press. We assume, perhaps, that Prospero's book is an illuminated manuscript full of occult material that somehow survived medieval suppression. Blessedly, the film goes on location. Prospero finds Caliban eating roots and subdues him. Ariel calls to Prospero from an unconvincing imprisonment inside a tree, and Prospero frees her. Ten years pass by in the time it takes to read the title card. Caliban woos Miranda, but Ariel, in the guise of a muskrat, chases Caliban away. The scene suggests the techniques of visual transformation that film would achieve later, as Jekyll became Hyde, a man changed to a werewolf or James Cagney felt his face grow marv'lous hairy as Bottom became an ass. Prospero creates a spell in a poof of smoke from which three doves fly forth. A ship, viewed through an opening in a cave, founders and sinks, much to Miranda's distress. Ferdinand, however, swims to shore, sheds his cape, and looks about, shading his eyes. Miranda sees Ariel (as the script suggests she does not) as Prospero sends his spirit off to fetch Ferdinand. In a series of dissolves that imitate Georges Meiles—the inventor of trick photography—Ariel plays a game of hide-and-seek with Ferdinand, who believes that Miranda will become the same diaphanous creature. She is real, though, and the two embrace at first sight. Prospero celebrates, then separates, the two. Ferdinand carries several small logs, then gives up. Miranda arrives and helps him carry a larger log a few feet. They pause to smooch. Prospero comes down the path, shakes hands with Ferdinand, and blesses the couple. Antonio's party, resting on the grass, is treated to a disappearing picnic. Prospero and this group become "Friends once more." Ariel is released and dances happily into the woods. Prospero shakes hands with someone we assume to be Ferdinand's father. A long boat slides in past the obvious flat and all climb aboard, except for Caliban, who wants to go with the departing people but is apparently exiled to the island.

What this film leaves out is, basically, the *evil* to which Prospero responds. "A genial Prospero forgives all," says Kenneth Rothwell (1990, 283), but for what? For all we know, he and the baby handed to him could be the first ones off a sinking ship. The film, however, is an interesting experiment in the simplification and visualization of the inherited story. Its use of location and special effects—like the disappearing and reappearing Ariel—demonstrates Stow's awareness that his new medium can free itself of stage conventions.

Dream in 1909

The American *A Midsummer Night's Dream* (1909) uses location shots exclusively—including the newly restored fountain in Central Park and parts of Prospect Park in Brooklyn—making it "more of a movie than a photograph of a play" (Ball 1968, 55). Its long opening title card emphasizes the lovers fleeing to the woods, as does the take that follows. The "Tradesmen" meet to discuss their play, and a splendidly hammy William V. Ranous mimes his desire to play all the parts. For some reason, Oberon is replaced by a "Penelope," who quarrels with Titania for possession of the Indian Boy. Rothwell speculates that the director might have feared "that the pedophile subtext...might upset the censorious classes" (1999, 10), but the strange substitution introduces an unmistakably lesbian relationship between Penelope and Titania. Puck's trip around the world and back is accomplished by a variation on Melies's *A Trip to the Moon.* Puck flies over a revolving earth and back again. A brief glimpse of Puck crash-landing is replaced by a more sedate shot of Puck handing the flower to Penelope. The best sequences are orchestrated by Gladys Hulette's delightful Puck: first the coming of the four lovers to a tree, where Puck mistakes Lysander for Demetrius, and then the resolution of the rectangle at the foot of another tree with a view of a lake in the background. The film demonstrates the value of an on-camera "stage manager" who at once makes things happen and mimes meanings to the audience. Ball reports seeing the "Pyramus and Thisbe" sequence (1968, 55), but this version ends with the lovers and nobles returning to the court from the woods.

While the "Penelope" insertion is confusing, this film is eminently worth adding to other versions of the play for its excellent Bottom and wonderful Puck.

Vitagraph's *Twelfth Night*

Rothwell suggests that the early films had to "struggle...to break out of the prison house of the proscenium stage...and make a film that does not look as if it had been photographed with a camera nailed to the floor in the sixth-row orchestra" (1999, 7–8). Charles Kent's *Twelfth Night* for Vitagraph in 1910 goes to the shores of Long

Island for the emergence from the sea of Viola and Sebastian and to a charming country-house garden, full of hedges, trellises, and midsummer vines, for most of the scenes at Olivia's.

Only at the beginning and the end does the film look like a filmed play. The effect is to bring the action back within a frame—as, for example, Olivier does with his film of *Henry V.*

The silents tend to isolate the love story in any given script, using the energy of late-nineteenth-century romances, which were available in colorful profusion on the newsstands, as a way for audiences to recognize the new medium. The 1910 *Twelfth Night* does not tell the gender story well. It does explain at the outset that Viola finds her brother's clothes in his washed-up trunk, as Trevor Nunn also does in his 1996 version. At the end of the silent film, however, we are confused about which twin is which. While such confusion is acceptable in *The Comedy of Errors,* here, the title card alone tells us that that's Sebastian with Viola. Visually, the final scene is a muddle. It looks as if Cesario is suddenly exchanging sword thrusts with Orsino. The film's condensation demonstrates how subtle and complicated the script really is. The madhouse scene, for example, is not in the film, so that the depth of Malvolio's humiliation is not plumbed, though he does appear with the forged letter at the end and does stalk angrily out. He is merely an object of ridicule here, not the focal point for questions about upward mobility or the lethargy of the ducal and county establishments.

The beruffed and busy court that swirls around the still point of Orsino is dominated by a huge painting of Cleopatra meeting Antony on the banks of the Cydnus, perhaps Orsino's effort to place himself within the tradition of tragic passion. If so, the painting contrasts with what the foreground will show. The film develops the "plucky Viola" tradition of the nineteenth-century stage. It relies on Florence Lawrence, who sighs over her love for Orsino, frowns when she sees how beautiful Olivia is, and slaps her knee in laughter when she realizes that Olivia has fallen for her. A portion of her response may signal that she has removed a rival for Orsino's love, even if she is now the object of Olivia's affection. Viola's counterpart is a sparkling Maria, who orchestrates the plot against Malvolio. The silent films work wonderfully when we watch a manipulator at work. If the situations are set up clearly, farce requires no spoken words. After Malvolio stomps away through the lovely country-house garden, misunderstanding his rebuff by Olivia, she gives Cesario a necklace. Toby watches and incites Andrew to challenge Cesario.

At the end, just before the film stops abruptly, Olivia and Sebastian hold each other camera right, while Orsino waits for Viola. She appears in her woman's weeds, shyly coming toward Orsino as the frame goes blank. It is a brief glimpse, but it fulfills the love story charmingly. This one-reeler is worth watching for its own sake, and certainly for its demonstration of the strengths and limitations of squeezing a *Twelfth Night* into twelve minutes.

King Lear

The Italian *King Lear* is beautifully tinted and mimes the language of the play. When Lear, for example, gestures toward Goneril's stomach, he is asking that sterility be conveyed therein. When he plucks a grass and holds it with trembling fingers over Cordelia's lips, he is hoping that it "stirs" from her breathing. At the outset, the Fool runs from the palace and sits in Lear's throne—a neat prefiguring of the foolishness to come. The beautiful Francesca Bertini as Cordelia, in a rose gown, is scornful of the opening auction. As she is disinherited, her sisters cackle and Kent remonstrates. Lear hurls Cordelia at "France" (an unidentified bystander here) and the Fool mocks Goneril and Regan. What one notices in an early film like this—without close-ups or reaction shots—is that we must read a range of responses across the screen. Our experience is somewhat like that of watching a play on stage. It is probably more difficult here, because the blocking is more one-dimensional and the lighting—whether on location or from the vapor lamps of the studio—cannot emphasize one character or create contrasts between characters. At the moment that Kent is unstocked, for example, we have a variety of reactions from Kent, the Fool, Lear, Regan, and Goneril. It is a challenge from which more advanced film technique has dishabituated us.

While no war or any invasion of Britain occurs, the film offers some superb visualizations—Lear as a white-haired martyr from an early Renaissance canvas; Lear riding a broomstick as, in his madness, he mocks his two unkind daughters; Lear feeling the pin prick, then wiping Cordelia's tears away. The final scene occurs on a windy day in front of an aqueduct—it is a nice anticipation of deep-field photography. We notice that the powerful Oswald, with his horned helmet, is present, suggesting that good and evil have been amalgamated in this confused kingdom, or, perhaps, that if Cordelia is dead, it does not matter who remains alive.

Rothwell says of this film that its "excessive" use of title cards "signals a failure in silent movie making" (1990, 130), but I found the film visually splendid and often moving. It creates mimed versions of the lines of the play. I don't think one has to know the lines to grasp what the actors are suggesting.

The Merchant of Venice

The Italian *Merchant of Venice* (1910) begins with plans for the elopement of Jessica and Lorenzo. Bassanio's hopes for Portia are merely a way of getting Antonio to Shylock. Ermete Novelli's Shylock is the Jewish villain, fulsome in public, salivating with the pleasure of his scheming in private. Shylock comically drops one of the three moneybags he gives to Bassanio. Antonio and Bassanio go off with him arm in arm to facilitate Jessica's escape. We notice that Lorenzo does not drop the casket that Jessica brings out from Shylock's house. Shylock returns with Tubal to discover the key that Jessica has dropped on the pavement in front of Shylock's house. As in the later Miller-Olivier television version (1969), Jessica's defection becomes the motive for Shylock's revenge, though he celebrated earlier as she looked at Antonio's bond. Portia is an ample matriarch, someone to whom Bassanio appeals on Antonio's behalf. Belmont is not a mountain across the waters beckoning with Jason's golden fleece but an opulent residence on one end of the Rialto. No casket sequence occurs. The strength of the film is in the beautifully tinted sequences, including one too-brief scene of canal and gondola, and in Francesca Bertini's winning Jessica. The trial scene moves quickly on a stagey set—the Duke on his throne camera left, Shylock at his feet, others camera right. Antonio, the Duke, and Portia ("disguised as a lawyer," says the title card, but obviously the dowager Portia) remonstrate with Shylock. Then, she shows the Duke the law that condemns Shylock. The latter, who has been whetting his knife on the left shoe he has removed, is easily defeated. The film ends abruptly there, with no ring sequence, no return to the stars and dawn of a new day in Belmont. The original apparently ended with Shylock's forced conversion (Ball 1968, 124). Ball notes that "too often the pictures merely illustrate the subtitles" (125). That is not necessarily a bad thing, assuming the subtitles accurately represent the action and that the illustrations are vivid. I would suggest that they are a visual augmentation. We should try to recall what an innovation film was in the early part of the twentieth century.

"Without subtitles the story could not be followed," Ball says (125). That may be true, but is it a condemnation? Subtitles were part of the film. They did require reading, certainly a different activity than looking at moving pictures, but they were part of a processing that people accepted before sound made title cards unnecessary, and before F. W. Murnau's *The Last Laugh* (1924), a silent film made without title cards.

The film demonstrates the problem of such brief depictions. They allow no gradual buildup of tension, no ebb and flow of action (as at the trial in the script) no nuances of motivation or characterization, only straightforward and uncomplicated narrative. This hollows out the script, of course, since the story is not just about what happens, but why, and, as so often—what *does* happen? No space is left for interpretation, for what critics used to call ambiguity, or for the post-modernist zone of "multiple signification." Such one- or two-reelers skim the surface, with no pauses, and, since neither the close-up nor the flashback is available, they tend to incorporate no moments of reflection on what any of this means or any depiction of past events that deepen and complicate the present.

Benson's *Richard III*

The 1911 *Richard III* is made up of separate scenes. This version, in which title cards take up about half of the footage, shows us how a pre–World War I play would have been staged at the Memorial Theatre in Stratford. It does not necessarily show us how a play would have been acted, since, as Ball argues, the actors provide "stage gesture amplified…neither appropriate to the theatre nor to the screen" (1968, 87). I suspect that an already over-elaborated style was exaggerated in front of the single camera that faces the obvious stage settings, in what Rothwell calls a "stagey movie" (1999, 9). The film does show how vigorous and exciting an actor Frank Benson must have been, even if we cannot hear him call for Richard's horse. Most of the scenes are introduced by a title card that describes what is going to happen and gives us an epigaph from the play. Scene eleven, for example: "Richard starts to meet Richmond, is met by his mother, Queen Margaret, and Queen Elizabeth. 'Therefore take with thee my most heavy curse / Which in the day of battle tire

thee more / Than all the complete armour that thou wear'st.'" It is
as if Benson did not trust the camera to tell the story, and, of course,
he is right, as Ball says: "The rigidly stationary camera is so far from
the fully pictured stage that the stage becomes the focus for the eye,
and the characters cannot easily be distinguished. The stage scenery
and appurtenances become obtrusive" (1968, 87). The scene does
feature an ironic Celtic cross on its generic medieval London street.
While Ball excoriates the appearance of the ghosts to Richard on the
morning of Bosworth Field ("It is not even good stage technique")
my response, as always, was of surprise at the number of victims:
Prince Edward, King Henry, Clarence, Hastings, the young Princes,
Buckingham, Anne. The film, like any version of this play, has been
a kaleidoscope of murder. It is not as bad as Ball says it is: "stage
film at its worst, theatrical rather than cinematic...a series of
incomprehensible illustrations of subjects described by titles, of
unrecognizable people doing unintelligible things" (88). If we know
the play, we fill things in, compensating for the film's lacunae. What
became of the king (Edward IV) that we saw crowned in the opening
scene? Why is Hastings dispatched? This silent film, more than any
other, demands language—as Benson seems to have been aware.
We needed to be in that theater. Since the film is episodic, lacking
continuity and the motives that Richard and Buckingham provide
in soliloquies, language added *to* the film, instead of coming in via
quotations on the title cards would not have helped. At times, the
film does resemble Rachael Low's description of it: "unwieldy
groups...brandishing swords, arguing and moving about on their
own obscure business" (quoted in Ball 1968, 87).

John Collick argues that the film is condemned because it is not
edited, as were the American films of the period. American films
reflected "a narrative-based manipulation of filmic space which is
intended to give the impression" of spatial coherence, so that "the
depiction of reality [is] the untimate artistic triumph" (1989, 43).
Collick suggests that those who view "the growth of film as a process
of natural development" will *naturally* condemn the Benson film. It
is not part of that evolution, particularly when judged from a further
remove, that is, from a stance takes in the "editing and spatial
organization [that] became enshrined as 'The Hollywood Codes of
Editing'" (42–43). Collick argues that two opposing traditions are
at work in the film. One is that "the directors are struggling to
maintain the central position of the text in a hostile environment"

(45)—thus the quantity of and the quotations in the title cards. Second, the film fits into the tradition of nineteenth-century illustrations of Shakespeare, as in Tree's Magna Carta scene in *King John*. The Benson *Richard III* must be considered "a series of tableaux vivants or 'living pictures,' a gallery of illustrations drawn from a famous Shakespeare play" (46). Collick concludes his argument by contrasting Benson's film with the Forbes-Robertson *Hamlet* of 1913, where "the accent is on naturalism" (46). Collick hardly saves the Benson film *as* film—we have been completely conditioned by "Hollywood" editing—but he does place it effectively within its historical context.

The Benson film is particularly instructive when contrasted with the virtually contemporaneous version of M. B. Dudley and Frederick Warde, a full-length film not included in the British Film Institute tape. Unlike the Benson version, the Warde does what Ball says silent film must do: "tell its story through significant moving pictures in a continuity which can be followed" (1968, 87).

Both Benson and Warde hand many of the mannerisms that they no doubt inherited from former Richards on to future Richards. Richard is an over-actor, as he knows, as well as an over-reacher, as he learns, so that we see in these films—in Benson's quicksilver changes of roles and in Warde's manic gleefulness—intimations of great Richards like Olivier's, Antony Sher's, and Ciaran Hinds's. Both films amalgamate material from *Henry VI*, Part Three. The murder of Prince Edward is deemed necessary to show the genesis of Richard's evil career.

Warde's *Richard III*

Warde's publicity claims that it took $30,000 to produce the film, 77 scenes, 1500 people, 200 horses, and a three-masted warship crowded with soldiers on real water. Ball, not having seen the film (it resurfaced in Oregon in 1996) tends to scoff at these figures (1968, 156, 158), but the film substantiates them. I counted two masts on the ship, but the water did look real. This is one of the first super-colossal films.

It begins with a marching army of hundreds in front of a fake wall and then shifts to Tewkesbury, where Richard kills Prince Edward. Richard rides to London down a country lane in Westchester County—one of the few that director Dudley could find that was "not disfigured by modern utilities.[T]hat would not do for England in the fifteenth century," as Warde reports (Ball 1968, 158). The shot, then, is one of the first location shots that ran into the almost-inevitable anachronisms of such projects—the television-aerial-behind-Al Capone's-1930-Cadillac problem. It is also an early "field of depth" shot, showing the length of the lane, then Richard galloping toward the camera. The camera does move a fraction to capture him riding out of sight.

Richard demands entrance to King Henry's cell in the face of a reluctant Keeper. Richard looks carefully at the Tower guards, either to remind them of their complicity in quasi-regicide, or to say "these be likely lads!" He insists that the elderly Henry kneel to him. Henry refuses and is stabbed. Then, in an economy of location, Richard rushes out onto the Tower's balcony and waves at his returning brother, King Edward IV. Richard returns to Henry's cell, stabs him several more times, looks at his sword, wipes it between thumb and forefinger, and flicks the blood down upon the corpse.

The scenes are fully developed, free of the necessity for condensation of the one and two reelers, and strong in depicting the religious and ceremonial elements of the inherited script. The wooing scene, for example, shows Lady Anne threatening Richard three times with the sword before dropping it and relenting to his suit. We see Richard give the "prophecy of a Wizard" to one of his henchmen and then watch as it is tossed in the window of Edward's throne room. We see Richard visit Clarence, feigning sympathy, then thrusting ink and warrant on the ailing king with which to condemn Clarence. Two vagabonds stroll conveniently by, and Catesby suborns them. They murder Clarence and are paid. In a splendid procession that wends through an impressive press of people, the princes, on ponies, arrive in London to be greeted by Richard. Richard, at his prayer book with priests, comes out onto the same balcony from which he had greeted his brother, and is entreated and consents to become king only after lengthy petition. Inside again, he flings the book joyously in the air—as Benson had done, no doubt continuing a long stage tradition. The use of the same balcony no doubt results from considerations of economy, but it does remind us of early moments in Richard's evil career. Richard has the princes kidnapped, torn in tears from their mother's arms. During the coronation scene, the camera does pan, past an apathetic Anne, to Richard ascending the throne. The effect is of Richard's controlling his enlargement of the scene, an effect augmented when he uses his scepter to sweep everyone out of the room, but Buckingham. Buckingham's reluctance to kill the princes is fully developed. Richard sees those two roving thugs outside his window, summons them, and has the princes murdered after their bedtime prayers. Their bodies are entombed, in accordance with the legend (apparently confirmed in the 1930s) that they were buried in a hidden vault in the Tower. The murderers are paid again and no doubt wander off to become squires. Richard woos Elizabeth, whose mother writes Richmond: "Your presence here is needful." He sails in a big two-masted ship with men in armor on horseback on the deck, is greeted by a kneeling clergyman, and rushes to Elizabeth. Richmond is a dashing swashbuckler, in contrast to the vigorous but heavy-footed Richard. Anne attempts to win Richard's favor. He hands her a dagger—with no need for instructions for how to use it—in a visual echoing of the wooing scene. He then has her bedtime drink poisoned. Lots of horses and men go off to meet Richmond at Bosworth Field. Richard deploys his captains, then has a dream in which all his ghostly victims point at him. Catesby apparently prevents Richard from stabbing himself with a dagger. The battle itself is a bit of a muddle. Two horsemen fight. Cavalry charges. Ambuscades occur. Richard is seemingly captured, but then he fights with Richmond in a scene almost identical to that in which Prince Edward was killed. Richard falls and the battle ends.

The original film was accompanied by a lecture and recitation by Warde: "While the eyes rest in the intermissions between the reels, Mr. Warde entertains the audience with a dramatic reading of famous passages in the play, elucidating them at the same time," says a newspaper account quoted by Ball (1968, 159). "In educational value, from the historical viewpoint, it is better than the presentation of the play itself. Indeed the offering is the best combination moving picture entertainment that has yet been brought to this city [Charleston, S.C.]. It is truly wonderful" (quoted in Ball 1968, 159). Warde appears, both at the beginning and the end of the film, an elegant middle-aged man in his lecture suit, taking bows in front of an imaginary audience. The film becomes a film within a lecture, or, more accurately, a film within a live performance—which is what many of the early films were. This one, though, represents an "integrated" evening.

With rare exceptions the camera is immobile, but things move within the frame, not, though, as if we are looking at a stage. The

Ludgate through which a newly crowned Edward rides in triumph lies just outside the tower in which his brother Gloucester has dispatched King Henry. Warde's Richard can run out onto a balcony, wave at his brother's procession, hustle back into the Tower chamber to stab Henry a few more times, then wipe his rapier clean. That ship floats in from Long Island Sound (as opposed to the English Channel) with Richmond and his rebels aboard—when only three years before a patently phony boat had sunk within sight of Prospero's island and had resurfaced, just as unconvincingly, as a Viking longboat.

The 1911 *Romeo and Juliet*

Perhaps the greatest of these early Shakespeare films is the Italian *Romeo e Giulietta* of 1911 It is not on the British Film Institute tape, either. Perhaps the Institute can be encouraged to produce another tape that includes it. Ball, who had not seen the film, shrewdly points out that "rather than expanding the opportunities of showing more of Shakespeare's narrative than a one-reel film could cover, by its rearrangement and elimination of characters this scenario actually simplified it...with greater concentration [on] the two principals" (1968, 126).

It begins with Romeo riding past a balcony just as Juliet drops her glove. Romeo dismounts and takes the glove up the steps to her. This is either their first meeting or, more probably, one contrived around the excuse of the dropped glove. The medium two-shot allows us to see facial expressions. She is fearful, he importunate. Their exchange occurs in front of a frieze of a fifteenth-century horseman, an image at once suggesting the movement of time and the forces that oppose the softer hours of love.

The film is visually beautiful. It is shot in Verona, and, as Rothwell says, the "lavish spectacle [is] true to the Italian operatic tradition" (1990, 246). The print I saw was mostly in sepia but included some brief scenes that were tinted. The settings are opulent—inlaid wood, chandeliers, and a Capulet garden with a heroic statue, behind which Romeo, Juliet, and Nurse hide as Capulet wanders out with the odious Tebaldo (the Paris-Tybalt figure). The scene in which Romeo sneaks along the Capulet wall to say goodbye to Juliet is superb. A reverse angle shot—the only one I could find in these films—shows Romeo disappearing over the wall from inside Juliet's room and then scrambling down the rope ladder on the outside of the wall. The pacing is superb—not only does the film move as it must within its half hour, but the pressure within the narrative is strong, as it must be for this script. The party at the Capulets' is designed to reveal the secret love of Romeo and Juliet to Tebaldo and, through Tebaldo, to Capulet. Capulet rushes out to challenge the Montagues so that the feud is motivated here, as it is not in the script. The public brawl meets the Duke's rebuke and elicits an immediate prohibition against dueling. Believing that Romeo is interfering with his own proper relationship with Juliet, Tebaldo challenges a reluctant Romeo, who merely wounds his rival in the left arm. Romeo falls under the Duke's interdiction, however, and is banished. Capulet simply refuses to permit Juliet to say no. Franchesca Bertini's Juliet is superb, consistently twisting so that her opulent figure crosses the camera to best advantage. Her gowns are magnificent, and, at the Capulet ball, she wears the chaplet of pearls that must have been standard issue for Juliet for several generations of actresses by then. Her appeal to us, the audience, lies not just in her love for Romeo but also in her loathing of the toad-like Tebaldo. She has, says Rothwell, a "gift for subtle facial expression" (1990, 246). The film's telescoping of the narrative works superbly as Capulet, Tebaldo, and the wedding party enter just after Juliet has taken the potion, so that her collapse and apparent death (in Tebaldo's arms) is sudden and public. Romeo drifts back to Verona and encounters Juliet's funeral procession, which is itself powerfully rendered, with monks, flower girls, and the bier swallowed up within the arch of the church entrance. Romeo follows, hides behind a crypt in the church, waits until the others have left the candle-framed bier, and stabs himself. Gustavo Serena is very good, with an expressive face and a controlled, rather than over-exaggerated, acting style. He carries the final sequence of the film, as he does in the play. Juliet awakens and they embrace for a moment before she stabs herself. The Nurse has been in on everything—the wedding, the visit to Laurence's cell, the vial—but neither she nor the Friar show up at the end to forestall the fatal ending. In this version, neither knows that Romeo is back in Verona.

The version I saw was greatly enhanced by the score of the Prokofiev ballet. The ballet premiered in Moscow in November 1936, so it *sounds* anachronistic behind a silent film, but it powerfully reinforces the visual rhythms of the film.

This film, were it available, would be an impressive addition to our many versions of *Romeo and Juliet* and, alone, would show how the archetype of love opposed translates to a powerful set of visual and auditory images. Not all silent films, of course, have a Prokofiev to enhance them.

Music always was part of film. Early film audiences expected it and, probably, were not overly conscious of it. Title cards were also part of early film and, if dull to us and cued to the slow readers among us, were no doubt accepted in the first decade of this century as a necessary element of what was a very exciting event. We make a mistake when we read back from our own sophistication toward what we consider a "cruder" technology. These films tell *a* story, as does any production—who would claim to know what *the* story of any of Shakespeare's plays is? At their best, the films tell a story well and invite further tellings, either by readers reading the text or by actors and audiences in other films or other media. These films are valuable as the first to use *film* as a narrative medium for Shakespeare's plays. They serve as a starting point for an exploration of the many films that have followed and also as points of comparison with the silent and sound films of the same script that have been made since these marvelous early works of art first flickered into the electric dark of the nickelodeon.

Frederick Warde as Richard III. 1912.

Chapter 6

Animated Shakespeare:
Second Season

No one would have predicted that the plays of Shakespeare would invade the space of the Saturday morning cartoon. They did, however, in a series of twelve half-hour productions in the early 1990s. As of 2001 they still appear, now and then, on HBO, but the wonderful second season is not available commercially. This essay is an effort to redress that shortcoming. Shakespeare's encounter with a sub-genre that emerged some three decades into the twentieth century is instructive. How can the complex materials of a tragedy be rendered in less than half an hour without being reduced to simplistic clichés? Even more basically (since plot summaries exist in other forms) how can the serious and complex quality of Shakespeare's plays escape trivialization in a cartoon format? Are we perceived as living within such televisual expectations that content has become irrelevant? The answer would seem to be that Shakespeare's plasticity dominates and enhances the tendencies of the genre and of our expectations of it. The space suddenly comes vitally alive and unexpectedly profound.

In a brilliant and definitive article on the first six productions in the Shakespeare Animated Tales, Laurie E. Osborne says that they "underscore the mechanics of film, particularly as it brings Shakespeare's poetry into illusory motion. In fact they prepare their audience to understand the plays cinematically rather than theatrically or literarily" (1997, 103). One important element that Osborne does not mention is the superb *speaking* of the lines by some of Great Britain's finest young actors. The series prepares students to *listen,* as well as to watch, so that the productions do incorporate a strong theatrical component and an invitation to enjoy the plays as spoken, not just as visualized. One reason why the voices are so effective is that they were recorded before the animation was done (Pendleton 1992, 37), and thus the films escape the often unfortunate effects of dubbing. As described, the process counters scriptwriter Leon Garfield's assertion that, in the theater, the actor "creates the part; in animation, it's the animator" (quoted in Buss 1992, 28). Those who advertise productions by U.S. actors claim that British accents are "hard to understand." My own experience in using these tapes with young U.S. students suggests that that claim is self-serving nonsense.

In a later article, Osborne suggests a link between the animations and the silent one- and two-reel films of the early twentieth century: each relies on "necessary abbreviation, the dominance of visual images, and a radically new representation of Shakespeare's films" (1998, 74). Of the three criteria, I would quarrel only with the second. While I would not argue that the visual image is not dominant in film—of course it is—the animated films have voices, often superb dramatic speaking, and narration, in addition to the visual images. The narration in the animations occurs while the image is described, so the *visualization* of these films accompanied by a voice is a constant. We have been conditioned to accept this simultaneity without thinking about it. In the silents, title cards tend to provide the scenario for what we are about to see. A few, such as the Dmitri Bukhovetsky–Emil Jannings *Othello* (1922), use quotations from the play as titles, and a few, like the Frank Benson *Richard III* (1911), combine description and quotation. We read, then watch. We see what we have been prepared to see, rather than watch an illustration of the narration or figures speaking. The animated films have far more visualization than the silents, particularly when the silent film takes as much time and footage for the titles as does the Benson *Richard III* ("almost half of the film"; Ball 1968, 87). Our experience of the visual images is very different in each medium. In the silents it is after the fact. In the animations, images are simultaneous with either the narration or the action. In the instances of the King John death scene, the Sarah Bernhardt duel scene from *Hamlet,* and the Benson *Richard III,* the films are new ways of recording Shakespeare performance but not really of representing it. But where film techniques are used (as opposed to a static camera) and where the various approaches to animation are applied to the inherited text, yes, they represent new and radical departures. The early silents teach us a lot about Shakespeare through his confrontation with a new medium that was to become the great art form of the twentieth century. The animations have much to tell us about the plays as well. They show us what some of us tend to forget—that the plays are meant to *entertain*. They demonstrate that the plays are narratives susceptible to visualizations that are reinforced by the spoken word. Terrence Hawkes is simply wrong to assert that "they are packages of stories based on the Shakespearean plots which themselves were not original. So they aren't going to provide much insight into Shakespeare" (quoted in Osborne 1998, 77–78). Any effort to produce the plays provides insight into Shakespeare. That few of the plots were original is irrelevant. For one thing, it is Shakespeare's version of the story that has become normative—I suppose that certain segments of the history of Cleopatra are exceptions—and for another, the retelling of the story, unless the narrative is coerced into a completely modern context, usually touches upon the archetype that explains why the story keeps getting retold.

I believe that the productions of season two are easily superior to most of those of season number one, which has an outstanding *Hamlet* but an over-narrated *Midsummer Night's Dream* and a melodramatic *Macbeth*. The puppet *Twelfth Night* and *The Tempest* seem to be more exercises in prettiness than anything else. Each of the productions of the second season would serve as an excellent introduction to its play as *script*, that is, as words to be formulated into a play as opposed to being read in a book. I believe that the plays of the second season would appeal to children even younger than the perceived 10-to-14-year-old group at which the series is aimed (with the probable exception of the *Othello*, and the possible exception of *Shrew*), and to students at any level. The more sophisticated, of course, can examine them on the basis of their condensations of the inherited script or scripts and of the techniques of animation themselves. I will describe each of the six productions, noting briefly what's in and what's out, and commenting on the capacity of the technique to express the script. The issue is, as always, Which of the possible stories that the script includes is told in this production? These are the "Animated *Tales*," and Osborne equates them to and distinguishes them from the stories written by Charles and Mary Lamb at the beginning of the nineteenth century. The productions emphasize what Osborne calls "the growing importance of narrative" (1997, 103), and it is not to much to claim, as Stanley Wells does, that "like many of the operas, ballets, and paintings based on Shakespeare, [they] transmute their raw material into something rich and strange in its own right" (1992, 6). As with the first six productions, which used cel animation, painting on glass (for *Hamlet*), and puppets (for *Twelfth Night)*, the second set employs the same techniques: puppets (for *The Winter's Tale* and *The Taming of the Shrew*), painting on glass (for *Richard III* and *As You Like It*), and cel animation (for *Julius Caesar* and *Othello*). Each approach has its advantages and disadvantages, of course. It is surprising to me that cel animation, which is normally employed in Disney fantasies or in slapstick Tom and Jerry or Roadrunner productions, can work powerfully as a medium for tragedy.

It is also surprising that puppets can be so effective in a play as somber as *The Winter's Tale*. The production begins with a landscape under snowfall and a palace to the left into which the camera moves. This is a parody of Hollywood "winter scenes"—Sonja Henie films, *Queen Christina, Swing Time, Holiday Inn*—so it achieves a neat, nostalgic "distance." In the courtyard, a boy cavorts in the snow, while a suspicious man watches a man and woman who are laughing as the man kisses the woman's hand. The first line, "Too hot! Too hot!" creates a verbal contrast to the wintry setting. For all of its visual cueing here, Leontes' "tremor cordis" comes suddenly, as it does in the play. The scene shifts to indoors and a fireplace. There Leontes enjoins Mamillius to "Go play, boy, play. Thy mother plays." A narrator, perhaps unnecessarily, tells us that Leontes has been stricken with "a sudden madness," and believes that Polixenes is the father of Hermione's unborn child. Snow swirls against a cliff as Leontes attempts to suborn Camillo. Camillo warns Polixenes. "I saw his heart in his face," says Polixenes, and the two depart on a waiting ship.

Inside, in a glowing scene borrowed from Veronese, Mamillius begins to tell his winter's tale. Leontes enters in a dark, Gestapo-like intrusion. "Is this sport?" Hermione asks. "Away with her to prison!" is the answer. Again, this action is swift, as in the play, reflecting Leontes' own o'rehasty conclusions. The question for the oracle goes off on a ship, prow against the snow, as Paulina brings the newborn daughter to Leontes. Furies swirl around his head, suggesting a self-invited gathering of judgment against him and preparing us for further visits from supernatural powers. The trial of Hermione occurs in an ornate room constructed of various types of marble that contrast with the deep Renaissance gold of the walls. She looks at a locket picturing her "father, Emperor of Russia." The oracle arrives. "Hermione is chaste!" Mamillius dies. Leontes recoils.

Herminone "dies" and the camera looks down "at what death is doing," suggesting the response of a "higher power." Antigonus begs for the child's life and takes it off, as Leontes orders, to a "desert place." Hermione's ghost, all in white, appears to him and names the child "Perdita." That this is Antigonus's dream is to be inferred perhaps, but if we don't know the play, the image reinforces our sense that Hermione is dead, as Osborne argues (1998, 80). It snows on the seacoast of Bohemia, and the camera moves quickly back and forth from Antigonus's depositing of the child, to the bear, to the Clown observing, to the ship crashing into the rocks, then to the Shepherd responding to the cries of the baby. It is a rapid coda signalling the end of time as agent of destruction. "Things dying" move to "things newborn," and an angel appears as Time, taking us through sixteen years and repeating the name "Perdita." The angel reminds us of Hermione's ghost—as it should. The "resurrected" Hermione is an agency in the triumph of time, along with Perdita, a major element in the play's movement toward the comic ending. Bohemia is also viewed through the prism of the old masters; a sketch of seacoast through the woods looks like the pale distance in the upper left of Breugel's *Icarus*. Autolycus is nicely delineated, with attention given to his picking of the Clown's purse. Autolycus is also amusingly pretentious as courtier. The buildup to Polixenes's unmasking and condemnation of all participants in the romance of Florizel (a young man out of Raphael) and Perdita (Botticelli's *Primavera*) is also carefully developed. Little festival occurs, of course, though we get glimpses enough to sense the pastoral antithesis of what has been an ugly vision of the court. It becomes the court of course, again in Polixenes's rage, the aristocratic parallel to Leonte's unreason earlier. Interludes such as the festival or Prospero's masque in *The Tempest* are victims of a format that condenses the narrative into some twenty-six minutes. Needless to say, the debate about nature and nurture is excised in this truncated version.

The major victim of time here is the statue scene. It occurs in a circular room, with small busts in niches under the ceiling, an appropriate chamber for the display of Italian sculpture, but Paulina rushes the ending, leaving no time for the miracle to develop. "Miracles can't be crowded," as Sheldon Zitner says of the BBC version (1981, 11). Nor can they be rushed. It may be that technique and script finally clash at this point. The slightly jerky moments of the puppets—they have to be moved minutely for each new shot—signal "fantasy" and are part of our pleasant experience of this production. But can a puppet be a statue? Easily, of course, but the point on stage, or in any medium using live actors, is that here is an apparent statue (which has been alive all along) coming to life for most of the characters in the fiction. We have to believe, with Leontes and Perdita, that it *is* a statue, or, and I suspect this is much more likely, that it really is Hermione who has been secreted away for sixteen years. Certainly we come to that conclusion before Leontes does, partly because of the dramatic conventions involved, partly because Leontes does not want to believe lest his belief be dashed. The scene resonates against the one in which Romeo describes a living Juliet but will not let belief take hold of him, and the scene in which Othello describes the pure Desdemona as statue ("smooth as monumental alabaster") before he kills her. In each case, we sense our impulse to intervene. In *Winter's Tale,* we don't have to "awake our faith," but we do have to suspend our disbelief and accept that Leontes thinks it's a stature. We do share his emotional response when he discovers that "She's warm!" but ours is a reaction to reunion and reconciliation, not to "miracle." Osborne says that the production "explores the magical boundary between stillness and movement. [Hermione's] appearance as the ghost, drawn into movement on behalf of her daughter, paves the way for the logic of her reanimation in the final scene" (1998, 78, 80). It is probably "too logical," even if we know that there's been no miracle and that, assuming that Hermione has been alive all along, none has been necessary once Leontes' inner attitudes have shifted so completely. The problem is that a puppet cannot "come to life" in a world already made up of puppets, unless we are witnessing a puppet version of the Resurrection. In some subtle way, our suspension of disbelief has been tampered with. Is it that the production insists on Hermione's death—the angel Time being just another manifestation of her ghost—or that stasis, puppet-as-just-puppet, is, at the end, more convincing than movement and that the production has left us on the still side of the magical boundary? I am not sure. Here, the ending verges on a parody of Pinocchio. I believe, however, that that difficulty is inherent in the puppet medium, which, the rest of the time, serves the script admirably.

The animated *Julius Caesar* begins with the narrator's "All Rome was wild with joy!" Caesar rides out of the sun on a black horse. He proceeds on foot to the capitol, an exaggerated structure of columns and steps borrowed from Joseph Mankeiwicz's 1953 film. "Beware the Ides of March," Caesar is told. Cassius tempts Brutus outside the Forum. They receive Casca's report. The storm drops down on Rome. The voice of Cassius echoes under the great arches as he furthers his conspiracy. Brutus reads Cassius's letter by firelight. The Conspirators appear in shrouds, faceless, looking like the Soothsayer. The pleas of Portia and Calpurnia are included briefly. Portia is a thin, pale woman, but Calpunia is vivid, giving Decius a look of terror as he arrives to flatter Caesar to the senate. Her depiction of a statue becoming quickly covered by a sea of blood plays against Decius's reinterpretation of the same image. Caesar's red robe becomes a shroud (which will later bleed down the stones of the capitol). We hear Brutus begin to speak to the crowd as Antony looks down at Caesar, asks pardon, and vows revenge. Brutus concludes and Antony appears with Caesar's body—a moment that shocks the crowd, and is also borrowed from Mankiewicz. As Antony speaks, the giant statue of Caesar dominates the sky behind him. The narrator takes us to Asia Minor and Philippi. The production provides a snippet of the quarrel between Brutus and Cassius and the former's revelation of Portia's suicide. Fire surrounds her pale face. The flames burn blue for Caesar's ghost. The production includes the brief exchange between Antony and Octavius, in which the younger Caesar insists that he does "not cross" Antony, but that he will have his way. Then we get a bit of the battle, and Cassius's suicide. Caesar rides in on a white horse down a fiery funnel from some other universe: the fifth horseman, Revenge. Cassius spins in white space and falls. Brutus dies less surrealistically, but Caesar rides again, this time into space, his ranging for revenge completed. Antony uses his own cloak to cover Brutus—it turns from blue to red—and delivers his eulogy. "His life was gentle" plays over the corpses on the battlefield, so that that seemingly obligatory eulogy seems to be undercut by the imagery surrounding it.

The production is filled with the omens that weave within the fabric of the play and of supernatural events and settings—fire, flaming caverns in the sky, statues and carvings that suddenly change their aspects into something fierce and dangerous within the marble. In this world even the stones of Rome can come to life, as Antony predicts in his oration. It is a frighteningly unstable world even while Caesar is alive, as the play suggests, since he himself "comes in triumph over Pompey's blood." In one spectacular image, an eagle takes off from the army of Brutus and Cassius and shatters into a flight of crows, fulfilling Cassius's foreboding images of carrion birds that substitute for the eagles that had accompanied them and create a "canopy most fatal."

This production is vivid and true to the major rhythms of the script. *Julius Caesar* is still used as an introduction to Shakespeare in many schools; it being the only script inoffensive enough to satisfy the rigid and anti-intellectual agenda of the religious right.

It is precisely because the play offers nothing in the way of sexuality; very little in the way of a bawdy, "downstairs" society; and mostly long speeches by males that it is not a good introduction to the canon. If used as an introduction to the play that introduces Shakespeare to so many, however, this production should overcome a lot of the problems. Shakespeare was not necessarily meant to be turned into an animated cartoon, but he was meant, and is meant to be experienced, as drama. This version fulfills that requirement very well.

As You Like It begins with the wrestling and the sudden infatuation of Rosalind and Orlando. It hits its stride when it gets to the forest and concentrates on the various lovers cavorting among the trees and fields. We get very little of the court here and thus not much of the contrast built into the script. The production looks as if it has been painted by Renoir, Cézanne, or Sisley. It certainly contrasts with the dark *Hamlet* and *Richard III*, which are also painted on glass, but look as if they had been "etched by Rembrandt" (Andreae 1993, 14). The style is a nice match for the play. Two brilliant moments occur when, first, Jacques's disquisition is illustrated by Elizabethan woodcuts of the stereotypical career he describes—including the DeWitt drawing of the Fortune—and when, later, Rosalind's description of married life is illustrated in bubbles that depict the unfortunate changes that occur when love turns into marriage. The line drawings contrast with the over-the-edge impressionism of the "inner" production. The effect—"art within art"—is akin to that of a play within a play. *As You Like It* is a very rhetorical play that involves a series of one-on-one confrontations on the forest pathways. Much of that language and action is, of course, not here, but the production is a pleasantly illustrated and engaging story about the several couples who finally come to the ark at the end of the play. This production comes the closest of any of those of the second season to resembling a picture book. A characteristic of the Shakespeare Animated Tales is the jumpiness of the animation itself, which is particularly noticeable in *As You Like It*. This is hardly the effortless fluidity of a Disney film, but a technique that calls attention to itself as craft. It is like watching the vase being made on the potter's wheel or the glass being blown. Our disbelief is suspended, of course, but our belief in the creation of the work of art before our eyes becomes a component of our pleasure in the art work itself. Osborne is correct to say that "the illustrated quality of this tale seems quite deliberate" (1998, 85). As the play dramatizes the dynamic process Rosalind encourages—as opposed to the static vision Jacques outlines and as opposed to the stereotypical, if mobile, negative images of marriage that accompany her words (it is a kind of exorcism)—so we experience the process of making the film, frame by frame. Animation, says Osborne, "enacts the basis of all film—the use of successive still images which create an illusion of motion. This effect is possible because of persistence of vision, that is, the ability of our retinas to retain an image as long as a tenth of a second, and its conceptual equivalent ... which allows us to perceive connections and relationships between such images" (1997, 107). The jerky quality of the *As You Like It* animation would be distracting in a regular film, but it works well here because of the further distance that animation imposes on the audience. What we experience in animation, as Lotman says, are "signs of signs; images of images" (1981, 37). This "non-reality" does not demand realistic motion; indeed, its effects are enhanced by the artificiality of the movement within the frame. We are constantly reminded of stillness overcome, of a physical movement simulating the emotional progress that Rosalind attempts to teach.

Richard III is the only history play in the entire series—unless we count *Julius Caesar*, which, with its concern with power and its shift from major player to player in the political drama, can be called a history play. *Richard III* concentrates from first almost to last on a single character and his manipulation of people and, through them, of events. I think that it is unfortunate that we begin here with "King Edward was sick and so was his kingdom." That is too facile. Let us begin with the supreme cynicism of Richard's "son of York." The narrative of this production does insist, though, that Richard must work quickly and sequentially to achieve his goals. The emphasis on alacrity becomes a metaphor for this greatly condensed rise and fall. The technique of painting on glass—where one image is wiped off before another is added—must be painstaking for the artists, but it is wonderful to watch. It has "all the attractive textures of a moving oil painting" (*Guardian* 1992, E14). It is done for this production mostly in black and white, with a few subtle colors—lime, gold, purple—lightly added. In one brilliant sequence, the camera observes through a stained-glass window the silhouette of Richard and Buckingham leaving to get the Princes at Ludlow , closes up on the window, which depicts soldiers fallen in battle, as the narrator tells us that the Queen's brothers have been killed; then shifts to a shot of Richard returning with the Princes and crossing Tower Bridge. The images reinforce the production's emphasis on plotting, fatality, and the speed with which Richard implements his schemes. In many of the frames, only a few elements—eyes, a face perhaps—move. Other images stay still. This technique becomes a metaphor for Richard, who controls moment *and* stasis through the action of his imprisoning will. The production demonstrates powerfully how conscience ultimately escapes from its prison within Richard and makes him the still recipient of its motion.

As with many of these productions, this one borrows from other films, reinforcing the education to film—specifically to Shakespeare on film—that Osborne claims for the series: "These connections serve to associate the cartoons more closely with Shakespearean films than with narrative children's versions or with Saturday morning cartoon[s]" (1997, 107). Here, for example, we see Richard looking down on a wan Lady Anne from a palace window, just as Olivier does in his 1957 film. The film also alludes to the *Hamlet* of the first season, which was also done on glass (directed by Natalia Orlova, who, I assume, is a sister of *Richard III*'s director, Natasha Orlova. Osborne assigns both the *Hamlet* and the *Richard III* to Natasha; 1998: 82). Interiors twist and swirl, suggesting that the very architecture colludes in evil (as in "The Fall of the House of Usher" and "The Haunting"). As in *Hamlet*, crows observe the action, and fly off as if reporting to unseen superiors. At one point, a crow dissolves into Richard, a reversal of the famous image from *Dracula*, where Dracula holds his robed arms out and becomes an ominous bird.

While the Hastings episode is nicely encapsulated, and while an effective fragment of the three ladies in front of the Tower is retained, and while the Duchess of York gets to curse Richard as he rides out to Bosworth Field, the production cuts Clarence's dream (which, I think, would have translated vividly to animation) and Buckingham's great "All Soul's day" speech (5.1.12ff). One wished for a *longer* production! As Osborne says, however, of the *Hamlet* production, the animation "resembles a series of slight jump cuts in its presentation of successive images [that] often echo excisions from the play" (116). The disaster that befalls Buckingham's army is reported and his execution narrated (so that he can be part of Richard's nightmare). At the end, Princess Elizabeth and Richmond pose iconically for a cheering and united England under two carved and intertwined roses. The frame had been prepared and awaited them to fill it.

The issue, of course, is not what is left out, but how the production is shaped out of the inherited script or scripts. Painting on glass involves an erasure of images that nicely coincides with Richard's technique ("When they are gone..."; 1.1.162. "To draw the brats of Clarence out of sight..."; 3.5.107) and the reappearance of images in the place of those wiped away. That latter aspect of the process coincides with the painting of the ghosts in and by Richard's conscience in his nightmare ("When such ill dealing must be seen in thought"; 3.6.14). The mode of production and the meanings in the script mesh powerfully. This production will be extremely useful, not only as an introduction to a play that can seem too long and complicated on the page, but in comparison to other good filmed versions—the Olivier, to which it alludes several times; the Dudley-Warde 1912 silent film; and Pacino's *Looking for Richard*, which dramatizes the making of a film of *Richard III*.

The animated *Taming of the Shrew* is one of the masterpieces of the series. It begins with the camera panning a pastel countryside with a small tavern at one of its woodland verges. Sly is tossed out of the door. "A pair of stocks, you rogue!" says an unseen woman within. The Lord comes upon the sleeping Sly, fat belly exposed and moving up and down above the grass. The Lord has his servants replace the boar they are lugging with Sly, who is reclothed, placed in a bed, and awakened by a hunting horn. *Shrew* is announced in script in front of a curtain that opens on to a proscenium-framed stage, where Baptista, Gremio, and Hortensio debate about Kate. A tiny, mouselike master of ceremonies moves in and out from Lord's house to play-within-play, serving economically as the Lord's master of the revels and narrator of the inner story, even a raiser of the curtain, à la *The Little Rascals*. The red-haired Kate wears a red dress, contrasting with the demure, blue-gowned, blonde Bianca. Petruchio "rides" in front of a moving background to arrive suddenly (to the apparent surprise of both "actors") at Hortensio's window. The flat representing the wall of Hortensio's house rumbles up to the flies, with Hortensio still in it, to reveal the scene in which Kate harasses Bianca. In keeping with the use of puppets, the production itself is "metadramatic." It keeps reminding us that the inner play *is* a play, and that the play-within-the-play is a shoestring operation that permits the audience to see how its tricks are performed. Other moving dioramas are employed for Kate and Petruchio's journeys to and from his country place. A very effective silence accompanies Petruchio's entrance up the steps to Baptista's house, and one notices the depth and three-dimensionality that can be captured with puppets. Kate and Petruchio exchange words. Petruchio vividly shows where he thinks a wasp wears its sting, but some of the debate is conducted by dance steps; as if two dancers or two musicians were competing in virtuosity. Here, it is a tie. Petruchio makes sure that Kate's eyes follow him. The mere fact of their movement within that proud face betrays her growing interest in this outrageous suitor. The wedding scene (particularly Petruchio's arrival) and subsequent banquet (particularly Petruchio's abduction of Kate) are carefully paced here. We get a good sense of the "waiting, and waiting, and waiting" of the former and of Petruchio's command of several roles in the latter as he runs the spectrum from solicitous husband to possessive male. Kate's initiation by mud, hunger, and deprivation is neatly developed and contrasted with Bianca's lessons back in Padua. Peter does tell us that "he kills her in her own humor." Petruchio turns directly to the camera to challenge the audience's ability to better tame a shrew. The ending suggests that the challenge is also delivered to Sly, though the camera does not show him responding at this moment. I was hoping that Garfield would retain the exchange between Petruchio and the Tailor about the making of puppets—it would have been a kind of in-joke that this amusingly self-aware production could have accommodated.

Before they return to Padua, Kate and Petruchio debate in front of a mantel on which sits a beautiful clock. It is a metonym for Petruchio's control of time. From the moment she accepts whatever version of sun or moon Petruchio prefers on the way back to Padua, Kate is moving to the pull of her own rhythms. She joyfully recognizes that she is no longer Petruchio's puppet or pulled by the strings of her self-defeating refusal to join the new society he offers her. The final contest is given an effective, relatively full treatment with Kate on a balcony and Bianca and the Widow below her on either side of the steps. We are reminded during Kate's final speech that it is part of a play. As her speech draws to a conclusion, the sleeping Sly is removed from the bed. The play-within-the-play concludes, as the Lord and his master of the revels applaud.

We look out from the stage at another stage at a fictional audience celebrating the fiction it has commissioned and assisted. The Lord's house, with its plaster and frescoes, contrasts, we notice, with the bourgeois setting of Baptista's home, with its leaded glass, woodwork, and laden table. Sly wakes up on the grass—this is a fragment of *The Taming of a Shrew* ending—remarks on what he believes to have been a dream, says "I know now how to tame a shrew," and immediately enters the tavern, knowing how to tame a shrew. He bounces out again and the same voice says "A pair of stocks, you rogue!" Sly's "dream," of course, has been an elaborate practical joke which finally plays its own joke on Sly, in a working out of the law of unintended consqeuences unforeseen by the Lord.

While we lose Petruchio's early speeches, the great role of Tranio, and the wonderful episode with Vincentio on the road back to Padua in this version, it raises all the right questions about framing—indeed it uses planes of fiction in effective and playful ways—and provides a surprising amount of the story of the play, particularly the competitions between Kate and Bianca and between Kate and Petruchio. Here, Kate does not surrender at the end. It seems to me that the production easily transcends the "Punch and Judy...punched Judy version of the marriage" that Osborne ascribes to it (1998, 81). Even if she does not wink at Bianca or at the audience during her final speech, Kate's face never loses its commanding expression. At the end, though, she seems to be in command of herself, as opposed to merely resisting the negative environments into which she has been thrust. She asserts her superior status by showing her love for Petruchio, as he shows his for her. The production demonstrates that the use of 9-inch tall puppets can create a likeness to stage productions, including many of the same values, particularly the incomparable benefits that accrue when the audience is acknowledged as a participant in the shaping of the fictions. While the production has its bawdy moments, it seems to me that this would be a superb introduction to the play—and to elements of Shakespearean dramaturgy—for young people.

The *Othello* is inconsistent and at times disjointed but remarkably powerful for an animated cartoon. The pictures themselves are consistently made up of grays, browns, and blacks, with each of those colors or non-colors finding itself in Othello's face, as if his skin pigmentation keeps changing. The idea, of course, is that he is not "constant." His black eyes roll like eight balls against the whites. Desdemona is a pale and diaphanous creature who tends to float, in contrast to the heavy, earth-bound Othello. That vivid colors are *not* employed mutes the "cartoon" feeling of this production, appropriately for this script.

The production opens with the title "Othello" standing against a rolling surf. The surf finally obliterates the letters. A narrator tells us that Othello and Desdemona have been married. The first words from the play are Iago's "I do hate him as I do hell pains." A montage shows Othello arriving by ship to a waiting Desdemona and Desdemona covering Othello's eyes with a handkerchief with one major strawberry in its center. This image suggests both her "deception" of Othello and the "happy ending," in which she produces that precise handkerchief on his demand (3.4.52). The couple kisses against a background of flames. "You're well tuned now," Iago says, borrowing a line from the first scene in Cyprus. The flames suggest both passion and jealousy—here, Iago's. The idea seems to be that he will transfer his own "hell pains" to Othello. The lines to the awakened Brabantio about the "old black ram" and "the beast with the two backs" (and later "her body's lust," "With her, on her, what you will," and "whore") are retained, augmenting the case for Iago's sexual jealousy. While the production may be aimed at early adolescents, it would likely be banned by the censors of the Christian right.

Visually, the production is fascinating. Othello's brief rendition of his previous career omits references to slavery, Cannibals, Anthropophagi, and men whose heads do grow beneath their shoulders, but behind his words, substituting for the open arches of Venice, are Uccello-like images of combat, seiges, and sea battles between giant galleys. This is the "tale" that would win the Duke's daughter. Another brilliant image—used only once—occurs when Othello shouts "Devil!" He looks up at the ceiling of a great cathedral, which cracks into fragments as if from an earthquake.

Othello's high-arched and seemingly indestructible faith in Desdemona is shattered. Since he is a "man of high estate" in the Aristotelian sense, his own fate is "not a single doom" but reaches out to the architecture of the state itself. The concept is briefly presented, not worked into the fabric of the production's visual and ideational texture. One instant that those who know Shakespeare films will recognize is Othello's undulating swing of his shoulders on "I'll tear her all to pieces," which is borrowed from Olivier's film version. The Iago in this production seems to have been modeled on Frank Finlay's cool and understated smirk of an Iago opposite Olivier. Even more obviously, the death of Desdemona's maid, Barbary, copies the scene in which Jean Simmons cruises down the river in the Olivier *Hamlet*. The links, of course, are her song "Willow" and the "willow" of which Gertrude speaks from which the hapless Ophelia tumbles into the water, which both women sing before they sink. Here, the Barbary episode arrives through Desdemona's hair, which becomes the willow tree. It is a kind of dream that moves us, and Desdemona, out of the play and out of the current situation for a moment, but that only reinforces Desdemona's dilemma by imaging and presaging the death of the hapless woman who loves a madman. The image of the drowning Barbary also foreshadows Desdemona's "passivity on her deathbed," as Osborne says (1998, 77).

The powerful cross-purposes of the "Cassio...Handkerchief" exchange between Desdemona and Othello are retained, and they help make her more of a protagonist than mere victim of male machination and misapprehension. At the end, Othello holds his hand in the torch illuminating Desdemona's chamber, quenches it, and reignites it. The image suggests his remarkable power and imperviousness to physical pain, as well as his claim that he has overcome his jealousy and is killing his wife for "the cause" (though that justification is not included here). Dying "upon a kiss," Othello pulls a curtain down. As it floats slowly in space, it captures Desdemona's precious frailty and, of course, the whisper of handkerchief that became such a heavy thing. The final scene, combining images of power and vulnerability with enough of Othello's potent double epithets to suggest the linguistic premises of his self-conception, even as he sees himself standing on the far side of tragedy, is superb. I wished only for Othello's apostrophe to Desdemona, "when we shall meet at compt ..." Surely Iago's earlier disquisition on wives, designed to heighten the tension in the time between the arrival of Desdemona on Cyprus and the coming of Othello's ship, could have been sacrificed for the sake of the later moment.

One of the advantages of the editing is that it avoids the issue of Othello's "peaking." On stage, the actor must balance on an uneasy equation between suspicion and certainty for a long time, from the middle of the long third scene of Act 3 to the illusory calm of "It is the cause..." just before the murder of Desdemona. Not so here, where the rush of torches and the sudden flash of swords along streets breaking lose from martial law are vividly depicted. Any moments of introspection—"Othello's occupation gone"—though, are sacrificed to the pell-mell pace of this production. The pressure of condensation seldom permits any rhythm other than "fast forward." While the flow of a Shakespeare production is—or should be—constant *between* scenes, one coming right in on top of the previous one—pauses can occur *within* scenes. Lady Macbeth pauses for a beat before she recognizes Macbeth coming from the murder chamber, then says, "My husband!" Coriolanus holds Volumnia "by the hand, silent," and silence circles Cleopatra's "O!" A problem for the animated version is that silence and pacing can be sacrificed to the constraints of time. That this is so seldom a problem is a tribute to the animators and directors, as well as to the skillful editing of Leon Garfield.

Teachers would be well advised to begin the tapes after the introductions by Robin Williams, which are for the most part stupid, in no way appropriate for the productions that follow, increasingly anachronistic, and likely to raise laughter from the injudicious.*

---

* Thanks to Professor Laurie E. Osborne of Colby College for making some of the productions available to me.

Chapter 7

Titus and the Genre of Revenge

Perhaps Montresor achieves the perfect revenge. "A wrong," he says, "is unredressed when retribution overtakes its redresser. It is equally unredressed when the avenger fails to make himself felt as such to him who has done the wrong." His family motto is *Nemo me impune lacessit*, as Fortunato learns. In search of that cask of Amontillado, Fortunato's luck turns to vinegar. He is entombed among the cobwebs of the Montresor catacombs, but not before crying "For the love of God, Montresor!"

Revenge on the Elizabethan stage almost invariably cost the revenger his life. Pickering's *Horestes* (1567) creates an allegorical Revenge, as Kyd would do. The casting out of Revenge permits Horestes to survive and become king. While the play "provides a virtual diagram of the Elizabethan perplexity about revenge," as Anne Barton says (1980, 13), Pickering's solution is "fundamentally anti-tragic" (14). Marston's Antonio, who says at the end: "a solemn hymn advance, / To close the last act of my vengeance," is another exception. More typical is Vendice in *The Revenger's Tragedy*, who brags that his revenges were "somewhat witty carried," is condemned, and says, "We die after a nest of dukes. Adieu!" The King's brother, Lysippus, at the end of *The Maid's Tragedy* tells us what the revenger can expect:

> May this a fair example be to me
> To rule with temper; for on lustful kings
> Unlook'd-for sudden deaths from God are sent;
> But curs'd is he that is their instrument.

The audience, says Fredson Bowers in his classic study, "hoped for [the revenger's] success but only on condition that he did not survive. Thus his death was accepted as expiation for the violent motives which had forced him to overcome the rules of God" (1940, 184). A benevolent revenger—one who forgave his enemies rather

than killing them—was, of course, permitted to survive. Marston's
Malevole-Altofronto elicits this confession from the usurping Pietro:

> O Altofront, I wrong thee to supplant thy right,
> To trip thy heels up with a devilish slight;
> For which I now from throne am thrown, world-tricks abjure;
> For vengeance, though 't comes slow, yet it comes sure.

Altofronto reassumes his dukedom as a result of a bloodless
coup. Another revenger, Heywood's Frankfort, finds that the angry
hand that would kill Wendoll is stayed by a servant girl. Frankfort
kills the unfaithful Anne "even with kindness." In *The Atheist's
Tragedy*, D'Amville raises the ax to execute Charlemont but strikes
out his own brains. Charlemont survives:

> Only to heaven I attribute the work,
> Whose gracious motives made me still forbear
> To be mine own revenger. Now I see
> That patience is the honest man's revenge.

A constant of the sub-genre of the revenge play is described by
Dame Helen Gardner: "The initial situation...is created by the villain.
The denouement also comes through his initiative. It is not the result
of a successfully carried out scheme of the revenger" (1963, 41).
Balthasar, son of the Portugese Viceroy, for example, requests that
Hieronimo "entertain [his] father...with...a show" in *The Spanish
Tragedy*. Hieronimo and Bel-imperia mine a yard below "the
entertainment" and translate it into a medium for revenge. The
revenge play invariably demonstrates a fatal cooperation between
villains and revengers. This economy of action and motive and the
pattern of discrepant awarenesses explain the Elizabethan-Jacobean
fascination with this type of play. The remarkable condensation and
"dramatic irony" that this configuration achieved are described by
an early critic of *Hamlet*, J. Drake, in 1699:

> Here was a Murther privately committed, strangely discover'd and
> wonderfully punished. Nothing in Antiquity can rival this Plot for the
> admirable distribution of Poetick Justice. The Criminals are not only
> brought to execution, but they are taken in their own Toyls .... The Moral
> of all this is ...that the Greatness of the Offender does not qualifie the
> Offence and that no Humane Power or Policy are a sufficient Guard
> against the Impartial Hand and Eye of Providence, which defeats their
> wicked purposes and turns their dangerous machinations upon their
> own heads (1950, 3–4).

Dame Helen uses *The Spanish Tragedy* as one of her examples,
along with Tamora in *Titus Andronicus*, who thinks she is

manipulating a powerless Titus, and the Duke in *The Revenger's Tragedy*, who makes certain that the rendevous he anticipates will be secret and "thus provides Vindice with the perfect place and time for his vengeance" (Gardner 1963, 42).

Other examples abound, and a few are worth adducing to suggest the pervasiveness of the pattern. Marlowe's Barabas brags to Ferneze about the trap he has set for Calymath:

> Here have I made a dainty gallery,
> The floor whereof, this cable being cut,
> Doth fall asunder, so that it doth sink
> Into a deep pit past recovery.

Barabas hands the knife to Ferneze, who will soon cut the cable and watch Barabas tumble into his own caldron. Ferneze attributes Malta's deliverance "Neither to fate nor fortune, but to heaven."

Marlowe's analogue goes back at least as far as the Psalms:"The heathen are sunken downe in the pit that thei made: in the net that they hid, is their fote taken. / The Lord is knowne by executing iudgement: the wicked is snared in the worke of his owne hands" (8:15–16. Geneva version).

An "entertainment" makes up the final scene of most revenge tragedies—"some pretty show, to solemnize / Our high installment— some music, masquery," as the evil Mendoza says in *The Malcontent*. In *Women Beware Women*, "an invention of" the Duke's, intended "to have honored the first marriage," is revived to celebrate his marriage to Bianca. But unlike Prospero's harmonious vision, where Cupid's malign intent is intercepted within the masque and where the masque itself gives way to the thwarting of "Caliban and his confederates," this one turns deadly. Livia, as Juno, is poisoned by the censer she swings. "My own ambition pulls me down to ruin," she says, dying. Bianca drinks from the poisoned cup she had prepared for the Cardinal that Ganymede had mistakenly given to the Duke. A Lord points at the "shift she has made to be her own destruction." Hippolito, shot down by the poisoned arrows of the masque's Cupids, draws the inevitable moral, which invariably comes too late (so there will be a play, of course):

> [Leantio's death]
> Has brought all this upon us—now I taste it—
> And made us lay plots to confound each other.

Piero, in *Antonio's Revenge*, invites the "sumptuous pomp": "with all my heart. / I'll fill your consort." The maskers kill him, of course, after showing him the severed limbs of his son, Julio. Andrugio's Ghost can say "'Tis done; and now my soul shall sleep in rest. / Sons that revenge their father's blood are blest." The revengers, Antonio, Pandulpho, and Alberto, survive, but retire to "the holy verge of some religious order, / Most constant votaries."

In *The Duchess of Malfi*, the Cardinal gives a fatal order regarding Ferdinand's raving: "And though you hear him in his violent fit, / Do not rise, I entreat you." He has poisoned his paramour with a venom-laced prayer book and wants "with better privacy [to] convey / Julia's body to her own lodging." The Cardinal is thus unable to summon help when Bosola arrives: "When thou killedst thy sister, / Thou tookst from Justice her most equal balance, / And left her naught but her sword," says Bosola. Marston's Dutch Courtesan, Franceschina, is undone by "her own vain strivings." And so on— the examples are manifold within this neglected canon.

The concept of a villain-crafted poetic justice is ingrained in early modern culture. Sir Philip Sidney talks of evil men "making theyr owne actions the beginning of their chastizements" (1962, II: 119). Sir Walter Raleigh, in his Preface to *The History of the World*, talks of the "forswearings, betrayings, oppressions, imprisonments, tortures, poysonings, and...politique subtlety [whereby] Kings [have] pulled the vengeance of God upon themselves...and seen an effect so directly contrary to all their own counsels and cruelties, as the one could never have hoped for themselves" (1953, 1127). Shakespeare's Buckingham, recognizing belatedly the power of the "high All-Seer, with which [he] dallied," acts out his tragedy on All Souls Day: "the swords of wicked men /...turn their own points to their masters' bosoms." A victim of unheeded prophecies, Buckingham's prediction will shortly apply to Richard's psyche. Macbeth recognizes that "this even-handed justice / Commends the ingredience of our poisoned chalice to our own lips." That happens to Claudius, of course: "He is justly served. / It is a poison tempered by himself."

O. B. Hardison suggests that the shift from cliché ("that poetic justice is a conscious or unconscious imitation of ideal justice," as Hardison says [1969, 9]) to dramatic convention means that the revenge plays demonstrate a moral universe at work, a working out of allegories perceived by the characters only at the very end of the play.

But against too-easy formulae, G. K. Hunter argues that the "surface language [of *Antonio's Revenge*] of moral concern is not merely detached from but largely contradictory of the underlying pattern of amoral ritual" (1965, xviii). A play such as *Titus*, emphasizing human activity and not providential design, moves out from under the category of poetic justice that a Sidney or a Bacon would impose upon literature. Still, however, a *play*, in which we participate individually and communally and within a zone of energy very different than that created by solitary reading, can create a powerful "shadow of satisfaction," as Hardison suggests: "The satisfaction comes from having one's deepest feelings about what is right confirmed by the action on the stage" (1969, 10). The ending of *Hamlet*, says Michael Goldman, "rarely fails to produce an overwhelming sense of excitement and satisfaction" (1972, 147). I would argue, however, that our enjoyment has resulted from our being taken on a journey into a forbidden realm, while all the time knowing that someone else—the heroic traveler—will pay for the trespass. Hamlet, as character, also probes our deepest feelings about what is wrong.

Unlike other revenge plays, *Titus* begins with an act by its protagonist—the sacrifice of Alarbus—that sets in motion the further fatal consequences that the play develops. Unlike other revenge plays, this one shows little if any moral universe evolving out of or reinforcing the revenge pattern, even as lip service to providence. Even this early, Shakespeare is granting to his spectator an indeterminate zone in which individual response must formulate itself.

It follows that *Titus* is a difficult script to deliver. It does not build up to that inevitable scene in which the villain—Barabas, Claudius, the Duke in *Revenger's Tragedy*, and others—constructs his own trap. Even *Richard II* pursues this pattern. Bolingbroke's effort to redress Gloucester's murder leads to the deposition scene, wherein Richard shows the new king how much has been *lost* in the exchange of power. That scene does occur in *Titus*, of course, as Tamora carelessly consigns her sons to Titus, then agrees to come to the meatpie party, but this play involves a revenge *for* a revenge. Other revenge plays involve revenge for a crime, which is often committed before the play begins. In Taymor's film, after Tamora plays the peacemaker and insists that Saturninus pardon Titus and company, Titus and Tamora face each other. The space between them flames. Alarbus's entrails are delivered again to the fire. His torso breathes aloud. This is as hokey as Branagh's horror-film Ghost in his *Hamlet,* but it works here because Taymor has established an eclectic style and because she is not treating the script with Branagh's deadly seriousness. Moreover, the death of Alarbus picks up the significance of a repeated ceremony, becoming a perverted eucharist. We can attribute some of the imagery in this film to imaginations informed by horror as cliché and our response to imaginations hollowed out by the clichés of horror films. Much of this is meant to be taken half-seriously, with, as it were, tongue in cheek.

The power of this film results from brilliant filmmaking and also from the genre underlying the film. The film gives images and specific narrative shape to Shakespeare's variation on a revenge story that goes back as far as Genesis and Greek mythology. The archetypal story and the way it was engineered for the Elizabethan stage work under the sensory experience the film provides. Our experience of the structure of the old story is abetted by Anthony Hopkins's uncanny ability to suggest that Titus is figuring out the pattern in which he is implicated as he goes along. Finally, he invents the format and symbology that suit his specific situation. *Titus*—like many revenge plays—changes the inherited pattern, but the pattern is there. In Taymor's film it organizes the depth structure of our psychology of perception and sets up our anticipation of what will happen and our satisfaction when our expectations are fulfilled. That argument is implicit in my desription of the film.

Taymor opens with a young boy playing with automated soldiers and getting so carried away that he trashes his own kitchen and destroys food that only the most surfeited of pre-adolescents would spurn. This is a combination of Saturday morning kid show and the spoiled-rotten product of such an indoctrination. An air raid begins outside, and the boy is carried off to an underground coliseum, where his house burns and one of his toys lies in the mud, but where the mechanized vision has expanded into a Rome in which soldiers do a robot dance (which simply looks silly) and where ancient weapons parade alongside post-modern machines stolen from *The Pentagon Wars.*

The boy—we assume him to be young Lucius, who doesn't appear in the play until 3.2—turns up now and then as an emissary from one self-destructive world to another. These appearances are disruptive, but only mildly so, as the film powerfully takes hold of us. At the end, though, young Lucius takes Aaron's tiny baby and wanders into the sunrise with the infant. The baby's black arm makes a mourning band on Lucius's right arm. We are meant to assume that young Lucius has learned enough to craft a new beginning. Given what has gone before, that assumption is not believable, and the film is hollowed out by this final sentimentality. I sought for some sense of undercutting irony here, but found none. The elder Lucius may have ended the endless chain of revenge—but has a new kinder, gentler ethic been installed? Doubtful. In Jane Howell's version for the BBC (1985), the events are the products of the "fearful slumber" of a young Lucius who observes everything with anachronistic specs. (see Maher 1985, 5–6). The end of the BBC version is more convincing than is Taymor's. Young Lucius looks sadly at the dead baby. This response *may* signal a new order to come when Lucius arrives at maturity, but it seems to suggest that compassion is a private and isolated moment, as ineffectual as anything Titus did until he decided upon the "rough justice" of revenge. It may be, as John Gillies says, that the elder "Lucius converts a typically tragic economy of 'violent reciprocity' into a typically comic order in which 'reciprocity' works for the good of the 'commonwealth'" (1994, 111), but the generic shift is heavyhanded as Taymor applies it. Far more compelling is what the film and script show, that Titus replaces "Rome's system of mutually beneficial, reciprocal relations...by imposing a symmetry of harm for harm," as Harry Keyishian says (1996, 46).

Taymor's opening sequence is further confused by a transposition wherein Saturninus and Bassianus vie for emperorship *after* Titus has turned it down. Saturninus enters the six-story imperial building, as if assuming his right to the throne. Would he compete with Titus for rule? We don't know, of course, since Titus acquieses so readily. It may be that Saturninus and Bassianus need to be introduced, as they are in the script. Here, they appear out of nowhere as competing politicians riding the streets with loudspeakers—Saturninus in a clear bulletproof case—similar to that used by the Pope, but perhaps meant here to signal Saturninus's paranoia.

Another problem with the opening is that Titus's sense of "service" seems incomprehensible, not just exaggerated, as it certainly is. He accepts the concept of eldest son inheriting, even if the eldest son, here, is a demented Alfalfa. The ideal of service itself, however, is even harder to credit than it might have been, say, sixty years ago. As Cynthia Ozick says, "For the modernists, the center notoriously did not hold; for us (whatever *we* are), there is no recollection of a center and nothing to miss, let alone mourn" (1996, 73). This insight emerges time and time again in the biographies of World War Two veterans in Tom Brokaw's *The Greatest Generation*.

The film really begins when Titus inspects the ranks. We have a leader established—as opposed to the puzzling lad who has been kidnapped to this underground space. Titus finally addresses the Romans. "Hail Rome, victorious in thy mourning weeds!" Soon, though, Titus encounters problems. In Shakespeare's late-fourth-century Rome, rituals are empty of their meanings. The film shows Titus filling the empty combat boots of his dead soldiers with dirt sifted from his hand. Titus shows no conviction in condemning Alarbus. It is a formula. Titus consumes some wine as the disembowelment is conducted, but the wine is not linked to the pagan ceremony of redress. "The signs of decadence, corruption, and loss of cultural confidence are everywhere," as Katharine E. Maus says of the play. "The distinction between legitimate and illegitimate behavior seems…remarkably indistinct" (1997, 375). Titus acquiesces in the burial of Mutius simply because it makes no difference what happens. He is not torn between ancient family-based values and an emerging civic order, as are Sophocles's Antigone and Aeschylus's Orestes, though he is in a position to effect this change and evades the responsibility. This play comes the closest in the Shakespeare canon to exploring the issues that the great Greek tragedians were probing within their evolving city-state. In *Titus*, though, the interrogation occurs during the period of decline and fall. Titus is a transitional figure, a fact particularly underlined in Taymor's film, since she first shows Titus in absolute command as he returns to Rome, then swings to the brawling factions of Saturninus and Basianus, then to Titus's weighting of the election to Saturninus. The problem with this transposition, of course, is that the play shows Titus returning in the middle of the ongoing election contest. Taymor creates so powerful and iconic a figure that Titus's preference for Saturninus seems like an incomprehensible surrender and a refutation of what the film has already established.

In *Titus*, old codes are a memory of the past, not a living guide to present behavior. Their observation, then, tends to violate a sense of "right" that may be evolving but has yet to be articulated. Tamora can only appeal for Alarbus on the basis of family, but that is also Titus's point: "These are their brethren [who] religiously...ask a sacrifice." Tamora must express what Titus is doing through oxymoron; "O cruel, irreligious piety!" By the time the play arrives at the "Antigone-Creon" conflict between Titus and the brothers of Mutius, the distinction between family and state is irrelevant. Rome, having taken in the Goths through Tamora's marriage to Saturninus, is shrouded in a moral murkiness similar to that that Dreiser explores in *An American Tragedy*, where a young man who may or may not be a murderer, but who certainly is a product of the tantalizing promises held out to him, goes to his death primarily because he found himself on the borders of that promised land. The only decision that we can applaud in *Titus* is Titus's to revenge. The play, then, is mostly a prologue to his freedom to make that decision. Once the film really begins—after its silly prologue—it provides "images and performances which are as good as anything in the history of Shakespeare on film," as Samuel Crowl accurately claims (2000, 1).

The acting is superb. Hopkins takes us on a compelling and effectively understated journey from potential healer to reviled outsider and from there into that thrilling zone wherein the revenger, realizing who controls the law, decides to kill them, and *also* to an existential space where laughter is the only response left. Titus's pleasure in his culinary skills took me back to Trevor Nunn's 1972 version for the Royal Shakespeare Company and Patrick Stewart honing his knife on a whetstone with that manic glee that Stewart can bring to his roles. After a portion of her initial plea is undercut by some unnecessary cello music, Jessica Lange's Tamora becomes so compelling in her combination of calculation, lack of compassion, and wrinkled, middle-aged lust that we yearn for her return to the camera. Harry Lennix's Aaron creates a zone of detached amusement that permits us to believe that he is as bad as he says he is. Taymor is careful to allow no trendy "race-blind" casting to diminish the fact of Aaron's blackness. The language about blushing is retained, as is the joke about the "fly that comes in likeness of a coal black moor." The retention of the racial—and racist—language helps us believe that Aaron does wish for an heir in this white and armor-plated world. Aaron's concern for his son may seem surprising until we remember that "Shakespeare's Goths and Africans apparently have no history, no myths, of their own: instead, they invoke and mimic examples provided by their conquerors" (Maus 1997, 73). Our willingness to accept Aaron in the role of father is conditioned by the ease with which Titus can say "no son of mine" after he has slain Mutius. Although Alan Cumming's Saturninus looks like the villain in an early silent film, he carries off two sequences superbly, first in making the transition from suggesting privately that Tamora be his mistress to publicly making her his wife. Later, he rants and rails in front of the senate about Titus's arrow-launched plea for justice, then snivels to Tamora about his lack of popularity. It is difficult, though, to believe that he has ever been able to walk among his citizens "like a private man," unless he wore a bag over his head, like the blue-eyed boy of the opening sequence. In a film as radically eclectic as this, it is simply beside the point to complain that "the British theatrical and American film styles don't mesh" ("Review," *New York Times*, 11 February 2000, B16).

The film is visually stunning. We notice the distinctive zones and backgrounds Taymor and her designers have made for her characters. The tombs in which Titus buries the dead heroes are modeled on the ovens at Dachau. The oversized throne on which Saturninus perches sits under a huge, metal wolf, which snarls through the clench of its ineffectual muzzle. It is intimidating but ironic above such an abject emperor. The floor of the room is fascist red and black. Titus's bald head plays against the Romanesque arches of the capitol. His wrinkled face echoes the cracked facades of older structures. This visual reinforcement suggests that he has achieved a craggy oneness with the institutions of his city. His returning soldiers, faces coated with gray clay, share his ethic. While they wash under huge culverts supplied by one of the eleven great aqueducts leading into the city, the clay is an emblem of the commitment of their flesh. The contrasting orgies of the new regime are conducted in a vast circular space with an open roof, a pool in the center, and bas-relief depictions of lust on the walls—as if the lovers's side of Keats's urn had been fast-forwarded a few moments. It is through the opening in the roof that Titus's archers sling their arrows, which, in a nice mingling of the old and the new, simulate V-2s soaring off in malign ballistic flight over the English Channel. One of the arrows punctures the left breast of a grotesque goddess of venery, floating in the pool. The orgy looks like a lot of fun and so does the shooting of the arrows. The camera's escape to the green of the countryside is illusory. It is not a Wordsworthian zone. A tiger roams the undergrowth and the sons of Tamora—often imaged as tigers themselves—control an environment that becomes nightmarish as the foliage blossoms and the sun shines "as it has to" on malice and the delight it brings to its perpetrators. The crossroads scene is perhaps the film's best. Taymor pulls out all the stops. The Roman officials march past Titus like figures in an expressionist painting. A wagon rolls over him, his sons caged inside. Trumpet-blowing angels slide around a sheep on a sacrificial block. A head appears on the sheep. It is Mutius, whom Titus has killed earlier. The two sons being killed now are just as innocent as Mutius was, but necessary sacrifices to the terror that Titus has done so much to unleash. An overhead shot zooms in on Titus, spread-eagled on the stones. Further bad news arrives: Lucius's exile, Marcus with the ravished Lavinia. The scene gives us a long perspective of a pre-Roman Stonehengian ruin. Taymor mutes her colors to achieve a visual depth that reinforces the increasingly ominous content of the scene. The lads—Chiron and Demetrius—have a club in the boiler room of the imperial building, complete with pool table, video arcade, and an old fridge for the beer. It is to this den that Aaron's baby is brought to him and it is here that the superb irony of his willingness to kill without conscience to protect his son is developed. Taymor can stop everything when a character decides to confide in us, as Tamora does when she says that she "will massacre them all." We are not in a world where time is a consistent medium. In one of the film's strongest scenes, Aaron climbs a ladder and places the noose prepared for him over his head but is not executed because his crimes confessed on this scaffold demand a death less quick and formal. He has placed himself outside the bounds even of standard capital punishment. At other moments, horror is domesticated. Aaron encloses Titus's severed hand neatly in a Baggie. Chiron and Demetrius are each gagged by gray slashes of duct tape. The perpetuation of horror is finally undercut by the presentation of the heads of Martius and Quintus. A three-wheeled carny wagon pulls up in front of Titus's place. A barker and his daughter get out. Titus. Marcus, young Lucius, and Lavinia sit down in chairs to watch the show. The small stage of the wagon opens to reveal the two heads in glass cases, with Titus's returned hand between them. This "distancing" creates the space for Titus's laugh, which is "not inexplicable or mad, but a sign of mental liberation, reflecting Titus' new understanding that he no longer owes Rome's rulers service...rather as much harm as he can inflict" (Keyishian 1996, 41). The final scene—Tamora putting her beringed finger in her mouth as she realizes what—who—she has been munching upon, Titus stabbing her in the neck, Saturninus frantically pulling a candle out of the chandelier with his teeth (a reminder of Lavinia carrying Titus's hand in her mouth) so he can impale Titus, Lucius forcing a long spoon down Saturninus's throat (Taymor's shrewd reference to feeding the devil) then shooting him with a suddenly available 45-caliber pistol—is funny. What else could it be? Was Shakespeare already satirizing the conventions he would bring to completion in *Hamlet*? Perhaps. Harold Bloom suggests that "Shakespeare knew [*Titus*] was a howler and expected the more discerning to wallow in it self-consciously" (1998, 47). Mark Van Doren calls it "parody…in the extreme degree" (1939, 33).

I find in the film no "blend[ing] of ancient Rome with Mussolini's Italy" ("Review," *New York Times* 11 Feb 2000, B16). Posters of the former Caesar may remind some people of Benito, but I see no jaw jutting from a balcony, no trains suddenly running on time, no sense that the state has been modeled around fascist premises. No beggars hold their hands out on these streets, but surely those be whores lurking near their stalls down in the area of the family tombs. Saturninus does have a taste for exotic uniforms, as Mussolini did, but the costumes here reflect the exoticism of the production, and do not imitate any moment that ever existed in history. Since the events themselves are non-historical, Taymor's yoking of bizarre images becomes appropriate for a translation that is limited only by her imagination. This script also fits a late twentieth century that has found no language with which to capture what has happened within it—indeed, where insight still strives to comprehend the experiences of over fifty years ago—and which produces, in its films, violence for the sake of violence, with no emotional or moral core to motivate it: *The Glimmerman*, for example.

The present film will not induce *Titus* into the classroom—it is "a play for some seasons," as Mariangela Tempera says (1999, 1)—but it should prove very popular with the consumers of violence, even if their teachers won't dare recommend it, even if it's unlikely to get to the provinces. The film, though, transcends its violence. Its depiction of an initial action, revenge for that act, and then the counter-revenge involves images that stay in the eye and the mind's eye. Of the scene that Titus and his bowmen interrupt, Taymor says, "It's shockingly beautiful" ("Review," *New York Times* 11 February 2000, B16). So is her film. It resolves a complicated paradox. A world so wildly unimaginable insists on our detachment from it, a stance akin to Titus's detachment at the outset. That withdrawn position, in turn, permits us to move with Titus toward the satisfaction of the ending—the satisfaction of something unimaginable until this brilliant film educates us to appreciate, even to enjoy, Titus's final, intimate supper.

The "space" that the film explores will be familiar to those who know Kevin Costner's *Revenge* (1990). The initial revenge is carried out by drug lord Anthony Quinn against Costner and Quinn's unfaithful wife. The "counter"-revenge is conducted by the wounded outcast Costner. Unfortunately, the second movement ends in sentimentality. The thesis-counterthesis structure, of course, is often present in Shakespeare's political plays. Richard's banishment of Bolingbroke elicits the latter's response. Macbeth's murder of Duncan insists on Malcolm's return. The power of Taymor's film results partly from the pervasiveness in our culture of the motivation of each of the major characters in the script—the desire to hurt those who have hurt them.

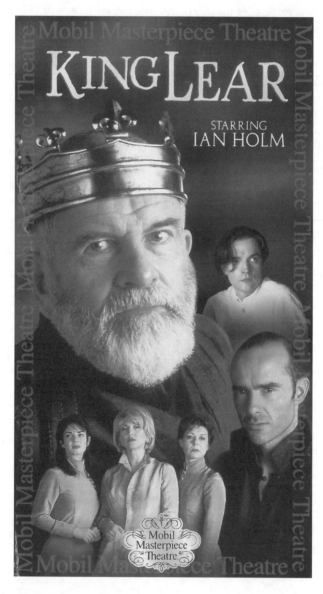

Cover for Richard Eyre's *King Lear. Photo courtesy of Mobil Masterpiece Theatre.*

Chapter 8

Two Recent *Hamlet*s: *The Branagh Shorter Version and the Almereyda*

The conceptual space of *Hamlet* is vaster and deeper than that of any other play. It is not just that the play comes forward from 1601 to be "a vehicle through which later cultures can reflect on pressing contemporary concerns" (Bate 1995, 162). It has a past: not the brilliantly fictionalized background that John Updike provides in *Gertrude and Claudius*, not the Oedipus myth to which Freud and Ernest Jones call our attention, but the accretion of meanings the conflated Shakespeare script inherited and developed—the slow growth of a pearl around the central molecule of revenge. Saxo gives us a brother's murder, an incestuous marriage, feigned madness, and revenge at last. Belleforest adds the crucial detail of the forfeit of the King of Norway's treasure to the King of Denmark, should the latter win the trial by combat. The latter wins and invades part of Norway, thus eliciting the expedition of Young Fortinbras. Belleforest twice mentions the ghost (*ombre*) of the murdered king, which becomes a speaking part in the *Ur-Hamlet* (the lost play, perhaps by Kyd, on which Shakespeare's version may be based). Shakespeare's play eliminates the hero's sojourn in England, which is prominent in Saxo and Belleforest, achieving an economy of action that is covered by Hamlet's letter to Horatio and Hamlet's offstage return to a plot-thick Elsinore. Shakespeare develops the Ghost and Fortinbras, thus adding a cosmic and a political concentricity around the inner drama.

The problem for the filmmaker is what to retain of this remarkably ranging playscript. Probably the most famous example of editing this text is the Olivier film, with its intense black-and-white depth of field and its deletion of Rosencrantz, Guildenstern, and Fortinbras. Hamlet ends up being king, knelt to by all survivors, but a silent king. In Zeffirelli's film, Mel Gibson's Hamlet lies dead on the throne room floor as the camera booms out and the credits roll. One assumes that the film has educated us not to ask, What happens next? On television, our medium of political closure, Fortinbras often appears at the end, as I have remarked elsewhere (1993). Formal cause seems more important to television than to film.

Neither the shorter Branagh film nor the Almereyda version do anything convincing with the cosmic dimension of the inherited script. Branagh exiles it to the category of special effects and chops the prayer scene completely. Almereyda gives us a haunted Pepsi machine and a Claudius deeply oblivious to issues of the spirit. Branagh overdoes the political issues, giving us a Fortinbras who violently invades a country waiting to hand itself to him. Almereyda reduces the theme of power to the politics of surveillance, so that much of the story seems to be coming at us from a camera automatically recording random movement. In editing his full-length *Hamlet* down to two hours, Kenneth Branagh faced a number of decisions, including what story he wants his shorter version to tell. He tells no story, really. The complete conflated *Hamlet* tells several stories, some of them competing with each other. The redundancy is repeated in Branagh's four-hour film. Bernice Kliman says, "Branagh ignores the interpretative imperative: interpretation drives textual choices" (quoted in Nichols 1997, 39). It was probably true that Shakespeare himself began with more than what was needed, as Stephen Orgel argues (Orgel, 1988, 7) and edited toward production. A *film* must edit out more of the language. In the full-length version, the actors must do a lot of tramping through the snow, while the camera tracks along like a pet retriever, as they discuss preparations for war in Denmark or theater wars in London, or as Laertes and Ophelia spar over her relationship with the Prince. The Gade-Neilsen silent film (1920) tells the story of a woman disguised as a prince and involved in a love triangle with Horatio and Ophelia. Olivier (1949) tells of a prince "who could not make up his mind," who is lost in the corridors of that mind and the dream castle of Elsinore. Ragnar Lyth's brilliant film of 1984 shows Hamlet as a spoiled rock or tennis star with a macabre sense of humor, as when Stellen Scarsgaard makes a ventriloquist's puppet out of Yorick's skull. Zeffirelli and Gibson (1990) depict a Hamlet more angry that his playmate mother is now cavorting with Claudius than at anything else. Gibson's Hamlet gets Gertrude back briefly as he clowns through his duel. Of the sound films, only Lyth retains

Kenneth Branagh. "…or not to be." *Photo by Pete Mountain, Courtesy of Shepperton Studios.*

Fortinbras; in this instance, a solid warrior more interested in taking over the polity than in learning how all former claimants grew so recently cold.

The Branagh Two-Hour *Hamlet*

All the editing decisions were made early. They, in turn, dictated the emphasis of the film. One can disagree with the interpretations (and certainly with my descriptions of them), but they incorporate the kinds of decisions that must be made as part of the process of translation from inherited script(s) to film. Trevor Nunn, for example, in filming *Twelfth Night* (1996), decided to break up Viola's soliloquy ("What means this lady?") and place it in segments throughout the film, so that it suggests moments of insight that arrive gradually, instead of an awareness dawning within a single monologue. The flexible medium of film permits the director a fluidity not available to him on stage. Branagh, beginning as he does with a stage script—or more—as *his* script, cannot achieve that flexibility in his longer version. He is stuck with that longer version as he edits it to a two-hour format. He can keep soliloquies in, as he must with the sequence of clichés in "To be, or not to be" (since he keys the soliloquy to the hall of mirrors—behind one of which Claudius and Polonius are hiding—and to his subsequent attack on Ophelia), or erase them (as he does with "The play's the thing," the competing soliloquies of the prayer scene, and "How all occasions"). In the shorter version of his film, he cannot break the play's many soliloquies up into smaller units without glitches in continuity, or having the words voiced over other action or placed in brief moments between actions. His technique of long takes greatly hampers his effort to condense his film. The long version inhibits the shorter. I wonder whether he was tempted—as one is when carving a soap sculpture that isn't working as it gets smaller and smaller—to abandon the project.

The shortened version of the film seems to be tailored to the videocassette. Only occasionally is one aware that it was originally a wide-screen rendition. The long tracking shots are gone, as is the distant view of Fortinbras's ant-like army in the snow. It would seem that the principle behind this edition is to give the main stars their moments on screen. Thus Polonius gets his "mad I call it" speech. Gertrude gets a full closet scene. Ophelia gets her songs. The shortened film strengthens Julie Christie's performance. No mother

wants to believe that her son despises her. Few wives want to believe
that their husband is the murderer of their former husband. Christie's
resistance and gradual awareness—Gertrude has never had to *think*
before—is brilliantly charted. She refuses to "follow" Claudius later,
a decision that pays off when she drinks the poisoned wine as a
demonstration of her freedom from his control. Derek Jacobi is still
superb as Claudius. We see him making the decision that, regardless
of whether Hamlet *is* mad, Hamlet will be "officially" mad for
Denmark. This Claudius realizes that Ophelia is a *political* danger,
even if the film seems not to know how she compromises the king's
power game. Claudius recognizes immediately what Hamlet has
been up to with Gertrude by glancing at the two lockets left behind
on her bed. He knows how close he came to being Polonius behind
that arras, thus giving a retrospective weight to Hamlet's question,
"Is it the King?" "But where is *he*?" Claudius asks about Hamlet.
The body of Polonius represents merely a sanitary problem, after
all. Jacobi's performance is what the film will be celebrated for in
future. Jack Lemmon's Marcellus is almost gone, and seldom has
an editor taken from us something we would more willingly part
with. Michael Maloney's cross-eyed Laertes conveys no sense of
danger, only the sense of an actor playing danger as a drama-school
exercise. Too much of Ophelia have we still. Kate Winslet is made
up with white face and a garish smear of lipstick, so that she
resembles a virtually consumed pie crust. Polonius forces her to
read her letter from Hamlet, but she can't go on and exits in tears.
She is pressed against those mirrors in the hall so that she looks like
a fish in a tank seeking microscopic food just above the weeds. She
gets the song "And will 'a not come again?" which consumes an
excruciating minute and thirty seconds. She mimes a sexual act while
recalling a romp with Hamlet (wouldn't it have been great if Branagh
had substituted Osric!). This editing is no service to the actor—
intelligent ways of depicting Ophelia do exist (see Coursen 1996,
205–208)—and does a disservice to the mentally disturbed by
reinforcing stereotypes. Ophelia also gets that profoundly silly
business wherein she has swallowed the key to her padded cell and
will escape! Does that mean that she has been feigning madness all
along so that she can get out to that frozen river and its miniature
icebergs? It takes too long for that ship to sink. Had this Ophelia
died of her cold-water therapy, then been the subject of Gertrude's
"official" version of her death, Branagh would have achieved a

brilliant sequence. Zeffirelli framed Bonham-Carter's very intelligent Ophelia, now mad, with the inner circle of the castle keep. It formed a crown around her sullen face. She became Queen Ophelia of Denmark as she called for her coach.

Although a lot of the "Swear" sequence is left in as the Ghost sinks down beneath the ghoul-haunted woodlands, Hamlet does not tell his companions that he will put on an antic disposition, so the film moves to a sudden discussion of something we don't know about. It is fairly sudden in the script as well, since we don't see Hamlet feigning madness until after his lunacy has been extensively considered. The film may ask us to believe that some time has passed since Hamlet's encounter with the Ghost and the court's concern with his "madness," but we are given no sense of transition.

Do we know a Ghost has appeared at the beginning of the play? No. The name "Hamlet" carved into the base of the statue appears as the clock is striking. A bird of the winter night is squawking. Francisco, in front of the gate as opposed to walking the parapets, is suspicious. He stares into the bleak distance. He swings his carbine around. We get an apparent angry clank of statue's hand on sword, heard by the single sentinel, Francisco. The camera cuts immediately to the wedding procession of Gertrude and Claudius. The implication is that the danger is from within, but that is only partly true. Horatio, Marcellus, and Bernardo appear to us for the first time after the wedding coronation scene to tell Hamlet of the Ghost's appearance. It is news to us, too.

The blue-eyed Ghost, with a mechanically reproduced voice and a setting that suggests that Elsinore is about to sink into the fault line of a Danish mudpie, is not the statue, so we can only be confused. The Ghost does narrate the story of his death with flashback to Claudius's incursion on his long winter's nap. Hamlet's "guilty creatures" soliloquy is cut, and Claudius hardly cracks up at the play scene. He does flash back to his murder of his brother. Hamlet's antics alone, however, are enough to break the thing up. Much more convincing is Jacobi's interposition upon the players in the BBC-TV version (1980), looking back as the structure of his play dissolves behind him. Patrick Stewart then reverses the Olivier film by holding a torch up to Hamlet's face. In the short version of the Branagh film, Claudius's "my offense" speech—and indeed all of the prayer scene— is cut. Horatio does not agree with Hamlet after the play—though he is more neutral than Robert Swan in the BBC-TV production, who disagrees with Jacobi's self-serving interpretation of Claudius's behavior. We have the Ghost's story, the Ghost's reinforcing flashback, and Claudius's corroborating memory as evidence here. In the script, even Hamlet is not sure of the truth of the Ghost's story until "Gonzago." We aren't sure, completely, until Claudius's effort at prayer—unless a production falsifies the script and shows Claudius fleeing in panic from the play. (Zeffirelli's powerful version had Alan Bates's Claudius holding his ear, suddenly aware of the terrible pain he had inflicted upon his brother.) Since the "guilty creatures" soliloquy is cut from Branagh's shorter version, there is no doubt about Claudius's guilt, so that we cannot share Hamlet's doubt. Gone is the excitement of the competing detective stories that climax at "Gonzago." We are given only Hamlet's explanation to Horatio that the play will imitate "something like the murder" of King Hamlet. The shorter film emphasizes the sentimental choices Branagh makes, as in his whiney "Seems madam" speech. Compare Jacobi's biting rendition in the BBC-TV version. Branagh and Winslet exchange a kiss just before she attempts to return his gifts. One or the other, not both. Since the effort to return the gifts is in the script, the tender kiss should have been reconsidered and excised.

Typical of the film's sentimentality in both versions is the aimless theme music. In the shorter version, it comes in under Hamlet after he has met the Ghost; counterpoints his "To be" soliloquy, therefore underscoring its conventional complaint; and plays under Ophelia's "out of tune and harsh," where surely, if music is needed, it is Schoenberg or Bartók, not Doyle. The music does work beneath the melancholy family reunion in Gertrude's closet, but it is totally out of place during the funeral scene, which calls for a "bell" perhaps but not for this sappy late-nineteenth-century score. The music generalizes the graveyard scene into the bland texture of the rest of the film. Compare the scene in Lyth, where Ophelia tumbles like a rag doll from her coffin as Hamlet and Laertes tussle. Again, in Branagh's film, the music hollows out the "fall of a sparrow" speech, making it a cliché Hamlet is uttering as opposed to something he may fleetingly believe or that he hopes is true. The film achieves a few good moments in Gertrude's closet. The room has trompe l'oeil wallpaper, suggesting the motif of appearance and reality. The Ghost does not speak in the shorter version. It would have been splendid had Gertrude gotten a glimpse of it, as in Barton's 1980 stage version, or had we been led to believe that she might have seen it. But this film, tied as it was in its original version, was also bound by the most conventional of interpretations. One good camera shot shows Branagh reflected in the pool of blood oozing from Polonius. That suggests Hamlet's implication in the bloodbath Denmark is experiencing. The ending continues a disaster. The duel goes on inside the vast throne room as Fortinbras and at least a regiment come stealing in. This is a variation without any tension of Griffith's technique, as in the 1918 *Hearts of War*, where the "Boy" and "Girl" (Lillian Gish) come close to getting killed in their little town even as an invading army closes in to save them (if it will get there in time, which it does). As if word and image have been severed from context, Laertes says "Have at you now" *after* his sword stroke wounds Hamlet. Shouts of "Treason" occur *before* Hamlet strikes at Claudius. No. The court is not, as yet, in on Claudius's guilt. As Horatio talks to Fortinbras about the "mouth" that has nominated Fortinbras for king, the camera looks at the dead Claudius. Again, that is just wrong. We get the silly *Scaramouche* business—the tossed rapier and swinging chandelier, a Hollywood of the 1950s for which even this wedding-cake setting has not prepared us. Fortinbras inspects his troops in the courtyard before the final attack—opening them up for a counter-attack or, at least, for sniper shots from the palace—then sends them charging in, the safety catches released from their rifles, against no one. The final attack isn't even a military exercise. The single sentry, Francisco, has been overwhelmed. Even ceremonial kingdoms post more guards. I was reminded of the beginning of the Loncraine *Richard III* (1996), where King and Prince have forgotten to post guards, even though they are at war. When one observes such movie-making, one simply suspends interest. At the end, King Hamlet's statue comes down. Claudius's reign has been a brief interregnum between military dictatorships. Ron Daniels's production of the late 1980s with Mark Rylance in Stratford, U.K., showed an armored Fortinbras coming in at the end as the armored Ghost had arrived in the early scenes. It was a return to the old order. Hamlet's effort to bring the concept of *future* to Denmark had failed. Here, the hokeyness of the ending merely contrasts uncomfortably with the blandness of what has gone before. I defended the longer version (Coursen 1999, 216ff.) in that it showed that Fortinbras is the only character who understands that language is merely an adjunct to *unspoken* purpose. Here, the editing takes that point away and emphasises what Lloyd Rose said about the longer version. "Hamlet is a Boy Scout whose tragedy is that he finds himself in a situation not covered by the handbook" (Rose 1997, G2). The shorter film demonstrates the problems inherent in editing a word-heavy film. So few moments exist when words are not being uttered! The shorter film, though, shows more vividly the problems inherent in making a word-heavy film in the first place. The main problem with the shorter film is that a longer version existed in the first place.

The Almereyda *Hamlet*

This is a low-budget film, and it shows. Almost everything potentially interesting in the inherited script suffers a grim reduction in this version. "Elsinore, Inc." is depicted as a company powerful enough to make the lead story in *USA Today*, but its people live very poorly. They have the obligatory stretch limo, but the Queen's bedroom is next to the fax center. They can't afford to repair the mirrored door through which Polonius has been plugged ("First thing, get that damned mirror replaced! Then, yes, look for the body."). Nor does the huge multinational Elsinore have its own fleet of planes. At a time when 60 percent of Fortune 500 companies have an aviation department and when most have planes of their own to avoid the frustrating hassle of commercial flight that mere mortals suffer, an outfit like Elsinore would have a Beechjet 400A to hop over to Albany to buy votes, a King Air B200 to get down to D.C. to buy votes, and a Hawker 800XP to whisk the son and heir out of the country after a brutal boardroom murder. Hamlet goes off to England via American Airlines: first class, true, but it's not British Airways, or even Virgin Upper Class. Hamlet's wanderings during the flight suggest that the rest of the 747 is virtually empty—again, the signature of a poverty project that cannot fill the cheap seats with extras. Perhaps it is the film's jab at American Airlines and at poor Hamlet, suggesting that other people know to avoid it. Ophelia's hideaway is in an insecure garret in a slum area. Hamlet wears a woolen cap, which I am told is very trendy these days, but he looks like he is more ready for a snowball fight than for any conflict beyond that. That Ethan Hawke prefers the Holden Caulfield Hamlet to Olivier's helps explain his version (Fierman 2000, 42). Certainly this Hamlet is "inconceivable as a leader," as David Denby says (2000, 106). Claudius the CEO, however, can afford neither a good tailor nor off-the-rack suits that fit. He dresses like a cop just promoted away from uniformed duty.

A vaguely criminal tinge clings to Elsinore, Inc., but none of the phony glamour of a real-life Gotti or a fictional Godfather. The Mafia approach, had it been attempted here, might have been interesting but, without more money or a more convincing wardrobe, it would have been invested with the same shabbiness that characterizes this seedy group. They would have been soldiers of the lowest fringes of the family. For how to do wealth, the director might have gone to *Executive Suite* or *Sabrina*, two oldies that convince us of the affluence of their inhabitants. The boss in the former has an office resembling a medieval keep, with vaulted ceilings, stained glass, and a gigantic fireplace. The boss in the latter (Humphrey Bogart) has a dictaphone in his limo and threatens playboy William Holden with a retirement pay of a dollar thirty eight cents a month. In the current effort, that threat would be a promise. For an opulent home, look at *Bunker Bean* (1936), where the boss's art-deco mansion makes one almost want to go back. Here, references to royalty seem satiric, and seldom has New York City looked so much like Buffalo. The film is "relentlessly urban," as Ann Thompson says (2000, 127). Elvis Mitchell claims that "the city's contradictions of beauty and squalor give the movie a sense of place," and falls back on the old cliché that "New York becomes a complex character"(2000, B23). If so, it is "naked city," a character Rudy Giuliani would banish from sight. Neither the "glitter and swank" of the city nor its occasional beauty—turning into the Park from the East Side, or the wall of buildings along the West Side of the Park as viewed from the air, or the New York Central building as one drives down Park at Christmas time—is even vaguely visible in this junkyard of a film. Liev Schrieber says that the *Hamlet* "is a real avant-garde film, so visual it's almost actorless" (quoted in Fierman 2000, 42). That is true—and it includes the city. (For how to "do" New York City, see Pacino's *Looking for Richard* or any episode of Wolf's *Law and Order*). Samuel Crowl, who finds the film a revival of Welles in its "jagged, ragged, inventive [and] radically imaginative film style," finds the city "souless and sinister" (2001, 1). I found it merely dull, but that was also because I found so little foreground against the background. Crowl neatly describes the film's mirroring effects (1–2), but I found almost nothing of interest in the objects and actions captured in all that glass.

"The movie," says David Denby, "is very downtown in its resentments and occasional squalor" (2000, 105). Mitchell says that the film "exudes an intoxicating masochism in which half the cast is battling despondency and the other half has the glint of imminent insanity" (2000, B23). But do not both the despondency and the glint of madness inhabit the single character of Hamlet? And is not Mitchell groping to describe something akin to bipolar disorder—what used to be called manic depression? Perhaps he is saying that only masochists could like the film. Denby says that the "movie is awash in replicated images, which produce an enormous sadness," because Hamlet is trapped in his narcissism and is aware of it (2000, 106). The psychological issues that Denby assigns to the film, however, radiate out to encompass the project, suggesting that no artistic distance informs it, or, as Denby says, "'Hamlet' could be taken as a confession of a filmmaker's despair" (106). Perhaps so, but if so, it argues the value of *private* confession. The vast reaches of the script itself remain untouched.

Director Michael Almereyda says that "nearly every scene in the script features a photograph, a TV monitor, and electronic recording device of some kind...creating a kind of overwhelming alternate reality" (2000, AR 22). No. That saturation by media merely makes the film gimmicky. *Hamlet* is a script in which not everything is recorded in black and white, where shadows become at best a Rorschach reality. Modern technology trivializes and literalizes whatever happens in *Hamlet*. A Pepsi dispenser swallows the Ghost. One moment that does link the old play with a post-modern world occurs when, on the flight to Heathrow, Hamlet replaces the diskette in Rosencrantz and Guildenstern's laptop, hits the delete button, and rewrites the King's command. That computer course he did not want to take at City College of New Haven pays off for Hamlet at last! And one does notice that the young Elsinorians drink Carlsberg and not low-budget Rheingold. Proof of the film's trendiness is that that great leaper-onto-trends, Stephen Greenblatt, finds it "gripping, intelligent, and alert to things that are deep in the play" (Fierman 2000, 42)—whatever they may be. "Shakespeare *has* to be about what we want now," Greenblatt continues. "We're not living 400 years ago" (42). That assumes that whatever *Hamlet* as script may be about, it would only make sense to people living almost 400 years ago. It also assumes a current need for instant gratification and a current ability to understand only what is *now*. Whatever became of historicism? It has been abandoned for something called instantism. That is not the same thing as what

Peter Brook means when he says of any production of a Shakespeare play "it has to make sense *now*" (1998, 53; his emphasis).

"Gonzago" is a film made by Hamlet. It seems to be a protest about the AIDS epidemic. Claudius leaves because he has better things to do. He could have said, like a father looking at his child's watercolor, "That's very nice." Instead, without false praise, he merely exits. Gertrude follows, apparently thrust by her awareness that she has spawned a talentless blockhead. "Gonzago," a work of staggering imbecility, is the only thing that could make the film surrounding it look relatively professional. In remarks after a showing in April 2000, Almereyda said that he had been inspired by Harold Goddard's *The Meaning of Shakespeare*. That cannot be true. Goddard's major point in his long essay on *Hamlet* is that Hamlet misses his great opportunity when he breaks up "Gonzago" and gives a guilt-plagued Claudius a chance to escape without proclaiming his malefactions. Here, the moment is reduced to abject insignificance.

Hawke delivers "To be" in the ubiquitous "Action" section of a video store. He cannot, it would seem, "lose the name of 'Action.'" That is heavy-handed, but it does give the camera something to dwell on as those clichés roll sententiously by. I have a hunch that Diane Venora—who, having played Hamlet and Ophelia, graduates to Gertrude—would have shone in a sumptuous context, or even in one as relatively affluent as that provided for Ruth Roman in *Joe Macbeth*. Shreiber's Laertes is believable as a brother who cares for Ophelia and as an angry young man whose unfocused rage is redirected by Kyle McLachlan's suave Claudius. At the end, however, Laertes's "Have at you now!" is accompanied by a pistol. It is the same pistol that killed Polonius and therefore would have been safely locked up at police headquarters. Hamlet and Laertes grapple. Laertes is shot. Hamlet gets hold of the gun and plugs Claudius. All die.

Almereyda misconstrues T. S. Eliot, who "noted years back 'Hamlet' is like the Mona Lisa, something so overexposed that you can hardly stand to look at it" (quoted in Almereyda 2000, AR 19). No. Eliot's 1919 essay alludes to the smile and its inscrutability. Almereyda's film is hard to look at, but all too scrutable. Crowl, who praises the film, agrees with me that "the graveyard scene and duel are poorly conceived and executed," that the musical score "is intrusive [and] at odds with the film's restless postmodernity" and

Julia Stiles in Michael Almereyda's *Hamlet. Photo by Larry Riley. Courtesy of Miramax Films.*

that "Hamlet's flight to England on American Airlines should have been cancelled" (2001, 6).

Elvis Mitchell claims that the "director's rigorous trimming has a boldness and vitality that make this version exhilarating while leaving Shakespeare's language and intent intact" (2000, B23). I suppose that trimming can be bold and vital—it sounds like an ad for a new diet—but I do not grasp how cutting language somehow also leaves it intact.

What works? The pouty Ophelia of Julia Stiles (fresh from *10 Things I Hate*) is permitted to be what the play says she is—a subversive force undermining the smooth operation of Claudius & Co. At one point—and it is a nice one—Bill Murray's Polonius stoops to tie the lace of her sneaker. This moment also, unintentionally, signals a shoestring operation. In a strong scene at the Guggenheim, her scream pierces down the ramps and twists its echoes back up from the atrium. She has to be hustled into an anteroom. This is one of the most potent Ophelias since Pernella Walgren's for Ragnar Lyth in 1984. Walgren's Ophelia breaks into a reception for visiting diplomats and causes great embarrassment for king and queen. Marianne Faithfull's superb Ophelia in the 1969 Richardson film was quietly but profoundly discomfiting, a mad jester taking Yorick's place in Denmark and destined for Yorick's grave. American films, it can be said, have learned to do the adolescent superbly, and Stiles is a case in point.

The film was shown at the Shakespeare Association in Montreal in early April 2000. Some asked whether it would do for *Hamlet* what Luhrmann did for *Romeo and Juliet*—that is, attract a new wave of young people to the cinema and to the play. I doubt it.

These productions are, for the most part, failures. That does not mean, however, that the script will not discover a filmmaker who will employ it to explore a present that the script will clarify for us sometime in the near future. Ironically, the *Odyssey* version of the play, televised in 2000, has an opulent setting worthy of a kingdom and an operative late-nineteenth-or early-twentieth-century context. While weak in many ways, the *Odyssey* production demonstrates the need for script and environment to interchange their energies in a way that permits the screen to articulate an authenticity that cannot be achieved by a shallow musical comedy atmosphere or a vast metropolis shrunk to the little measure of a tourist's camera.

Chapter 9

Kenneth Branagh's *Love's Labour's Lost*

The summer of 1939 was one of the most glorious that Europeans could remember—crystalline days, rainfall after midnight, clouds dissolved by dawn, no oppressive patches of muggy heat and no long stretches of industrial smoke nestling in the valleys and erasing the sight of the mountains. This Camelot summer of 1939 reminded older people of the summer of 1914. Nor was the ominous parallel lost on anyone in Europe. The mobilizations of August 1914 had dropped those languid months into the trenches that lasted for years to come, elicited the black rows of names of those killed in action in the *Times,* and evoked the comment by one of Hemingway's characters that "maybe wars don't end anymore." The summer of 1939 would end with Hitler's panzers responding to an "attack" from Poland and sweeping toward Warsaw.

In the decades between the wars, of course, the Western world had experienced its ups and downs—the Roaring Twenties and the Great Depression. The latter (and I use the images I remember from the U.S. side of the Atlantic) included men in impeccable business suits and fedoras selling apples on the streets of New York; veterans of the Great War being rousted out of their shanty town within sight of the U.S. Capitol by MacArthur and his adjutant, Eisenhower; and the stark photographs of Dorothea Lange and Walker Evans. According to Henry Allen, one saw "fewer cars in town, just the stoplights rocking in the wind. You don't hear as many whistles, factory or railroad. You don't hear babies crying. People are afraid to have them" (1999, 10). It was the time of the Joads and *The Grapes of Wrath.* But against this grim physical and emotional landscape, Packard limos with those built-in spare wheel wells on their sides purred into the circular driveways of oceanfront hotels, and tennis balls continued to be thunked across red clay and grass by men and women in crisp all-white outfits who called "love" back and forth to each other. Someone could afford that 1935 Duesenberg convertible that Branagh's film shows us.

Richard Loncraine also puts his *Richard III* into the late 1930s, imagining for us a fascist takeover in Great Britain. Given Edward VIII as a traitor king, the Hitler-adoring British fascists Oswald Mosley and his wife, Diana, and the sentiments traced in as a kind of misunderstood subtext for the butler in *Remains of the Day*, the concept of an alternative history is plausible. Indeed, Britain under Hitler was not only possible—Operation Sea Lion was the greatest military campaign never undertaken—but on the Channel Islands it was realized in microcosm. The problem for the *Richard III* is that the modernization betrays the script. Richard is not the hypnotic leader of a mass movement based on concepts of racial purity or impurity—"to be as blonde as Hitler, as thin as Goering, as tall as Goebbels, as keen-eyed as Himmler," as they used to say—but a shrewd, behind-the-scenes loner whose public persona affects to shy away from any thought of power. *Richard III* emerges from the medieval—Augustinian—premise that a man can gain the whole world and lose his soul, and know it. Loncraine's vividly imaged 1937 cannot take us to where the play goes—to Richard's sweaty soliloquy on the morning of the battle of Bosworth Field, to a man trapped between wakefulness and the unconscious, torn within a debate between body and soul, between temporal success and eternal damnation. As Ron Rosenbaum has brilliantly demonstrated, Hitler has yet to be fitted to the dimensions of morality play (1998).

The coming of World War II also ended the first and probably greatest era of the movie musical. The musical was a situation comedy—often barely that—in which minor complications gave rise to song. In Cole Porter's *Anything Goes*, for example, an overnight incarceration gives rise to the plaintive "All Through the Night," a song a situation was hastily invented to contextualize. Between MGM's *Hollywood Review of 1929*, which included a brief Technicolor moment for Norma Shearer and John Gilbert's balcony scene, and 1939's *The Wizard of Oz*, the musical movie flourished, as a space of movement captured by inventive camera angles and newly perfected sound, which drew millions of people to the theaters that every small town boasted. World War II changed that. The films became grim allegories of struggle against vicious enemies. The songs told of bluebirds over "The White Cliffs of Dover" and "The Last Time I Saw Paris." The United States raised concerns about fidelity: "No

Love, No Nothing," "They're Either Too Young or Too Old" ("When you are off in India, / I'll still be what I've been to ya"), and "Don't Sit Under the Apple Tree" were hits, and for those who remember when it first came out, "White Christmas" will be forever associated with the separations imposed by World War II. Branagh leaps into that zone where, as Russell Jackson says, "love makes us do...daft things. ...People suddenly bursting into sonnets—well, we burst into song" (quoted in Thompson, *EMLS*, May 2000). It is the "magic world," as Robert Solomon suggests of the "love-world" (1981), that is ludicrous unless we accept its conventions, which include sudden launchings into lyricism. The difference between Branagh's interwar moment and Loncraine's is that the former's does not depend on historical parallels bound to break down under the most superficial analysis. The 1930s were a decade of economic depression but also a time of compensatory fantasy, of Hollywood films flying us down to Rio, or simply opening the doors to art-deco luxury in which William Powell and Myrna Loy traded witty comments or in which Fred and Ginger cavorted to captivating songs. It is not too much to say that the songwriters of the 1930s created more music that is still heard by the discerning listener to small jazz groups or to the stations that play old 78-rpm records than any decade ever. From the Gershwins: "Embraceable You," "But Not For Me," "I Got Rhythm," "Who Cares?" "Summertime" (with DuBose Heyward), "Love Walked In," "They Can't Take That Away from Me," and "Love Is Here to Stay." From Ira Gershwin and Vernon Duke: "I Can't Get Started." From Vernon Duke: "Autumn in New York." From Duke and E. Y. Harburg: "April in Paris." From Cole Porter: "Night and Day," "Anything Goes," "Begin the Beguine," "I Get a Kick Out of You," "Just One of Those Things," "Easy to Love," "I've Got You Under my Skin," "In the Still of the Night," and "I Concentrate on You." From Richard Rodgers and Lorenz Hart: "Blue Moon," "Where or When," "My Funny Valentine," "The Lady is a Tramp," and "My Heart Stood Still." From Herman Hupfield: "As Time Goes By." From Irving Berlin: "Cheek to Cheek," "Easter Parade," and "Let's Face the Music." From Duke Ellington: "Mood Indigo" (with Albany Bigard and Irving Mills) and "Sophisticated Lady" (with Irving Mills and Mitchell Parrish). From Harold Arlen and Ted Koehler: "Stormy Weather." From Dorothy Fields and Jimmy McHugh: "Don't Blame Me," and "I'm in the Mood for Love." From Dorothy Fields and Jerome Kern: "The Way You Look Tonight." From Hoagy

Carmichael and Frank Loesser: "Heart and Soul," and "Two Sleepy People." From Count Basie: "One O'Clock Jump." From Maxwell Anderson and Kurt Weill: "September Song." From Harold Arlen and E. Y. Harburg: "Paper Moon" (with Billy Rose), and "Over the Rainbow." From J. Fred Coots and Haven Gillespie: "Santa Claus is Comin' to Town" and "You Go to My Head." From Brooks Bowman: "East of the Sun." It is to this moment that Branagh's comedy takes us. It is a zone that repels any history but its own, but it invites the kind of game-playing that goes on in Shakespeare's play and that was going on in the 1930s, in spite of empty smokestacks and dust-filled midlands. As in Shakespeare's play, some of the "happy endings" were deferred in 1939 because of another Great War. Some of the endings were not happy.

Branagh is even more specific. His film begins on 1 September 1939. The newsreel speaks of imminent war and shows what looks like a Dornier flying through a murky black-and-white sky—a diving Stuka would have been closer to the mark—but, in historical fact, Hitler is invading Poland at the moment that the King of Navarre announces his academy. The film, then, occurs within some fold in the space-time continuum, in a never-never land in a never-never time, along a misty River Cam where people pole in punts lighted by the glow of paper lanterns. The play is freer from history than any play Shakespeare wrote—unless we insist, with scholars of a previous generation, on finding therein Raleigh, Chapman, Florio, Nashe, and a host of Elizabethan personages of the mid-1590s, or claim that the play emerges from Henri of Navarre's meeting with Marguerite de Valois at Nerac in 1578. The film opens with an innocuous overture, like that those that played under the credits of many musicals, and the 1930s cliché of the film's title handwritten across a field of undulating silk. The script lifts silkenly out of time and, as Branagh says, is "a play not many people are familiar with" (guildpath press kit, 5/25/2000). Most people won't know that Berowne is well read to reason against reading, that the Gentlemen deliver Petrarchan poetry in their "infant play" and not the Gershwins' 1930 song, "I've Got a Crush on You" (hardly their strongest), that the Gentlemen visit the Ladies disguised as Muscovites, that Rosaline has a wonderful put-down of Berowne ("Sans *sans*, I pray you"), that the comic characters depict the Nine Worthies of Antiquity and are mercilessly mocked by the Gentlemen (who see their own reflection in the ludicrous play-within-a-play), or that the play ends with a song about spring and winter, hot blood and wisdom. None of this is in the film. The final song is one of the last of the great Gershwin-Gershwin collaborations (itself a poignant fact), "They Can't Take That Away From Me," and Armado's final line, capable of a variety of interpretations on the stage, is skywritten at the Princess's request by an unusually aerobatic DC-3: "You that way; we this way." The final moments, of course, intend to remind us of the ending of *Casablanca,* and the allusion resonates powerfully. Another allusion, subtly tucked within the film's visual texture, is suggested by the switch from the black-and-white "Kansas" of newsreel and headline to the vivid colors of this "Land of Oz." *The Wizard of Oz,* of course, was being seen by millions even as those panzers pounced on Poland during that Technicolor late summer of 1939. The King's retreat with his friends into monasticism is "news," of course, but it is of the lighter variety with which Movietone interspersed its grim and grainy images of blitzkrieg and buildings crumbling like castles of sand as the dogs of Europe barked along the length of that September. The newsreels preceded the feature films, but Branagh's film suggests that the newsreel will supersede the musical comedy, as it does at the end of the film. Other references to films range from overhead shots of dances, meant to recall Busby Berkeley, to underwater shots, intended to evoke the bubblepics of Esther Williams. With the exception of the "Onetime" newsreels, this is shot in color—which musicals of the 1930s did not use (except for the fashion-show inset in *Vogues of 1938* and *The Wizard of Oz*)—and in the dimensions Branagh obviously savors, the widescreen format of the 1950s, when film was trying to get bigger and bigger to combat television.

This is a musical, and a musical of the 1930s at that. The genre called for a plot based on mistaken identity or some other minor complication as a means of getting the songs in. Sometimes the plot involved putting on a musical show, so that, for example, Mickey and Judy could sing without the necessity of a cue in the dialogue. For Paramount, the musical incorporated foreign adventure (the *Road* series), Bob Hope's one-liners, and Bing singing a song to Dorothy ("Moonlight Becomes You," for example). The emphasis was on the music and, in the case of MGM, the dance sequences. In RKO's *Showtime,* Ginger Rogers's favorite among the ten films she made with Fred Astaire, Fred is a dancer come to New York and she, conveniently, is an instructor at a dance academy. When Fred gets Ginger fired, he insists that she and he demonstrate to the boss how much she has taught him. The boss is impressed. The "plot" centers on Fred's need *not* to earn the $25,000 required to return to Ohio and marry his high school sweetheart. He's fallen for Ginger, you see. That is sillier than anything in Shakespeare's comedies, because it *is* plot, and not an immaturity in character that must be resolved for the comic ending. These films were entertainment. They still are. They are silly until they swing into a Hermes Pan or Busby Berkeley dance routine, with music by Porter, Berlin, Kern, or the Gershwins. With an unknown play like *Love's Labour's Lost* blended into the easygoing genre of the musical film, additions and deletions don't matter here, or, rather, deletions don't matter very much. I wished that Richard Briers's Nathaniel, suffused with the wistful eyes and voice that make Briers such a wonderful actor on stage, had been given more space here, though his autumnal romance with Geraldine McEwan's Lady Don is movingly delineated. The line about daughters having learned under Holofernes, however, is hardly as potent when it becomes "sons." I also wished that Natascha McElhone's luminous and deft-tongued Rosaline had been privileged over Alicia Silverstone's pudgy Princess, even if the latter does have some 100 more lines in the 1598 quarto, and, admittedly, the crucial rejection of Navarre and directions for departure at the end. After all, she's Queen, a status the film gracefully acknowledges. Suffice it that Silverstone's efforts to "naturalize" the poetry only make it (and its speaker) awkward. It isn't that her "sexy tongue isn't made for iambic pentamenter" (quoted in "Review," *Rolling Stone*, 8 June 2000, 36), it is that she has not learned to speak it. By way of contrast, McElhone's performance shines. She glances sharply at the Princess, when the latter boasts that "Berowne hath plighted faith to me," a look that suggests that some fault lines exist in this sorority. McElhone dominates her final moments with Berowne, as the script suggests she does and as Branagh's generous direction permits her to in the film. This is one of those "intimate moments" that "often sparkle" (*Rolling Stone*, 8 June 2000, 36). Another vivid woman is the tall and angular Stefania Rocca in the small but visually and emotionally significant role of Jaquenetta. I think she gets all of her seventeen lines. Berowne does get the great apotheosis to love, set among those dust-gathering books of the King's library, as a centerpiece to the film, and we are grateful for it. Branagh obviously has a great time riding that rhetoric on by, and the speech balances the music, giving us a sense of how much this play treats of language and the limits of language. In a play "about" words, the plot is indeed not as basic an element as Aristotle would make it. The camera follows Berowne as he circles the library, simulating the "motion sickness" of infatuation (what the boys call "love"), and contrasting with the static lectern the king had set up in the same room earlier. While not much of the language of this rhetorical script escapes into the film, Debra Tuckett is correct, I think, when she says that Branagh succeeds "by adhering to the spirit rather than the letter of the play" (2000). In a testy review, Richard Corliss says of Branagh that "we must look elsewhere for an actor of classical grace and modern power" (2000, 82)—whatever "modern power" may be—but even Corliss, who must have been smiling in the darkness of the theater, admits that "some of the dance numbers work up to a pleasing tension" (2000, 82). The *Rolling Stone* reviewer says that the film "comes right up to the edge of disaster but stubbornly refuses to leap in. Charm keeps peeping through this thin excuse for a plot" (8 June 2000, 36). A. O. Scott compares the film to the kind of makeshift production that Branagh has already satirized in the charming *A Midwinter's Tale*: the film displays "the gusto of a man playing a tuba with a bass drum strapped to his back while his pet monkey leaps around with a squeeze box. It's not art exactly, or even music, but it's entertaining…even after the song is ended the melody lingers on" (*New York Times*, 9 June 2000, B12). The "amateur hour" is meant to capture the spontaniety of eight lovers suddenly letting themselves go within a parenthesis in reality between the King's abandoned decree and the sober news of death and warfare heading for Navarre. The enjoyment flows partly because that's *not* Fred Astaire and Eleanor Powell up there.

The music that Branagh imports into the film is cued—as in 1930s musicals—by the merest hint. "I'd Rather Charleston" is a response to the King's prohibitive charter. The song, I would guess, is from the 1920s—"Charleston" was one the big hits of 1923. By the 1930s, the foxtrot was the step of choice. The coy 1935 "I Won't Dance" emerges from the King's refusal to let the Ladies enter his court, in spite of the rekindled and reciprocated attraction of each Jack for his Jill. Berowne's "heaven" insists that he contemplate the word and find himself "in heaven," dancing cheek to cheek with a photograph of Rosaline. The four men fly to the ceiling in their ecstasy. It's a funny moment—four Peter Pans, leaping free of their academy, now wishing to stay in their newer never-never land of infatuation. Most of the musical sequences are brief, so that they don't slow the narrative, which is slight in Shakespeare's original script, but not as thin as in a 1930s musical, say *Anything Goes*, where the plot is a scarcely visible string on which the songs are threaded. Armado's "I Get a Kick Out of You" is meant, I assume, to verge on the ludicrous—it is a parody of a song that parodies love songs—but the music itself carries it through. The lovely "The Way You Look Tonight" gets a quavery treatment from McEwan, but the autumn mists of its setting and the version of Bergmanian danse macabre that it motivates give the song a poignancy it has not enjoyed since Astaire sang it to Rogers. Perhaps the film's best musical interlude is a dream sequence, more "Slaughter on Tenth Avenue" than "Out of My Dreams," in which the lascivious instincts of both Gentlemen and Ladies are imaged in a scantily clad, finger-slithering, tongue-licking release of libido. Since it is a dream, it represents a containment of desire, the prelude to sexuality that is the theme of comedy and its situational shadow, musical comedy. The song is one of Berlin's best ballads and also one of Astaire's finest numbers—"Let's Face the Music and Dance" from 1936. The dancing isn't bad—indeed Adrian Lester's Dumaine takes a couple of brilliant turns, à la Donald O'Connor—and the singing does what singing in the 1930s did. It gets the lyrics across. Astaire, as he knew, did not have a great singing voice, but he introduced "Night and Day." Bob Hope, who also was no singer, introduced "Delovely," "Penthouse Serenade," and "Two Sleepy People." The Worthies are replaced by a "production number" of the 1946 "There's No Business Like Show Business," in which Nathan Lane gets to imitate Jackie Gleason. This isn't a bad number, though it adds nothing to the film—except possibly to build up another fiction within a fiction, which Mercade's message of death (he, too, floats darkly in, like that Dornier of the opening newsreel) and the intrusion of World War II on this seemingly timeless latter summer idyll must shatter.

Had I been any god of power, I would have argued for "Where or When"—with Lorenz Hart's lyrical evocation of déjà vu—for a moment after the Gentlemen and the Ladies meet (they've "met before"), and for "I Concentrate on You"—with its proof that "wise men can be wrong"—as an homage to new insights toward the end. But then, I am not complaining.

What the film does superbly is to dramatize what John Kerrigan calls the play's design of "organized disagreement" (1982, 17). The ending, though, gives me some pause. I thought, as I watched, that Branagh might render a third version of *Love's Labour's Lost*. The conventional sense—at least among my students—is that the four couples will get together at the end of that year. A minority—and if they are adolescents a year can still be a long time—know that way leads on to way. They suggest that the four lovers are saying goodbye for good. The song for the falling off of infatuation would be "It Was Just One of Those Things." What I thought the film could show is that sometimes human intention is irrelevant, that greater powers than we can contradict can dictate what happens to mere mortals, even to kings, queens, and noble people. In other words, "We may never never meet again on the bumpy road to love"—the never-never land of Lear's repeated trochee. What we get instead is a montage, in which Berowne, working, it seems, in a field hospital, must comfort himself with a photo of Rosaline, where the King hands out Red Cross packages, where the Queen is interned by French fascists, where Rosaline cannot stay with a dying Boyet because the enemy is closing in (someone has to die, and poor Boyet is odd man out), where air-raid wardens work among the shattered stones of London, and where some, behind barbed wire, are beyond succor. A sequence of headlines and actual combat film, like the view from a landing craft of Sword Beach on D-Day, brings us to troopships returning, women struggling through crowds to their men, Armado holding up his and Jaquenetta's son (who has Armado's Dali mustache), and the happy ending of 1945—too long for a play, no doubt. Certainly this ending is questionable, particularly because it mixes two film genres, as Ralph Berry argues: "The events of the war, alluded to in newsreel black and white, are altogether overwhelming for the admittedly sombre conclusion of the play...I like 1930s musicals, but 1940s war movies are something else" (2000, 31). It is a different world that has to be traversed before *Loves's Labour's Won* can begin. As the credits roll, the film reprises rhythm and dance, the songs of Apollo after the dark music of Mars. The film (particularly through Rosaline and Berowne) establishes the love—and desire—of the four couples for each potential partner. Rosaline, after all, is willing to accept Berowne even if he cannot discard "sans." The closing sequence suggests that he learns that mere wit is "loose grace" and that he will be wiser hereafter.

The film also serves to create "audiences...ready to view [Shakespeare] films as entertainment and not as intelligence tests," as Branagh says. (guildpath presskit, 5/25/00, 1). The film nestles gently into its chosen moment—a moment outside of history—as neatly as an engagement diamond given in 1939 snugged into its Tiffany setting . The "Dearly beloved, we are gathered here..." had to wait through years of shadows. In spite of my own adumbration of another closure, the film earns its happy ending.

Conclusion

The Shakespeare script teems with options. How a line is read at any given moment argues who the actor believes his character to be at that moment in relation to his understanding of himself, to the other characters in the play, and to the situation driving him and the other characters. These possibilities can be variously interpreted, and can alter radically, given other variables. When Simon Russell Beale was replaced as Richard III by Ciaran Hinds in the Warehouse production of 1993, the laugh lines, which had been a function of Beale's calculatedly bumbling Richard, did not accrue to Hinds's menacing, fascistic version. Suddenly, Buckingham was the comedian. Film can reinterpret single moments—the growth of Viola's awareness of her complicated status, the development of Othello's conviction that Desdemona has been unfaithful—by breaking them into the separate units and placing them throughout the film, as opposed to in one soliloquy or scene. Film, then, increases the number of options available, by adding its own techniques to the script, particularly the plasticity of time that film can employ in ways not available on stage. Those techniques are not completely visual, however. The filmmaker needs a "literary" sense of the script, as I have argued, and as Parker proves by overly and unwisely editing his *Othello*, and as Branagh proves by not editing *enough* in his full-length *Hamlet*. The play has a shape, a dynamic, a rising action, a climax, and a denouement (although critics will disagree about the specifics in any given script) that a filmmaker flattens out at his peril. He must edit the language, but carefully; not just toward cutting down on all those words but toward retaining those that reinforce both the visual and intellectual elements of his or her production, not just the sight of Othello plunging from his own secure premises, but the *why* as well. If that element gets into the film, it augments its power with profundity, with a sense of the archetype, the configuration that underlies the specific activity the script depicts, that insists that we are more than just observers of that activity. At times, of course, the language is unnecessary. The young lovers of Luhrmann's film need not speak (one wishes they would not!). The world around them—the self-infatuated parents, the adolescent rivalries, the crushing metropolis and its empty icons—tells us what must happen to their effort at exception. All of that is done visually, and the archetypal story emerges from any need for linguistic formulation. We sense the tragedy from the stance of doomed lovers, failed parents, or both.

We can also sense the comedy in the Romeo and Juliet story—its pressure toward completion in marriage, not stasis in death. Film has conditioned us to that expectation. One day, out of sheer ennui, I was watching a 1936 film called *Bunker Bean,* with Owen Davis, Jr. and Louise Latimer ("how soon they forget!"). This one is about a boy who falls in love with the boss's daughter, over the objections, of course, of her parents. The mother learns that Bunker is not a social-register Bean, but one of the numerous "Boston Beans" and is her husband's secretary to boot. She turns up her well-turned nose. They are the Capulets. The young lovers succeed, after the usual complications, and Owen, Jr. and Louise ride together into the sunset in a '36 Lincoln Zephyr. In the film, the fortuneteller asks, "After all, what's in a name?" I am not saying that the film is in any way consciously modeled on *Romeo and Juliet.* I am suggesting that my enjoyment of the film was based at least partly on the archetype at work under the conventional story.

The linkages with a stage history that I cited at the outset are useful for the *actors.* Familiarization with the lines (so that the lines retained for the film can be reworked to emerge like normal speech) and with the character (so that the actor's conception of the character can function with other actors in a very different atmosphere from that of stage) will help. But stage—where audience and actors share the same space and where we have agreed to suspend our disbelief—and film—where light shines through a carefully arranged sequence of rapidly moving images onto a screen—are so radically different that the contrasts are greater than any comparisons, even if the same script is the basis for production, even if a stage production gives rise to a film. It makes no sense to say, for example, that "McKellen's performance [as Richard III] is far more successful on film than in was on stage, in part because the proximity of the camera breaks through the surface armor of his icy characterization " (Loehlin 1997, 75). One might prefer the film over the stage production (I greatly preferred the latter), but performances within the separate media serve distinctly different audience expectations in a production designed for its medium. Had there been the kind of "breaking through" in the stage production that Loehlin describes (as when, in the film, Richard turns to us and says, "I am not made of stone!"), the continuum that was being built between stage and audience would have been shattered. A small moment did occur in the stage production, a moment of insight, not of the breaking down of barriers between characterization and audience, when, in Richard's dream, Richmond cut in on Richard, who was dancing with Anne. A brief flash of jealousy hit Richard. Suddenly he valued something that he had discarded. Dreams will do that kind of revaluating for us. The film seldom came close to anything like this brilliant instant, so intent was the film on its fidelity to 1937.

Where film should imitate stage is in the *rhythm* of production. A good stage production recognizes such a thing as rising action, climax, and denouement. Film sometimes does not. *Henry V* incorporates two episodes in Agincourt that undercut its glorious reputation. Pistol bargains for LeFer as Davy Gam, Esquire dies nearby. Then LeFer is caught in Henry's general order to kill all the prisoners. The battle, meanwhile, is the subject of reports and casualty lists. Olivier shows the French charge in a magnificent, mile-long tracking shot, the longbow arrows taking off like so many Hurricanes, the sudden confusion in the French armor, the English yeomen dropping out of the trees on the French like Robin and his Merry Men, Henry and the Constable squaring off *mano a mano*, riderless horses plunging across a field of corpses, and a book of hours tableau that fixes the moment in an iconic posterity. Shakespeare's stage cannot show all that, but the Technicolor camera can, and few have blamed Olivier for giving us what the stage asks us to imagine. Olivier might have been wise to end his film sooner than he does; 1944 may have needed the allegory with which he reinforces Burgundy's speech about war, but does the film? Still, the return to the Globe at the end, the reenclosing of this convincing moment in "history" within its fictive frame is brilliant. Olivier reminds us that it has been a play even after he has convinced us otherwise. Seldom has the relationship *and* contrast between stage and film been as exquisitely poised.

Branagh—with his soundstage format—goes too far in making the script a film. A great moment—the English looking at the French charge as if it is a tidal wave about to break—nicely qualifies the King's quiet talk about brotherhood. The camera has closed in, concentrating on Branagh's King, as his troopers are doing, as opposed to booming out to incorporate the army, as Olivier's voice rings out to the sentinels at the farther edges of the encampment. Then, however, Branagh gives us that long mudbath, borrowed from Welles's black-and-white Shrewsbury in *Chimes at Midnight*. That is punctuated by Welles's Falstaff in his rotund armor leaping from bush to bush to avoid battle. A comic leitmotif plays through Welles's ten-minute orgy. After Agincourt, Branagh's interminable *Te Deum* creates such a strong sense of closure that his film can scarcely get going again. On stage, it would have been a greater disaster, perhaps, because it would have substituted one kind of show for another. The filmmaker must acknowledge the rhythms the script suggests. That does not mean he gives us a filmed play. It does mean that he gives us the shape of the drama, that he imitates on film the action imitated in the play. At moments, as in the Parker *Othello*, that means including language when the words alone convey essential meanings, as in Othello's speech on landing at Cyprus, which makes himself the pagan hero of his own grand narrative when he should be kneeling to thank the God in whose name he has recently been baptized.

Peter Hall is right to say of film that "what is said in front of the camera needs to convey to the cinema audience the sense that it has not been written, that the language...is being invented by the character in the situation spontaneously at that moment. We must not be aware of the writer" (Crowdis, 1998, 50). In some way, however, as we are aware of suspense physically, without our *saying* as much, we, the spectators, should be aware of the director cooperating with the dramatist, the editor working with the inherited script, translating word to image, to shape a completed action and to involve us in its dynamics. Yes, he can do what the camera does and the stage cannot do. He must, but he or she also must do what the play does, that is, to move us through an emotional and imaginative experience, based on the ancient Aristotelian formulae, that makes the material our own at the end of that experience. We should share a sense of archetype with our fellow auditors, of an experience deeper than the rendering of performance, which is existential, existing in time and place and with an audience that will be very different the next night, even if, inevitably, our articulation of the experience is different from that of the people sitting next to us at the same production. Our language is different, our experience has been different before and during the performance, but we will have shared something—some fragment of what it is we share as human beings. If that sounds like an essentialist argument, I simply point at how much we are sharing through these wonderful films that keep coming our way.

The *televised* stage play can be very effective in bringing a sense of the event—audience and actors together in a theater—to an electronically connected audience. Caldwell's *Macbeth*, the Papp and the Epstein *A Midsummer Night's Dreams*, and the Papp *King Lear* are examples. Furthermore, the small stage production remounted for television can be brilliant—Nunn's *Macbeth* and *Othello*, the Warner-Shaw *Richard II*, and the Eyre *King Lear*, for example. The size of the stage is similar to the size of the studio, so that production values tend to be simple, probably metaphoric, and scaled to the smaller screen. Furthermore, acting style tends to be pulled back so that it works within the intimate confines of a small theater and, it follows, within the close-up, two-shot, reaction-shot grammar of the television cameras. It is simply a matter of space coinciding with space. Failures can occur in the remounting process, particularly if it involves translating a large auditorium production to television—as in the case of the Kevin Kline *Hamlet*, where, for whatever reasons, the camera inhibited the wonderful sense of humor that Kline's Hamlet had exhibited on stage. But successes also come, as in Trevor Nunn's superb remounting of *Antony and Cleopatra*, where metaphor—pillows and gauzy curtains for Egypt, columns and marching feet for Rome—characterized the zones in which we found their aboriginal characters, Cleopatra and Octavius. Peter Hall says, "I would love to make a film of *The Merchant of Venice* in Venice, with Dustin Hoffman" (1998, 55). He had the chance to make a superb television production out of the understated version he directed with Hoffman at the old Mermaid Theatre in London's West End seven years ago. This would have been excellent as a televised stage play or as a television production transferred to a studio. The production had a unity of design and coherence of costume and property that would have given us a version of the play that I think would be considered easily the best we have on screen.

I understand, here in the winter of of 2001, that Kenneth Branagh is considering *As You Like It* as his next film (perhaps with Helena Bonham-Carter as Phoebe!). I have written to Branagh that he consider doing the script as a history of film, with early segments in silent sepia with title cards ("The Wrestler, Charles, who krushes all komers"). The film would move into more sophisticated silent screen techniques—as at its brief apogee in the mid-1920s—achieve sound at the Forest (where all those one-on-one confrontations and debates occur with and about language), at some point burst into color, perhaps at the Duke's feast, where Jacques's disquisition could be rendered in cartoon bubbles (the lover being Mickey Mouse, the soldier, Donald Duck), and then, maybe for the wedding sequence expand to a widescreen format. Having created the big bang of recent films, Branagh deserves to be its Stephen Hawking.

Bibliography

Allen, Henry. 1999. "Brother, Can You Spare a Dime?" *Washington Post National Weekly Edition*, 25 October, 10–11.

Almereyda, Michael. 2000. "A Live Wire to the Brain: Hooking Up 'Hamlet.'" *New York Times*, 7 May, AR19, AR22.

Andreae, Christopher. 1993. "'Animated Tales' of Shakespeare." *Christian Science Monitor*, 6 January, 14.

Anon. 1992. "Animation: A Visual Symphony." *The Guardian*, 23 November, E14.

Anon. 1998. "Midnight at the Oasis." *Shakespeare Magazine* 2, no. 3, Fall, 1-6.

Anon. 2000. "Review." *New York Times*, 11 February, B16.

Anon. 2000. "Review." *Rolling Stone*, 8 June, 36.

Bacon, Francis. 1955. *Selected Writings*, ed. Hugh D. Dick. New York: Macmillan.

Ball, Robert H. 1968. *Shakespeare on Silent Film*. London: George Allen & Unwin.

Barton, Anne. 1980. "Introduction." In *The Tragedy of Hamlet, Prince of Denmark*, ed. T. J. B. Spencer. London: Penguin.

Bate, Jonathan. 1995. "Caliban and Ariel Write Back." *Shakespeare Survey* 48: 155–162.

——— . 2000. "Shakespeare in Less Than 10 Minutes." *New York Times*, 13 February, Arts 26.

Berkowitz, Gerard. 1983. "Shakespeare in Edinburgh." *Shakespeare Quarterly* 34.

——— . 1996. "*Richard II*." *Shakespeare Bulletin* 14, no. 2, Winter, 9.

Berry, Ralph. 2000. "Shakespeare at the Inns of Court." *New Straits Times*, 29 March.

Birkerts, Sven. 1994. *The Gutenberg Elegies: The Fate of Reading in an Electronic Age*. London: Faber and Faber.

Bloom, Harold. 1998. *Shakespeare: The Invention of the Human*. New York: Riverhead.

Blos, Peter. 1952. *On Adolescence*. New York: Free Press.

Bobbin, Jay. 1998. "Shakespeare's *Tempest* Brews Anew on NBC." *TV Week*, 13–19 December, 2.

Boose, Lynda E. and Richard Burt. 1997. *Shakespeare the Movie: Popularizing the Plays on Film, TV, and Video*. London: Routledge.

Bowers, Fredson. 1940. *Elizabethan Revenge Tragedy: 1587–1641*. Princeton: Princeton University Press.

Branagh, Kenneth. 2000. "On the Play." Guildpath Press Kit (25 May).

Brokaw, Tom. 1999. *The Greatest Generation*. New York: Random House.

Brook, Peter. 1998. "Shakespeare in the Cinema." *Cineaste* XXXIV, no. 1.

Buchman, Lorne. 1991. *Still in Movement: Shakespeare on Screen*. New York: Oxford University Press.

Bulman, James C., ed. 1996. *Shakespeare, Theory, and Performance*. New York: Routledge.

Buss, David M. 2000. *The Dangerous Passion*. New York: Free Press.

Buss, Robin. 1992. "A Palpable Hit." *Sunday Independent: Review*, 8 November , 33.

Canby, Vincent. 1998. "Help Wanted." *New York Times*, 26 July, 2.

Collick, John 1989. *Shakespeare, Cinema and Society*. Manchester: Manchester University Press.

Corliss, Richard. 2000. "Branagh Faces the Music." *Time*, 12 June, 82.

Coursen, H. R. 1984. "Why *Measure for Measure?*" *Film/Literature Quarterly* 12, no. 1: 65–69.

———. 1992. *Shakespearean Performance as Interpretation*. Newark: University of Delaware Press.

———. 1993. *Watching Shakespeare on Television*. Madison: Fairleigh Dickinson University Press.

———. 1996. *Shakespeare: Whose History?* Athens: Ohio University Press.

———. 1999. *Shakespeare: The Two Traditions*. Madison: Fairleigh-Dickinson University Press.

Crowdis, Gary. 1998. "Shakespeare in the Cinema: A Film Director's Symposium." *Cineaste* 24, no. 1.

Crowl, Samuel. 1992. *Shakespeare Observed: Studies in Performance on Stage and Screen*. Athens: Ohio University Press

———. 1994. "A World Elsewhere: The Roman Plays on Film and Television." In *Shakespeare and the Moving Image*, ed. Anthony Davies and Stanley Wells. Cambridge: Cambridge University Press.

———. 1996. "*Othello*." *Shakespeare Bulletin* 14, no. 1, Winter, 41-42.

———. 2000 ***

———. "*Titus*." *Shakespeare Bulletin* (forthcoming 2001).

———. "*Hamlet*." *Shakespeare Bulletin*. (forthcoming 2001)

D. D. 1999. "Review." *The New Yorker*, 21 May.

Davies, Anthony. 1988. *Filming Shakespeare's Plays*. Cambridge: Cambridge University Press.

——— and Stanley Wells, editors. 1994. *Shakespeare and the Moving Image: The Plays on Film and Television*. Cambridge: Cambridge University Press.

Denby, David. 2000. "Flesh and Blood." *The New Yorker*, 15 May, 105–106.

Dessen, Alan. 1986. "The Supernatural on Television." *Shakespeare on Film Newsletter* 11: 1, 8.

Dobree, Bonamy. 1961. "The Last Plays." In *The Living Shakespeare*, ed. Robert Gittings, 147–160. New York: Fawcett.

Drake, J. 1950 [1699]. "Antient and Modern Stages Surveyed." In *Readings in the Character of Hamlet*, ed. Claude C. H. Williamson. London: Allen & Unwin.

Eliot, T. S. 1932. "Hamlet and His Problems." In *Selected Essays: 1917–1932*. New York: Harcourt, Brace.

Fierman, Daniel. 2000. "A New Version of *Hamlet*." *Entertainment Weekly*, 2 June, 39–42.

Fineline Productions. 1996. Press Notes for *Twelfth Night*.

Gardner, Dame Helen. 1963. *The Business of Criticism*. Oxford: Oxford University Press.

Gillies, John. 1994. *Shakespeare and the Geography of Difference*. Cambridge: Cambridge University Press.

Goldman, Michael. 1972. *Shakespeare and the Energies of Drama*. Princeton: Princeton University Press.

Graham, Renee. 1995. "Another View of Henry V's Triumph." *Boston Globe,* 19 February, B25, B30.

Gussow, Mel. 1998. "Onstage Music with Water." *New York Times,* 28 July, B1.

———. 1999. "Tom Stoppard in Love With Shakespeare." *The New York Times,* 12 January, B1–B2.

Hamill, Pete. 1990. "Crack and the Box." *Esquire* (May).

Hardison, O. B. 1969. "Three Types of Renaissance Catharsis. *Renaissance Drama,* New Series 2: 3–22.

Hawking, Stephen. 1988. *A Brief History of Time.* New York: Bantam Books.

Heilman, Robert. 1948. *This Great Stage.* Baton Rouge: Louisiana State University Press.

Herbert, T. Walter. 1977. *Oberon's Maz-ed World.* Baton Rouge: Louisiana State University Press.

Hodgdon, Barbara, ed. 1997. *I Henry IV.* Boston: Beacon Books.

Holden, Stephen. 1996. "There's Something Verboten in Illyria." *New York Times,* 25 October, C10.

Hortmann, Wilhelm. 1984. "Shakespeare in West Germany." *Shakespeare Quarterly* 35.

Howe, Desson. 1999. "A Pleasant 'Midsummer Night's Dream.'" *Washington Post National Weekly Edition,* 12 May.

Hunter, George K., ed. 1965. *Antonio's Revenge.* Lincoln, Neb.: Bison Books.

Hytner, Nicholas. 1998. "Entering Shakespeare's Dreams." *New York Times,* 12 July, C4, C20.

Jackson, MacDonald P. 1999. "'A Wood Near Monte Athena': Michael Hoffman's *A Midsummer Night's Dream.*" *Shakespeare Newsletter* 49, no. 242, Summer, 29, 27, 38, 44.

Jackson, Russell. 1999. "Surprising Find in British Archive." *Shakespeare Bulletin* 15, no. 4, Fall, 39–41.

Jorgens, Jack. 1977. *Shakespeare on Film.* Bloomington: Indiana University Press.

Kennedy, Dennis. 1993. *Looking at Shakespeare.* Cambridge: Cambridge University Press.

Kerr, Derren. 2000. Interview with Russell Jackson. *Early Modern Literary Studies* 5 (May).

Kerrigan, John 1982. "Introduction." *Love's Labour's Lost.* London: Penguin.

Keyishian, Harry. 1996. *The Shapes of Revenge: Victimization, Vengeance, and Vindication in Shakespeare.* Atlantic Highlands, N.J.: Humanities Press International.

King, Rosalind. 1999. "Review." *Yearbook of English Studies.*

Klawans, Stuart. 1999. "Oscar Who?" *The Nation,* 15 March, 35.

Kolin, Philip C. 1995. *"Titus Andronicus": Critical Essays.* New York: Garland.

Lane, Anthony. 1996. "Tights, Camera, Action." *The New Yorker,* 25 November, 64–77.

Lardner, John. 1999. "Close-up on Will." *Newsweek,* 15 February, 62–64.

Loehlin, James N. 1997. "'Top of the World, Ma': *Richard III* and Cinematic Convention." In *Shakespeare: The Movie,* ed. Lynda E. Boose and Richard Burt. New York: Methuen.

Lotman, Yu. "On the Language of Animated Cartoons." In *Film Theory and General Semiotics,* ed. V. V. Ivanov, Yu M. Lotman, and A. K. Zholkovsky. Russian Poetics in Translation. vol. 8.

Lyall, Sarah. 1998. "The Muse of Shakespeare Imagined as a Blonde." *New York Times,* 13 December.

Maher, Mary. 1985. "Vision in the BBC's *Titus.*" *Shakespeare on Film Newsletter* 10, no. 1, December, 5–6.

Maslin, Janet. 1995. "Fishburne and Branagh Meet Their Fate in Venice." *New York Times,* 14 December, C11, C20.

———. 1998. "Shakespeare Saw a Therapist?" *New York Times,* 13 December, B16.

———. 1999. "Movie Guide." *New York Times,* 21 May, 29.

Maus, K. E. 1997. "Introduction to *Titus Andronicus.*" *The Norton Shakespeare.* New York: W.W. Norton.

McLuhan, Marshall. 1964. *Understanding Media.* New York: McGraw–Hill.

Meltz, Marty. 1999. "Blocked Bard Writ Large." *Maine Sunday Telegram,* 24 January, E1, E5.

Miller, Sue. 1999. *While I Was Gone.* New York: Ballantine.

Mitchel, Elvis. 2000. "Film Guide." *New York Times,* 2 June, B23.

———. 2000. "Review." *New York Times,* 11 February, B16.

Montrose, Louis. 1996. *The Purpose of Playing: Shakespeare and the Cultural Politics of the Elizabethan Theatre.* Chicago: University of Chicago Press.

Moyers, Bill. 1995. "Commentary." Public Broadcasting, 10 January.

Nemerov, Howard. 1964. *Poetry and Fiction.* New Brunswick: Rutgers University Press.

Nicholls, Graham. 1986. *Measure for Measure: Text & Performance.* London: Macmillan.

Nichols, Nina. 1997. "Branagh's *Hamlet* Redux." *Shakespeare Bulletin* 15, no. 3, 38–41.

Orgel, Steven. 1988. "The Authentic Shakespeare." *Representations* 21: 5–25.

Osborne, Laurie E. 1997. "Poetry in Motion: Animating Shakespeare." In *Shakespeare: The Movie,* ed. Lynda Boose and Richard Burt. London: Routledge.

———. 1998. "Mixing Media in Shakespeare: Animating Tales and Colliding Modes of Production." *Post Script,* Winter/Spring, 73–89.

Ozick, Cynthia. 1996. *Fame and Folly.* New York: Knopf.

Pendleton, Thomas A. 1992. "Animated Shakespeare on HBO." *Shakespeare Newsletter,* Fall, 37, 40.

———. 1998. "Shakespeare…with Additional Dialog." *Cineaste* XXIV, no. 1: 62–67.

Price, Joseph. 1977. "Recalling Four Past RSC Productions." *Shakespeare Quarterly* 28, no. 2, Spring, 257–262.

Rafferty, Terrence. 1991. "Zeffirelli's *Hamlet.*" *The New Yorker,* 11 February.

Raleigh, Sir Walter. 1953 [1614]. *History of the World.* In *Tudor Poetry and Prose,* ed. J. William Hebel, et al. New York: Appleton-Century-Crofts.

Ranald, Margaret Loftus. 1999. "Review." *Shakespeare Bulletin* 17, no. 1, Winter, 46.

Rochlin, Margy. 1999. "Ally McBeal Dusts Off Her Shakespeare." *New York Times,* 2 May, MT44.

Rose, Lloyd. 1997. "*Hamlet.*" *Washington Post,* 24 January, G1–G2.

Rosenbaum, Ron. 1998. *Explaining Hitler.* New York: Random House.

Rothwell, Kenneth S. 1990. with Annabelle H. Malzer. *Shakespeare on Screen.* New York: Neal-Schuman.

———. 1999. *A History of Shakespeare on Screen.* Cambridge: Cambridge University Press.

———. 1998. "Orson Welles: Shakespeare for the Art Houses." *Cineaste* XXIV, no. 1: 28–33.

Rutter, Carol. 1997. "Fiona Shaw's Richard II." *Shakespeare Quarterly* 48, no. 3, Fall, 214–224.

Saccio, Peter. 1988. "The Historicity of the BBC Shakespeare Plays." In *Shakespeare on Television*, ed. James Bulman and H. R. Coursen. Hanover: University Press of New England.

Scott, A. O. 2000. "What Say You, My Lords? You'd Rather Charleston?" *New York Times*, 9 June, B12.

Scott, A. O. 2000. "Review." New York Times, 9 June, B12.

Schwarzbaum, Lisa. 1999. "What the Puck?" *Entertainment Weekly*, 14 May.

Searchlight Pictures. 1999. *A Midsummer Night's Dream*. Press Kit.

Shakespeare, William. 1982. *Love's Labour's Lost*. ed. John Kerrigan. Harmondsworth: New Penguin.

———. 1997. *Titus Andronicus*. In *The Norton Shakespeare*, ed. Walter Cohen, Jean E. Howard, and Katharine Eisaman Maus. New York: Norton.

Sidney, Sir Philip. 1904 [1595]. "Apology for Poetry." In *Elizabethan Critical Essays*, ed. G. Gregory Smith. Oxford: Oxford University Press.

———. 1962 [1593]. *The Acadia*. In *The Prose Works of Sir Philip Sidney*, ed. Albert Feuillerat. Vol. II. Cambridge: Cambridge University Press.

Solomon, Robert C. 1981. *Love: Emotion, Myth, and Metaphor*. New York: Harcourt, Brace.

Tempera, Mariangela. 1999. *Feasting with Centaurs*. Bologna: Libraria Universitaria.

Thompson, Ann. 2000. "Review." *Early Modern Literary Studies*, Special Edition (May).

Traister, D. 1999. "Review." *Choice* (September).

Tucker, Cynthia. 1994. "Editorial." *Atlanta Constitution*, 22 October.

Tuckett, Debra. 2000. "Review." *Early Modern Literary Studies* 5 (May).

Van Doren, Mark. 1939. *Shakespeare*. New York: Doubleday Anchor.

Varnell, Margaret A. 1998. "Review." *Shakespeare Bulletin* 16, no. 1, Winter, 22–28.

Wells, Stanley. 1991. "Shakespeare Performances in England." *Shakespeare Survey* 42.

———. 1992. "Shakespeare's Been Reframed." *Daily Telegraph: TV and Radio*, 11 June, 6.

Wheeler, Elizabeth. 1991. "Light It Up and Move It Around." *Shakespeare on Film Newsletter* 16, no. 1, December, 5.

White, Hayden V. 1973. *Metahistory*. Baltimore: Johns Hopkins University Press.

Williams, Wendy. 1998. "Fonda Takes on *The Tempest*." *Satellite TV Week*, 22–28 November, 2.

Wolf, Matt. 1997. "Cornering the Market on Ardent Young Swains." *New York Times*, 15 November, 2A, 4.

Wright, William. 1998. *Born That Way: Genes, Behavior, Personality*. New York: Knopf.

Zitner, Sheldon. 1981. "Wooden O's in Plastic Boxes." *University of Toronto Quarterly* 51, Fall, 1–12.

Credits for Productions

Richard II. BBC-2. 1997. Color. 130 minutes. Directed by Deborah Warner. Music: Arturo Annecchino. Sets/Costumes by: Hildegard Bechter. With Fiona Shaw (Richard), Graham Crowden (Gaunt), Richard Bremmer (Bolingbroke), David Lyon (Mowbray), Paola Dioniscotti (Duchess of Gloucester), John Rogan (Carlisle), Julian Rhind-Tutt (Aumerle), Kevin McKidd (Percy), Jem Wall (2nd Gardener), Henry Ian Cusick (Green), Nicholas Gecks (Bushy/Surrey), Donald Sinden (York), Sian Thomas (Queen), Danny Sapini (Bagot), John McEnery (Willoughby/Gardener), Struan Rodger (Northumberland), Roger Sloman (Ross/Abbot/Exton), Jude Akuwudike (Scroop), Elaine Claxton (Lady/Soloist).

Henry IV. BBC-2. 1995. 170 minutes. Directed by John Caird. With Ronald Pickup (Henry IV), Jonathan Firth (Prince Hal), David Calder (Falstaff), Rufus Sewell (Hotspur), Corin Redgrave (Worcester), Joseph O'Conor (Northumberland), Josette Simon (Kate), Jane Horrocks (Doll), Paul Eddington (Shallow), Jonathan Cullen (Poins), Elizabeth Spriggs (Quickly), Geoffrey Hutchings (Bardolph), Simon McBurney (Pistol), Tim McMullen (Blunt), Daniel Worters (Page), Graham Hubbard (Mouldy), Toby Jones (Wart), John Dallimore (Feeble), Paul Hamilton (Bullcalf), Clive Kneller (Shadow), Peter Jeffrey (Silence).

Silent Film Credits. *The Tempest* (1908). Directed by Percy Stowe. *A Midsummer Night's Dream* (1909). Directed by Charles Kent. With Walter Ackerman (Demetrius), Charles Chapman (Quince), Maurice Costello (Lysander), Julia Swayne Gordon (Helena), Gladys Hulette (Puck), William Ranous (Bottom). Rose Tapley (Hermia), Florence Turner (Titania). *Twelfth Night* (1910). Directed by Charles Kent. Julia Swayne Gordon (Olivia), Charles Kent (Malvolio), Florence Turner (Viola). *King Lear* (1910). Directed by Gerolamo Lo Savio. With Francesca Bertini (Cordelia), Ermete Novelli (Lear). *The Merchant of Venice* (1910). Directed by Gerolamo Lo Savio. With Francesca Bertini (Jessica), Ermete Novelli (Shylock). *Richard III* (1911). Directed by Frank Benson. With Eleanor Aickin (Duchess of York), Frank Benson (Richard), Mrs. Frank Benson (Anne), James Berry (Henry VI), Alfred Brydone (Edward IV), Harry Caine (Hastings), Wilfred Caithness (Stanley), Murray Carrington (Clarence), R. I. Conrick, (Rivers), John Howell (Brackenbury), H. James (Tyrrel), Betty Kenyon (Richard, Duke of York), James Maclean (Norfolk), Victor McClure (Surrey), H. O. Nicholson (Murderer), Alfred Wild (Catesby, Murderer), With Kathleen Yorke (Edward, Duke of Wales), J. Victor (Mayor). *Richard III* (1912). Directed by M. B. Dudley. Frederick Warde (Richard). *Giulietta e Romeo* (1911). Directed by Gerolamo Lo Savio. With Francesca Bertini (Juliet), Gustavo Serena (Romeo).

Measure for Measure. BBC. 1994. Directed by David Thacker. 110 minutes. Produced by Simon Curtis and Peter Creggeen. Designed by Bruce Macadie. Costumes by Lyn Avery. With Tim Wikinson (Duke), Corin Redgrave (Angelo), Juliet Aubrey (Isabella), Ben Miles (Claudio), Rob Edwards (Lucio), Margot Leicester (Mariana), Sally George (Juliet), Henry Goodman (Pompey), David Waller (Escalus), Ian Bannen (Provost), Sue Johnston (Mistress Overdone), David Bradley (Barnadine), Robert Demeger (Abhorson), Romy Baskerville (Francesca), Geoffrey Beevers (Friar Thomas), Kristin Hewson (Kate).

A Midsummer Night's Dream. 1996. Directed by Adrian Noble. Designed by Anthony Ward. Music by Howard Blake. With Osheen Jones (Boy), Alex Jennings (Theseus, Oberon), Lindsay Duncan (Hippolyta, Titania), Desmond Barrit (Bottom), Barry Lynch (Puck, Philostrate), Alfred Burke (Egeus), Monica Dolan (Hermia), Emily Raymond (Helena), Daniel Evans (Lysander), Kevin Doyle (Demetrius), John Kane (Quince), Marc Letheren (Flute), Robert Gillespie (Starveling), Howard Crossley (Snout), Kenn Sabberton (Snug).

A Midsummer Night's Dream. 1999. Fox Searchlight. 115 minutes. Directed by Michael Hoffman. Produced by Leslie Urdang. Designed by Luciana Arrighi. Music by Simon Boswell. With Kevin Kline (Bottom), Michelle Pfeiffer (Titania), Rupert Everett (Oberon), Stanley Tucci (Puck), Calista Flockhart (Helena), Anna Friel (Hermia), Dominic West (Lysander), Christian Bale (Lysander), David Strathairn (Theseus), Sophie Marceau (Hippolyta), Roger Rees (Quince), Max Wright (Starveling), Gregory Jbara (Snug), Bill Erwin (Snout), Sam Rothwell (Flute), Bernard Hill (Egeus), John Sessions (Philostrate), Heather Parisi (Bottom's Wife), Annalis Cordone (Cobweb), Paola Pessot (Mustardseed), Solena Nocentini (Moth), Flaminia Fegarotti (Peaseblossom), Chomoke Bhuiyan (Changeling).

Titus. A film by Julie Taymor. Fox Searchlight and Clear Blue Sky Productions. Color. 163 minutes. Released for a limited engagement in the United States on 25 December 1999. Produced by Jody Patton, Conchita Airoldi, and Julie Taymor. Directed by Julie Taymor. Cinematography by Luciano Tovoli. Designed by Dante Ferrenti. Costumes by Milena Canoneero. Music by Elliot Goldenthal. Edited by Françoise Bonnot. Choreographed by Giuseppe Pennese. Art direction by Dominco Sica and Carlo Gervasi. With Osheen Jones (young Lucius), Anthony Hopkins (Titus), Jessica Lange (Tamora), Jonathan Rhys Meyers (Chiron), Matthew Rhys (Demetrius), Harry Lennix (Aaron), Angus Macfayden (Lucius), Alan Cumming (Saturninus), James Frain (Bassianus), Colm Feore (Marcus), Laura Fraser (Lavinia), Geraldine McEwan (Nurse).

Hamlet. 2000. Double A Films. Miramax. 122 minutes. Directed by Michael Almereyda. Costumes by Luca Mosca and Marco Cattoretti. Music by Carter Burwell. With Ethan Hawke (Hamlet), Kyle MacLachlan (Claudius), Diane Venora (Gertrude), Liev Shreiber (Laertes), Julia Stiles (Ophelia), Bill Murray (Polonius), Karl Geary (Horatio), Steve Zahn (Rosencrantz), Dechen Thurman (Guildenstern), Sam Shepard (Ghost).

Love's Labour's Lost 2000. Adapted and directed by Kenneth Branagh. 95 minutes. Produced by Branagh and David Barron. Music by: Patrick Doyle. Cinematography by: Alex Thomson. Design by: Tim Harvey. Costumes by: Anna Buruma. Choreography by: Stuart Hoops. Casting by: Randi Hiller and Nina Gold. Literary Advisor: Russell Jackson. With Kenneth Branagh (Berowne), Richard Briers (Nathaniel), Richard Clifford (Boyet), Carmen Ejogo (Maria), Russell Jackson (Man with Newspaper), Nathan Lane (Costard), Adrian Lester (Dumaine), Matthew Lillard (Longaville), Natasha McElhone (Rosaline), Geraldine McEwan (Holofernia), Emily Mortimer (Katherine), Alessandro Nivola (King), Stefania Rocca (Jaquenetta), Alicia Silverstone (Princess), Timothy Spall (Don Armado), Jimmy Yuill (Dull).

Index

STUDIES IN SHAKESPEARE

Edited by Robert F. Willson, Jr.

This series deals with all aspects of Shakespearean drama and poetry. Studies of dramatic structure, verse and prose style, major themes, stage or performance history, and film treatments are welcomed. The editor is particularly interested in manuscripts that examine Shakespeare's work in its American setting—in the academy, on stage, and in popular culture. Inquiries and manuscripts should be sent to the series editor:

Robert F. Willson, Jr.
Department of English
University of Missouri-Kansas City
College of Arts & Sciences
106 Cockefair Hall
Kansas City, MO 64110-2499

To order other books in this series, please contact our Customer Service Department at:

(800) 770-LANG (within the U.S.)
(212) 647-7706 (outside the U.S.)
(212) 647-7707 FAX

or browse online by series at:
WWW.PETERLANGUSA.COM